Jack Coombs

Jack Coombs
A Life in Baseball

John P. Tierney

McFarland & Company, Inc., Publishers
Jefferson, North Carolina, and London

LIBRARY OF CONGRESS ONLINE CATALOG

Tierney, John.
  Jack Coombs : a life in baseball / John P. Tierney.
      p.   cm.
  Includes bibliographical references and index.

  ISBN 978-0-7864-3959-1
  softcover : 50# alkaline paper ∞

  1. Coombs, Jack.   2. Baseball players — United States —
Biography.   3. Pitchers (Baseball) — United States — Biography.
I. Title.
GV865.C673 T54   2008
796.357092 — dc22   2008038254
[B]

British Library cataloguing data are available

©2008 John P. Tierney. All rights reserved

*No part of this book may be reproduced or transmitted in any form
or by any means, electronic or mechanical, including photocopying
or recording, or by any information storage and retrieval system,
without permission in writing from the publisher.*

Cover photograph: Coombs warms up on Coombs Day at Colby
College, 1912

Manufactured in the United States of America

McFarland & Company, Inc., Publishers
  Box 611, Jefferson, North Carolina 28640
    www.mcfarlandpub.com

For Donald and Nelson Wentworth

Acknowledgments

Don and Nelson Wentworth are great-nephews of Jack Coombs. They were extremely generous in offering me access to newspaper clippings, family photos, and the diaries of Coombs' uncle, Jessie Snow. We spent many enjoyable hours discussing their personal remembrances of their "Uncle John." I particularly enjoyed our breakfasts and lunches in Kennebunkport.

Pat Burdick at the Colby College Special Collections, Waterville, Maine, Tom Harkins at the Duke University Archives, Tracy Baetz at Kennebunk's Brick Store Museum, and all the staff at the A. Bartlett Giamatti Research Center at the National Baseball Hall of Fame were very helpful in providing access to research materials.

Bobby Plapinger has been a terrific source for old baseball books for many years. Research is so much easier when you have dozens of classic baseball books at your fingertips.

The Society for American Baseball Research (SABR) does a tremendous job of fulfilling its mission to "foster the study of baseball past and present." Even if you are simply a baseball fan with no intention of ever doing any research, I would still highly recommend becoming a member of SABR. The wonderful SABR publications alone are worth the cost of the annual dues. Besides, it will probably be your only opportunity in life to say that you belong to the same organization as Stan Musial.

Douglas J. Muzzio is a professor of political science, a newspaper and television commentator, and native New Yorker. He offered thoughtful, balanced commentary on drafts of the text.

My two sons, Brian and Kevin, have helped give me perspective and insight throughout this project. Brian graduated *summa cum laude* from Colby College in 2006, one hundred years after John Wesley Coombs' graduation.

He has constantly demonstrated to me in words and actions just how much joy there is in playing baseball "the right way." Kevin graduated *magna cum laude* from Middlebury College in 2008. He has constantly demonstrated to me in words and actions that there is more to life than baseball.

This book would not have been written without the active encouragement and support of my wife, Kathleen. For more than thirty years she has gone to innumerable baseball games in all kinds of weather, and cheerily withstood endless discussions about the infinite wonders of the national pastime. She has become an expert at knowing just when a pitcher should be removed from a game, a skill that could be put to good use by Red Sox management. No man could ask for a better friend.

Table of Contents

Acknowledgments	vii
Preface	1
Prologue — September 1, 1906	3
1. The Colby Carbine	9
2. "So that's how they throw them in the big league"	23
3. A Second Ty Cobb	37
4. "No pitcher ever did more for a manager"	47
5. A Willingness to Work	66
6. Mack's Greatest Team?	88
7. "Jack Coombs is a sick man"	101
8. "Old Jack Coombs"	118
9. "You can have this glove; I won't need it anymore"	135
10. The Coombsmen	150
11. Professor Coombs	164
Epilogue — "The times have certainly changed"	176
Chapter Notes	189
Bibliography	195
Index	199

Preface

I joined the Society for American Baseball Research (SABR) in 1989. A wealth of fresh information pertaining to baseball was opened to me, rekindling an interest in the history of the sport I had enjoyed since childhood. Unlike some of the more celebrated SABR members, such as Bill James, my focus was not necessarily on the statistical measures of the game. Rather, I particularly enjoyed reading about the people who contributed in ways large and small to the development of the national pastime. As a youngster, I had read every baseball biography contained in the local branch of the Brooklyn Public Library.

My membership in SABR led to a strong interest (my wife would say fanaticism) in collecting books on baseball. My baseball library now numbers in excess of a thousand volumes, and my children have questioned the actuarial odds of my living long enough to read them all. While accumulating this collection, I developed a measure of guilt over the fact that I was becoming a consumer of other people's research while not making any contributions to the supply of baseball literature. For a while, I toyed with the idea of writing a biography of Mel Ott, who had been my father's childhood hero. While I was busy contemplating, other people were researching. Two brief but interesting biographies of Ott were released; one by Fred Stein in 1999 and the other by Alfred M. Martin in 2003. I decided to look elsewhere for a subject.

My eldest son matriculated at Colby College in the fall of 2002. While reading about the history of the school, I came across the name of John Wesley "Colby Jack" Coombs, undoubtedly the college's most famous athlete. I realized that Coombs' well-written text on baseball was among the volumes in my collection. Further research led to the realization that Coombs had been a quality major league pitcher in the early twentieth century, particularly while pitching for the Philadelphia Athletics during their run of four World Series appearances in the five-year period from 1910 to 1914.

The history of the Philadelphia Athletics is intertwined with the life of Connie Mack, who managed the team for fifty years, starting from its inception in 1901. In fact, when Putnam published its series of hardcover histories of the sixteen major league franchises then in existence in the 1940s, the history of the Athletics was titled *Connie Mack: Grand Old Man of Baseball*. While there is no separating Connie Mack from the success and failures of the Philadelphia Athletics franchise, one must recognize that the Athletics also employed a number of talented, successful ballplayers during Connie Mack's reign. Waddell, Plank, Bender, Collins, Baker, Foxx, Grove and Cochrane were great ballplayers who ultimately made their way into the Baseball Hall of Fame. In Mack's view, Jack Coombs was every bit as important to the success of the franchise as these other star players, and Mack believed that Colby Jack was worthy of induction at Cooperstown.

In the fall of 2005, an Internet search on Coombs provided the push necessary to stop contemplating and start researching. Through this search I found Nelson Wentworth, a great-nephew of Coombs who had written to Colby College's alumni magazine to inform the editor of an error the magazine had made regarding Coombs' family history. In short order, I was having breakfast in Kennebunk, Maine, with Nelson and his brother Donald. Through their stories Jack Coombs became more than just a successful ballplayer. Jack Coombs was intelligent, articulate, generous, loyal, and dedicated. Subsequent research confirmed this view; Coombs was respected and admired by all who knew him, friend and foe alike.

Coombs' life and career have to this point only been described in essays contained in biographical compilations. This is the first full-length biography of Jack Coombs. I hope I have done justice to my subject.

Prologue: September 1, 1906

Saturday, September 1, 1906, was a magnificent day in Boston, Massachusetts. The sky was a clear bright blue, with the temperature in the low 70s, touched with a light breeze, an unusually comfortable day for a city accustomed to muggy summer weather. Among the outdoor amusements available for Bostonians to enjoy on this perfect day was a baseball doubleheader between the defending American League champion Philadelphia Athletics and the hometown Boston Americans. The opening contest of the twinbill was scheduled to begin at 1:30 P.M. at Boston's Huntington Avenue Grounds.

Between them, the two teams had won the previous four American League championships, Boston having won in 1903 and 1904, and Philadelphia capturing the pennant in 1902 and 1905. Neither team was destined to win the championship in 1906. At the time Boston was mired in last place, where the team ultimately finished the season as a result of losing 105 of 154 games played. The Americans, who would not be known as the Red Sox until the 1908 season, had emphatically established themselves as non-contenders back in May, setting a dubious league record by losing twenty straight games, nineteen of them in a single homestand. Philadelphia, under the leadership of forty-three-year-old Connie Mack, was in third place, 5½ games behind the league-leading and eventual pennant-winning Chicago White Sox. While technically still in the hunt for the league championship, the Athletics were fading, their veteran roster lacking the verve to make the push necessary to bring them back to the top of the league in the final month of play.

Despite the Americans' dismal record, the combination of beautiful weather, a three-game Boston winning streak, and a doubleheader against the defending league champions brought an unusually large number of Bostonians out to the Huntington Avenue Grounds that day. The 18,084 fans who paid their way into the ballpark had no idea that they would not get to see the second game of the scheduled doubleheader, but none who witnessed the day's dramatic events would feel shortchanged for having been limited to only one contest.

Joe Harris was pitching for the Americans in the scheduled first game. Harris, a twenty-four-year-old native of nearby Melrose, Massachusetts, had joined the Boston club from Fall River of the New England League in September of the previous year. Having won twenty-five games against nine defeats for Fall River, he finished the 1905 season for Boston with a record of one win and two losses. More so than any other pitcher on Boston's 1906 staff, he had suffered from the team's anemic offense and weak defense. At one point in the season, he had lost fourteen consecutive games; in six of those games his teammates had failed to score a single run in support of his pitching. Heading into this start he had won just two games all season, the most recent being a 1–0 shutout against Cleveland on August 8.

Opposing Harris was a tall, strapping rookie pitcher named John Wesley Coombs. Coombs had graduated from Colby College in Waterville, Maine, in June of 1906, and joined the Athletics immediately thereafter. While he had shown significant promise in his previous outings, including a complete-game shutout against Washington in his inaugural appearance, his win-loss record was only 5–6 going into this day's action. He had started a game against Boston just two days earlier, but Connie Mack had quickly yanked him from the mound with the bases loaded and only one out in the first inning.

Given the records of the teams and their pitchers, there was no reason for the crowd, which numbered around 5,000 at the start of the game, to expect anything beyond an ordinary match engaged under extraordinary weather conditions.

The game started routinely, with both teams retired in order in the first inning.[1] In the home half of the second, Boston threatened to score first, with runners on first and third and only one out. First baseman Myron "Moose" Grimshaw, the runner on first, dashed for second base, hoping to draw a throw from the catcher that would allow Hobe Ferris, the runner on third, to take off for home plate. Grimshaw's tactic drew the anticipated throw from Philadelphia catcher Doc Powers, but Ferris stood transfixed at third as Grimshaw was easily thrown out.

Philadelphia scored its first run in the third. With one out, Coombs hit a slow roller down the third base line that Harris was unable to field in time to catch the speedy rookie at first base. Coombs again put his legs to good use by stealing second, and then scampered on to third when the next batter grounded out. He scored on an infield single by center fielder Bris Lord. Even in the era of "scientific" baseball, it was unusual for a team to manufacture a run on the legs of its starting pitcher.

As the game continued, the crowd kept growing, forcing the opening of the seating in the center-field bleachers for the first time since the Fourth of July. The horde continued to swell over the next few innings, as defense dominated the game, and no runners crossed the plate. By the sixth inning, the crowd had become so large that ropes were put up in the outfield to handle those who were still arriving. Balls hit into the overflow crowd were designated a triple by ground rule.

In the bottom of the sixth inning Boston shortstop Freddy Parent tripled to right field, to the thunderous cheers of the patrons. He was brought home on a single by center-fielder and manager Chick Stahl, tying the score. (Stahl had been named acting manager of the Americans on August 27, when manager Jimmy Collins had abruptly left the team, culminating an ongoing feud between Collins and team owner John I. Taylor. The Americans had won three of the first five games that Stahl had managed.)

Following the sixth inning, both pitchers settled into a rhythm. Each team had scoring opportunities, but smart defensive plays on both sides kept runners from crossing the plate. The contest continued into extra innings, and the crowd became increasingly energized with the growing tension of the well-played game.

In the top of the fifteenth inning, Coombs was presented with the opportunity to win the game. With one out, John Knight, the Athletics third baseman, hit his second triple of the game. (Those two triples were his only triples of the season.) Following a fly out to short right field, Coombs then hit a hard ground ball towards third base, where Boston third baseman James "Red" Morgan was able to block the ball and get off a quick throw to first to nab the swift Coombs. The crowd erupted in ground-shaking applause.

The Athletics almost threw the game away in the bottom of the fifteenth, as shortstop Cross started the inning with a throwing error, allowing Grimshaw to reach second base. Grimshaw was then sacrificed to third, and Boston manager Stahl opted to send Buck Freeman up to pinch-hit for catcher Bill Carrigan. With Harris on deck, Connie Mack waved his scorecard to his catcher, Doc Powers, signaling him to walk Freeman to get to the weak-hitting Harris. After three pitches sailed wide of the plate, Freeman decided he did not want to be denied the opportunity to heroically end the game. He lunged across the plate to swing at the next outside pitch, resulting in a weak grounder back to Coombs. With two outs, Harris then struck out to end the threat. The *Boston Globe* the next day described Freeman's impatient lunge as "the dumbest play ever made at the Huntington Avenue Grounds."[2]

In the bottom of the eighteenth, Boston put runners on first and third, with only one out. With Stahl coming to the plate, Mack again ordered an intentional walk, setting up the force at home plate. The force never came into play, as Coombs calmly reached back and struck out Ferris and Hoey, each on three pitches. At this point, the Boston crowd was so moved by the drama of the game that all feelings of partisanship evaporated, and Coombs was given a rousing standing ovation for his work under pressure.

The game moved on, and neither team advanced a runner past second base for the next five innings. When the game went into the twenty-first inning, it established a major league record for the longest game, exceeding the twenty inning contest played the previous season by the same two teams. On July 4, 1905, Rube Waddell of the Athletics beat Cy Young of the Americans by a 4–2 score, with both pitchers going the distance. Young, thirty-eight years old at the time, did not walk a single batter during his twenty innings of work.

At the start of the twenty-third inning, the scoreboard operator wrote the word "skidoo" under the numeral 23, but despite his exhortations neither the players nor the fans were quite ready to leave. Knight of the Athletics was the only batter to reach base for either team in that inning, but he was erased at second on an attempted steal.

At the end of the twenty-third inning, both teams approached umpire Tim Hurst, suggesting that the game should be called on account of darkness. The diminutive, pugnacious Hurst had once commented on the work of an umpire, "The pay is good, and you can't beat the hours — three to five."[3] He had a reputation for calling games on account of darkness when the sun was still shining, just so he could assure himself of being on time for a theater performance. In this case, however, sunset was only 10 minutes away, and having already invested much more than his standard workday in the game, Hurst was not interested in going anywhere without a resolution. He ordered that the game be continued in the gathering twilight.

With one out in the top of the twenty-fourth inning, Athletics left fielder Topsy Hartsel singled and stole second while Bris Lord struck out. Ossee Schreckengost was Philadelphia's next scheduled batter. Usually a catcher, "Schreck" had replaced Harry Davis as the Athletics' first baseman in the eleventh inning. Schreckengost quickly found himself behind in the count. But he lined the two-strike pitch past Harris straight up the middle of the field, sending Hartsel home with the go-ahead run. The letdown of having finally allowed a run after twenty consecutive scoreless innings seemed to unravel Harris. The next two batters hit ground-rule triples into the overflow crowd, increasing the Athletics lead to 4–1.

The Americans attempted a comeback in their half of the twenty-fourth, as Grimshaw singled with one out. Third baseman Knight dropped Morgan's ensuing pop-up, but was able to force Grimshaw at second. Coombs then induced Criger to ground out to short to end the contest.

The fans had witnessed a tense, dramatic game, and none were disappointed that they had missed the opportunity to see the scheduled doubleheader. The twenty-four innings had lasted 4 hours and 47 minutes, or only two minutes more than it took the Boston Red Sox and New York Yankees to play a regulation nine innings in August of 2006.

Both teams sent more than eighty batters to the plate. Coombs struck out eighteen batters, which constituted a major league record at the time, while Harris struck out fourteen. Of the players who played all twenty-four innings, only Boston third baseman Red Morgan went hitless, finishing the day with no hits in seven official at-bats. Aided by the

A young John Coombs poses for a formal portrait in his Athletics uniform early in his career (courtesy Wentworth Family Personal Collection).

ground rule associated with balls hit into the overflow crowd, there were six triples in the game. There were also seven stolen bases, including two by winning pitcher Coombs.

Pitch counts were not tracked during those times, but one can reasonably conjecture that each pitcher threw more than 300 pitches in the game, perhaps as many as 400. The two pitchers were not the only "iron men" on the field — Tim Hurst was the sole umpire for the contest, and Philadelphia catcher Doc Powers caught all twenty-four innings, throwing out five of six potential base stealers during his day's work.

The *Sporting News* described Coombs' effort in glowing terms. "That performance ... has made the name of Coombs a household word, and no matter what he does from now out, the fact will never be forgotten that Coombs, just out of Colby College, pitched and won the longest complete-game ever played."[4] While there have since been major league games exceeding twenty-four innings in length, Coombs is still the record holder for longest complete game victory, a record unlikely ever to be approached in the future.[5]

Taciturn Connie Mack was sparing in his praise of his rookie pitcher.

As Coombs came off the field, Mack slapped him on the shoulder, saying, "My you had a mighty long day, Jack. That was a great job."[6] Chick Stahl tried to cheer up the hard-luck Harris, telling him, "That game made you, Joe. Keep on pitching like that, and you'll stay in the league a long time."[7]

Coombs saved the baseball used to record the last out of the game. A year later, he donated it to President White of Colby College, even though he had been offered as much as $50 for the ball. White then offered it to the school's athletic department as the initial contribution to a new trophy display. "I want to give this baseball to someone who will prize it properly," he said. "Put it in your trophy room in a glass case as one of the dearest treasures of Colby athletic history."[8]

Despite Stahl's encouragement, Harris' future in the game was limited. In fact, he did not win another game in the major leagues, losing the rest of his starts in 1906 and going 0–7 in 1907 before Boston finally released him. In his brief major league career, he posted a record of 3–30.

While Harris had an unfortunate major league baseball career, he lived a long life, dying at the age of eighty-two in his native Melrose, Massachusetts. Other players on the field that day were not so fortunate. Emotionally overwrought to begin with, and unable to handle the rigors of managing, Boston's Chick Stahl took his own life by drinking a bottle of carbolic acid during spring training of 1907, three days after abruptly resigning as the Boston manager.[9] Doc Powers, the Athletics' catcher, died from intestinal peritonitis in 1909, just two weeks after catching the inaugural game of Philadelphia's Shibe Park.[10] Ossee Schreckengost, who drove in the winning run in the game, died of complications relating to tuberculosis in 1914 at the age of thirty-nine.[11]

Coombs and Harris shared more than the fame associated with their marathon pitching performance. Both contracted typhoid fever, an infectious disease much more common a century ago than it is today. Harris was stricken immediately after the 1906 season, a mere footnote to what was in so many ways a forgettable year for him. Coombs contracted the disease in early 1913, and in his case the illness was much more than a footnote. Typhoid fever derailed for two full seasons the career of a man who many then considered one of the finest pitchers in the game of baseball.

1

The Colby Carbine

John Wesley Coombs was born on November 18, 1882, in La Grand, Iowa, a small town about fifty miles northeast of Des Moines. He was the first child of Frank H. Coombs and Ellen J. Snow Coombs, who had married in 1880. Both Frank and "Nellie" were natives of Maine, but they had moved to Iowa in 1881 in search of greater economic opportunity. They settled on a small farm under the provisions of the Homestead Act.[1]

Frank Coombs earned his living as a blacksmith. He was a large man of incredible strength and durability, traits that his firstborn inherited. Frank Coombs was born in Brunswick, Maine, and learned his trade as a child, purportedly making his first horseshoe at the age of eleven. Nellie Snow, two years older than Frank, traced her ancestry back to Stephen Hopkins, who came to America on the *Mayflower*. Despite this pedigree, she was an unsophisticated, hard-working woman devoted to her husband and her family.

That family grew rapidly in the next four years, as two additional sons, Curtis (1884) and Ernest (1887), were born. Having spent the five years necessary to claim title to the land, Frank sold the farm and moved back to Maine in late 1887, settling in Pownal, near Kennebunk, where he set up shop as a blacksmith. In the next few years, Nellie gave birth to two more children, a son, Harry (1889), and a daughter, Alice (1891).

Kennebunk is located in southeastern Maine, about twenty-five miles southwest of Portland. It was first explored by Europeans in the 1660s. With the Kennebunk and Mousam rivers running through the region, it was primarily a seafaring community. By the time Coombs and his family moved there, the area had also developed into a resort destination, providing summer residences to wealthy New Englanders. Author Kenneth Roberts was a

John Coombs (right) poses with his younger brother Curtis around 1885 (courtesy Wentworth Family Personal Collection).

native of Kennebunk, and Pulitzer Prize winner Booth Tarkington maintained a summer home in the area.[2]

John Coombs experienced an ordinary childhood in Maine. An intelligent, energetic, extroverted youth, his time was consumed with his studies, his chores and play. His father supposedly crafted him a baseball at an early age, and young John took to throwing that ball almost immediately. Frank Coombs claimed in later years to have spent part of his own youth playing ball, and actively encouraged John in his athletic interests.

Although he would become famous as "Jack" Coombs, he was called John by his family and close friends throughout his life. Even in later years, he was more likely to sign his name "John W. Coombs" than "Jack Coombs."

Coombs entered Freeport High School in 1898, and because of his intelligence and aptitude, he was enrolled in the school's college course of study with the expectation that he would be attending one of Maine's leading colleges. Coombs was willing to put his intellectual skills on display, writing for school publications and participating in public debates. The athletic fields were the forum where his talents stood out; he played football in the fall and baseball in the spring. Freeport High School was a small school, and it was difficult to field competitive teams against typically larger competitors. In his freshman year, the football team did not win a game, and the baseball team managed only two victories.[3]

Coombs' athletic talents were apparent in high school. He was tall with broad shoulders and great strength. He was so strong that his pitches occasionally knocked over his catcher. And he was tireless, always eager to join in a spirited contest. His reputation as an athlete quickly spread, and while still in high school he was recruited during the summers to pitch in semi-professional town leagues. His pitching caught the attention of Dr. J. F. Hill, an 1882 graduate of Colby College. Dr. Hill encouraged Coombs to bring his intellectual and athletic talents to Colby, and towards that end Coombs transferred from Freeport High School to Colburn Classical Institute in his senior year of high school. Colburn Classical was located in Waterville Maine, and served primarily as a preparatory school for Colby, also located in Waterville.

Waterville was a small city located about twenty miles northeast of Augusta, Maine's state capital. Located on the Kennebec River, early residents engaged in shipbuilding, but by the time of Coombs' arrival, the principal economic focus of the community was on small manufacturing. The most famous products were Hathaway shirts, which were made in Waterville until the early twenty-first century.[4]

Coombs graduated from Colburn in the spring of 1902, and spent the summer pitching for the Waterville baseball team, earning $25 a week to help pay for his Colby education. While tuition at Colby was "only" $90 a semester at the time, this was a sizeable sum for a blacksmith's son. As a result, Coombs worked during his college career, usually by pitching semi-professional baseball during the summers. This was not an unusual practice for college athletes at the time. Under today's rules, Coombs' pitching for money to defray his college expenses would make him ineligible for intercollegiate sports.

When Coombs matriculated at Colby in the fall of 1902, the school consisted of approximately 200 students, half of them women. At the time, it was unusual for a school to be co-educational. Most institutions of higher learning, if they offered an education to women at all, segregated the females into different colleges with separate faculty and curriculum. The intermingling of men and women in a single college at the time was considered a detriment to Colby's ability to attract male students. As a result, male enrollment declined slightly in the early part of the twentieth century.[5] There is no record of Coombs being "repelled" from Colby because of the "large" number of women there; he was attracted instead by the opportunity to pursue a disciplined course of study in science and play on a competitive baseball team.[6] Since playing college baseball was at that time an uncommon jumping point to the major leagues, particularly at a small co-educational institution such as Colby College, Coombs' principal focus in going to Colby was to attain a quality education that would ultimately lead to a professional career. His chosen course of study was chemistry.

Colby was first chartered in 1813, making it one of the earliest colleges established in the United States. It was founded as a Baptist institution, initially named the Maine Literary and Theological Institution. It was the second college established in Maine, and intended as an alternative to the Congregationalist focus provided by its antecedent, Bowdoin College. While both of Coombs' parents were Baptists, there is no indication that he attended Colby for its religious foundation. Although attendance at daily chapel was a requirement for all undergraduates, Coombs took advantage of a liberal "allowance for cuts" and missed chapel twenty to forty times a semester.[7] In later life, when asked about his religious affiliation, Coombs identified himself as a Quaker.

As a student, Coombs excelled in the sciences, earning As and Bs in physics, biology and chemistry. His course notes in the sciences were well organized and meticulous. Languages appeared more challenging for him, as he earned Cs and Ds in French and German. While Colby had offered courses in the sciences for a number of years, it was not until 1906 that the school conferred a bachelor of science degree. Two 1906 graduates earned such degrees, and by virtue of being first alphabetically, John Wesley Coombs owns the distinction of being the first Colby graduate to be conferred with a bachelor of science degree.[8]

Even though he was accidentally left out of the listing of the freshman class in *The Colby Echo*, the college newspaper, Coombs received campus-wide notice immediately thereafter by pitching a shutout in his first inter-class athletic event. Of greater note, he tried out for the varsity football team and became the starting halfback due to his quickness and strength. The team went 5–3 for the season, including victories over rival Maine colleges Bates and Bowdoin. Coombs scored a touchdown in a victory over New Hampshire. At the conclusion of the season, Coombs moved from the gridiron to the basketball court, where he was the starting center on the varsity basketball team that went 8–4.

Football and basketball were just preludes, giving Coombs an athletic challenge while he waited for baseball season to arrive. Not surprisingly, he

Coombs' father Frank stands in the doorway of his blacksmith shop in 1908 (courtesy Wentworth Family Personal Collection).

made the varsity baseball team, where he played second base and center field whenever he was not pitching. His collegiate pitching career began in a rather humiliating fashion, as the Colby team traveled to Cambridge, Massachusetts, on April 11, 1903, to play the Harvard varsity team in front of nearly one thousand spectators at Soldiers Field. Harvard overwhelmed the men from Colby by a score of 15–3. Harvard scored eight runs in the third inning from a combination of six hits and "stupid fielding and errors" on the part of the Colby defense.[9] At this point Coombs was relieved from his pitching duties and moved to center field. Overall, the Colby team made seven errors in the game, an effort described in the press as "listless."[10] In a baseball career filled with notable victories against formidable opponents from all the major league clubs, Coombs was never able to beat the Harvard varsity baseball team, losing three straight years.

Things were different nearly two weeks later when Colby played the Lewiston Athletic Club, an aggregation of ballplayers with recent collegiate experience. Colby pounded out a 15–1 victory over Lewiston, with Coombs striking out eleven of the first twelve batters he faced. He added to this memorable performance with three hits in six at-bats, including a triple, a stolen base and three runs scored. Two days later, he faced a rival Maine college for the first time, appearing in relief in a 10–5 victory over Bowdoin. *The Colby*

Echo reported that "Coombs in the box showed he is the peer if not the superior to any college pitcher in Maine today."[11] While the reporter might at first be suspected of biased hyperbole, Coombs' performance for the year suggested that even as a mere freshman he was setting the standard of pitching excellence in the New England collegiate ranks. In one game he struck out nineteen batters while gathering two hits, including a triple, in five trips to the plate. In another, he recorded ten strikeouts, and went three-for-seven at bat, including two stolen bases. Unfortunately, the Colby team again committed seven errors behind him, as they lost the game in the sixteenth inning.

Coombs excelled in all aspects of the game, batting well over .300 as a switch-hitter, and displaying power, speed, and excellent defense. The team finished with a record of eight victories and seven losses for the season, and Coombs was selected for the all–Maine inter-collegiate team.

Coombs stayed in Waterville for the summer, playing baseball primarily for the Waterville town team as well as other all-star aggregations in various exhibition games. The summer schedule started with a series of games played in St. John, New Brunswick. The Waterville lads made such an impression on the natives, particularly the young ladies, that they were invited back to play in the late summer. Unfortunately for the young ladies of St. John, the team's schedule did not permit such a diversion. The ladies penned a public letter expressing their disappointment, weaving the names of their favorite players into the letter. "We girls have decided the next time you *Coombs* to St. John you will receive a *Cowing* down. We expected to have a *Goode* time for we all had *Taylor*-made suits for the occasion, and now we are all *Phelan* blue sitting in the cozy *Connors* under the *Britt*-ish flag."[12]

Throughout his collegiate career, Coombs encountered young ladies who showed an interest in him. And on the surface at least, it appeared that he returned the favor, having given a fraternity pin to a few different young women during the course of his four years at Colby. But Coombs' principal focus was his studies and athletics, and the attention of females was but an interesting distraction. Years later, in a speech to the Colby Alumni Association, he offered his views as to where the priorities of a young collegian should be, claiming "that a young man at college had far better be on the athletic field building up a sound body and resulting strong mind, than to be wandering through village lanes hand in hand with some girl."[13]

The culmination of the summer league was a Labor Day weekend game played in Waterville, pitting Waterville against Fairfield. The activities for the day included bicycle races, automobile races, a hot-air balloon ascension, and a contest to capture a greased pig. But the highlight of the day was the scheduled baseball game, in which Coombs drove in two runs and scored the winning run in a tense 4–3 contest witnessed by nearly 2,000 holiday revelers.

Describing Coombs' contributions to the team's success, a local paper commented, "The more he plays the better Waterville likes to see him in a tight place. In the box or at the bat he always does his best work when things are going dead against him."[14] This proved to be true throughout Coombs' professional baseball career, as his greatest achievements always seemed to take place in the toughest games against the strongest competition. In the parlance of the time, John Coombs was at his best "in a pinch." His performances during the summer led to the inevitable descriptive nicknames in the press. Particular favorites were "The Colby Carbine," "Long John," and "Cy," in comparison to the legendary major league pitcher Cy Young.

In the fall of 1903, Coombs again played for the Colby varsity football team, switching to the left tackle position. The team was mediocre, winning only one game while losing five, with Coombs contributing to the sole victory against Bates with a blocked punt. In a loss against Maine, he again blocked a punt, and "all on one wild dash" ran the ball in for Colby's only touchdown.[15] He was occasionally called upon to kick extra points, using the drop-kick method in vogue at the time. For his efforts on the gridiron, he was named to the all–Maine inter-collegiate football team.

Coombs returned to the basketball court that winter, captaining and centering for a team that won five of eight contests.

Expectations were high for the Colby baseball team that spring. Coombs was considered "as good as the best of them," and was named as co-coach of the team.[16] The team did not get off to a good start, however, as Coombs displayed for the first time a penchant towards misfortune that would shadow him throughout his baseball career. The team's season opened with a doubleheader. In the first game, base runner Coombs was hit in the head on an attempted pickoff throw and apparently knocked unconscious. He recovered sufficiently to pitch in the second game, striking out eleven Amherst batters. In May, on Friday the thirteenth, prior to a game against Maine, Coombs was inspecting the new seats that had been installed at Colby's baseball diamond. He fell from the grandstands and his ribs were severely bruised. A doctor was called to the scene to tend to the pitcher. *The Colby Echo* reported, "[C]overed with sticking plaster, John appeared on the spot and pitched as good a game as will be seen this year."[17] This time the paper was guilty of understatement, as Coombs struck out sixteen batters in the game and contributed to his own cause with a hit, a run scored, and four assists in Colby's 3–0 shutout over Maine. A local newspaper reporter was so impressed with Coombs' performance, he suggested that, "Hereafter, when Colby has a hard game ahead, Coombs's special training is to consist of a drop from a four story window so that he will strike on his head on a brick pavement. Then he will be rolled with a steam road roller and pounded back into shape with sledge hammers."[18]

Coombs and the team slumped during the next three games. Despite his sore ribs, he pitched the next day following his accident. The team committed six errors, leading to five runs in one inning and a 6–0 defeat at the hands of Bowdoin. A week later, they were shut out by Harvard, with no Colby base runner advancing beyond second base.

With two victories against six defeats, the season was developing into a disappointment. But then Coombs and the rest of the Colby nine kicked into high gear. Coombs pitched and won all five of the remaining scheduled games, including three against Maine rivals. The highlight of the streak was the final game against Bates. With the Maine inter-collegiate championship on the line, Coombs struck out ten Bates batters and went three-for-four at the plate, including a long home run that traveled like a "runaway automobile."[19] Colby finished with the state championship for the thirteenth time in twenty-six years, posting a record of four wins and two losses against Maine rivals Bates, Bowdoin and the University of Maine. Coombs pitched all six of those games, recording fifty-three strikeouts and a batting average of .455. In the Maine league he led all batters in runs, hits, total bases, and batting average, and was again named to the all–Maine baseball team.

Following the season Coombs was named the Colby team captain for his junior year. *The Colby Echo* reported, "John will make an ideal captain — he has the respect and confidence of every man on the team and has a fine knowledge of the game."[20] To enhance those skills and knowledge, and to earn additional money, Coombs spent the summer following his sophomore season pitching for a newly formed team in Northampton, Massachusetts. The Northampton team provided him with the opportunity to hone his pitching skills, as the team played more than sixty games during the summer. Coombs was responsible for twenty of Northampton's forty-one victories. One of his teammates on the Northampton team was John Hoey, who at the time attended Holy Cross. Hoey would later be the Boston left fielder in the twenty-four-inning marathon game as well as Coombs' strikeout victim to end Boston's bases-loaded threat in the eighteenth inning.

That summer Coombs experienced another on-field injury in a game, but recovered to secure a victory against a team from Rockville, Connecticut. The local newspaper reporter, in the heroic style of the day, emphasized the drama of the story.

> The game, besides being exciting, had other features that strained the spectators' nerves to the utmost. In the eighth inning Coombs, the giant pitcher, who has made more personal friends in the city than probably any pitcher that has ever been here, in running for a foul fly, collided with a boy whom the Northampton management had delegated to care for the visitors' bats and gloves. Two men were out, and the big pitcher made a brilliant dash after the foul. As he reached the

visitors' bench he failed to see the youngster till it was too late, catching the little fellow's head square on the temple as he stumbled over him. He stopped, drew himself up to his full height, threw his two hands to his head, staggered to the end of the bench and fell, rolling under the end of it unconscious. The visiting players and spectators pulled him out onto the grass, and with the aid of water revived him after about two minutes work.

O'Gorman, a new pitcher, just obtained, started to warm up, and the hopes of the crowd fell. O'Gorman they had never seen play, and with Old Ironsides injured, none knew how badly, there was little joy in their hearts. Then the people on the grand stand saw the big pitcher's form rising from the ground, the little knot of nurses separate and the big fellow stepped shakily out, not for the diamond, but over to the little fellow who was now weeping on the bench, more scared than hurt. After quieting the trembling little fellow, Coombs started slowly toward the box, and the entire crowd went crazy. Manager O'Donnell went up to Coombs, just before he reached the diamond, and said, "Hadn't you better rest?" "Not on your life," was the game reply. "If I go off the field, I'll go feet first. I'll be all right as soon as I start to work." The next two men landed safe hits and reached second and third. Coombs seemed weak but when the next batter faced him he settled down into the crouch he uses in delivering the ball, and there was only a streak of brown as the ball sizzled for the plate. Before the crowd could realize it the batter had fanned and the teams were filing across the diamond.[21]

This performance, reminiscent of the heroics of contemporary fictional characters exemplified by Frank Merriwell, was witnessed by a crowd of 581. Unfortunately, despite the competitiveness of the Northampton team, attendance was generally poor, and when Coombs decided to pitch in the more competitive Northern League the following summer, the attendance dropped even further, and the team disbanded midway through the schedule.

Coombs branched out from athletics in his junior year at Colby, taking a turn at acting. His irrepressible, extroverted personality made him a natural on the stage. He was one of the lead characters in that year's theater production, "Comrades," a farcical comedy. The reviews were favorable. "Coombs, '06, as Simon Stone, 'jack of all trades,' furnished the fun of the evening. The part seemed to have been made expressly for John. There was never a dull moment in his courting Nancy from the time he was presenting her with candy until he, as a member of the 'Ring,' was offering her rings."[22] Despite the fact that Colby was a coeducational institution with what was considered a large number of women, all of the female roles were played by men.

Coombs was also increasingly active in the Delta Upsilon fraternity, which he had joined as a freshman, attending the national convention as one of Colby's representatives. He was part of the organizing committee for the junior promenade and awarded the class prizes at the 1905 commencement. With the possible exception of chapel, if there was a communal activity on the Colby campus, John Coombs seemed to have a hand in it.

The performance of the baseball team in the spring of 1905 was disappointing, as expectations were high for another Maine championship. The team record was a mediocre six victories against seven defeats, with a 3–3 record against its Maine rivals. The season included the annual humiliating defeat at the hands of Harvard, this time by a score of 16–5, with the game called after five innings by the agreement of both teams. Coombs was involved in a controversy in a game against Maine. Carrying a 1–0 lead in the fifth inning and having held Maine to no hits, Coombs was involved in a baserunning collision with a Maine infielder. Maine claimed that Coombs had interfered with the fielder, an opinion not shared by the umpire. In the debate that followed, the Maine team became so incensed with the umpire's steadfast insistence on the appropriateness of his call that it left the field, forfeiting the game to Colby, and depriving Coombs of his opportunity for a no-hitter.

The team defense was particularly suspect that season, as exemplified in a game against Bowdoin, which Colby won by a score of 11–6. Although Coombs struck out fourteen batters, Colby committed four errors on defense, leading to five of Bowdoin's runs. Going into the last game of the season, the team had a chance to tie for the Maine championship with a victory against Bates. Coombs pitched ten shutout innings, but the Colby offense could not put any runs across the plate against the Bates pitcher. Finally, in the eleventh inning, two Colby errors led to a single run and the loss.

The summer of 1905 found Coombs pitching for the Inter-City Athletic Association in the independent Northern League. The Inter-City team represented the Vermont cities of Barre and Montpelier. Coombs was presented as the marquee attraction for the team, described on posters as "Mr. Coombs, the Maine wonder."[23] Coombs' pitching and hitting (he generally batted cleanup) helped lead the team to a first-place finish in the league.

The Vermont League was a four-team "outlaw" league, operating outside of the jurisdiction of organized baseball, but employing talent comparable to some of the established minor leagues. Future major league stars such as Eddie Collins and Ed Reulbach played in the league. Six of Coombs' teammates in 1905 went on to appear in the major leagues.[24]

The season was marred by a controversy instigated by one of Coombs' teammates, Sammy Apperius. A native of Selma, Alabama, Apperius refused to play against the team from Burlington because its shortstop, William Clarence Matthews, was black. Apperius feared "social ostracism" for himself and his family if he were to appear on a baseball diamond with a black man.[25] Most fans in the Green Mountain state had little sympathy for Apperius, who claimed that Northerners simply could not appreciate the intensity of the feelings that Southerners had regarding blacks.

William Clarence Matthews was also from Selma, Alabama. As a youngster he attended the Tuskegee Institute prior to attending the exclusive Phillips Andover Academy in Massachusetts. From there he enrolled at Harvard College, where he was arguably the best player on the team. He had feasted on Coombs' pitching in Coombs' first start for Colby back in 1903, gathering four hits, including a double and a triple. Earlier in 1905, Matthews had clouted two home runs off Coombs in Harvard's five-inning slaughter of Colby.

Having graduated from Harvard in 1905, Matthews was interested in a career as a ballplayer, and had joined the Northern League hoping for an opportunity to catch the attention of a major league club. His skills came to the attention of Fred Tenney, first baseman and manager of the Boston franchise in the National League, who had once played ball in the Northern League. Tenney was in need of an infielder, and Matthews fit the bill. However, a black ballplayer had not played at the major league level since 1884, when the Walker brothers briefly played for the Toledo franchise of the American Association. When word leaked out that Tenney was signing a black man to his roster, Southern-born players throughout the league made it known that they would not tolerate the mixing of the races on the field of play, and rumors emerged of the formation of a rival southern league where the racial purity of the rosters would be maintained. Buckling to the pressure, Tenney backed away from his offer to Matthews, and major league baseball continued to exclude black players from employment for another four decades.

Matthews abandoned his aspirations for a career in baseball and instead pursued a degree in law. He passed the bar in 1908, rising to a position in the district attorney's office in Boston. He eventually became an assistant attorney general in the Coolidge administration.[26]

Eddie Grant was a teammate of Matthews at Harvard and played in the Vermont League the summer of 1905 for Inter-City. The second-best player on the Harvard team next to Matthews, but not burdened with the handicap of Matthews' skin color, Grant reached the big leagues, playing for four different franchises over a ten-year career. In 1918, Grant was killed in the battle of the Argonne Forest during World War I, becoming the only major league ballplayer to die in the war.[27]

It was apparently during the summer of 1905 that Coombs' talents were brought to the attention of Tom Mack, the brother of Philadelphia Athletics manager Connie Mack.[28] Various people have been credited with bringing Coombs to Tom Mack's attention, including Dr. Hill, who had recruited Coombs to Colby College.[29] Tom Mack spoke to Coombs about the potential for a career in major league baseball upon the completion of his studies at Colby. Having now been acknowledged as a potential major league talent, Coombs returned for his senior year at Colby.

Football was for the first time not part of Coombs' regimen in the fall, as he recognized the potential hazards the sport could present for his last collegiate baseball season. While avoiding the dangers of the gridiron, Coombs was willing to take some risks with a rifle in his hands. In the fall *The Colby Echo* described him leaving the campus as he "shouldered his new double-barreled breech loading shotgun and started for the woods. In the evening he returned with five plump partridges."[30] Hunting would be a passionate hobby for Coombs throughout his life, and one that on occasion proved detrimental to his well-being.

He continued to play center on the basketball team his senior year, "throwing his horseshoes from all over the field."[31] He was also involved in Colby's annual theater production, another comedic farce, titled "Trouble." Coombs played the lead role, General Benjamin Darrell, "a retired general of a dyspeptic temperament."[32] The review of the performance at the Waterville Opera House was glowing. "Coombs, as the dyspeptic old general played his part to perfection, doing the different stunts called for, in a manner that would have done credit to an old timer on the stage. He made the success of the evening. His work was all that could be desired throughout the play, but the manner in which he did the difficult 'jim-jams' stunt in the third act was especially good."[33]

Coombs had participated in track and field events during his Colby career. His performance in the spring of 1906 was particularly impressive. In Class Day activities, he finished first in the 100-yard dash, the broad jump, the 220-yard dash, and the pole vault. He set the school record for the hammer throw, with a throw of 119 feet, 7 inches. In the Maine inter-collegiate meet that spring, he was the only Colby athlete to win an event, finishing first in the shot put.

The 1906 Colby baseball team proved to be the strongest of Coombs' collegiate career, finishing with a record of twelve victories against six defeats. For the first time, at Coombs' recommendation, the school hired a professional coach for the team; Coombs had been the co-coach the previous two years. On May 30, he pitched a no-hitter against Portland, recording nine strikeouts along the way. In the next game, on June 2, he pitched a one-hitter against Maine, this time fanning seven batters. An interesting note of the season was that Harvard cancelled its game against Colby, depriving Coombs of an opportunity to even the score for the past humiliations at the hands of the Harvard nine.

Notwithstanding its strong overall record, the team lost two games late in the spring against Maine rivals. The first loss was a 1–0 defeat at the hands of Bates, despite the fact that Colby had ten hits to Bates' four. The Colby team displayed poor baserunning, depriving itself of scoring opportunities.

In the last game of the schedule, Bowdoin defeated Colby by a score of 4–0. The team made three errors in one inning, leading to three runs, and Coombs threw a wild pitch allowing, the fourth run to score. He also struck out to end the sixth inning, stranding two base runners. The defeat at the hands of Bowdoin left the two teams tied for first place in the Maine inter-collegiate league.

Coombs was frustrated with his performance: his pitching had been substandard when presented with the occasion to clinch a second state championship against Bowdoin. He was given the opportunity for redemption, as a championship game against Bowdoin was scheduled in Portland for June 25, on graduation weekend. Coombs redeemed himself by throwing a five-hit shutout, contributing to his own cause with a pair of doubles. For the second time in three years, Colby was the Maine collegiate champion.

Colby College graduation picture of John Wesley Coombs, class of 1906 (courtesy Colby College Special Collections, Waterville, Maine).

The team returned to a hero's welcome in Waterville just in time for graduation weekend festivities. Two days later, on June 27, during commencement ceremonies, Coombs did his best to entertain his classmates with jokes during the procession leading to the presentation of his bachelor of science degree in chemistry. His original plan for his post-graduate life was to attain a graduate degree at the Massachusetts Institute of Technology and ultimately pursue a career as an analytic chemist. But Tom Mack had kept diligent track of Coombs' exploits on the diamond, and used his "art of Irish persuasiveness" to convince his brother Connie to come to Maine to meet the young prospect.[34] Connie Mack made his sales pitch. "Chemistry is a hard and tiresome road to independence," he told Coombs. "It will take years for you to acquire anything near the competence that a few short seasons on the diamond will promise you. Take my advice and join the Athletics, and you will never regret the move."[35]

Coombs took Mack's advice, signing a contract with the Athletics for $2,400 a season. This was an impressive sum for a prospect who had never played in the minor leagues, a rarity in those times. Coombs boarded a train for Philadelphia immediately after graduation. Chemistry would have to wait; Colby Jack Coombs was on his way to Philadelphia and the big leagues.

2

"So that's how they throw them in the big league"

Jack Coombs left for Philadelphia immediately upon completion of his graduation ceremonies at Colby. This was a major adventure for him, as he had never traveled to a major city other than Boston, and that trip had been in 1903 in the company of Fred Tenney, first baseman for the Boston Americans. (Coombs' most vivid memory of the Boston trip was that the teams had no shower facilities, and that each player was provided with only a "little tin tub, the kind used for bathing babies," for cleaning up after a game.)[1] Arriving in Philadelphia at the conclusion of the three-day trip, Coombs found himself crisscrossing the big city on various trolley lines, trying to find the one that would take him to Columbia Park, the Philadelphia Athletics' home field. With the aid of a policeman he finally arrived at the ballpark several hours late.

Rushing into the park, he met Connie Mack, the manager and part-owner of the team. Mack did not waste any time, telling the nervous rookie to get into a uniform, meet him on the field, and start throwing to Doc Powers, one of the Athletics catchers. They were followed onto the field by another player, unknown at the time to Coombs. In his book, *Connie Mack: The Grand Old Man of Baseball*, Fred Lieb described the tryout as follows.

> So Coombs started to toss a few preliminary pitches to Powers, limbering up his shoulders and body muscles, which were stiff from his long trip. The big fellow who had come late into the clubhouse joined them and also started to take a few kinks out of his arm. Pretty soon Jack started to let out and put some zip behind his throws; the big man followed suit. But the harder Coombs threw, so did the big man. Finally Jack gave it all he had, but his delivery looked like a slow freight compared to the fast express the other sent roaring into Powers' glove. Per-

spiration stood on Coombs' brow, and dreary thoughts ran through his mind. 'So that's how they throw them in the big league,' he concluded, thinking of returning to the farm and getting back to college in the fall and concentrating on chemistry, which he had thought of making his life's work.

Then Connie walked over and said rather sharply to the big fellow: 'Reuben, what are you trying to do, show that boy what a fool you are? He will see that speed often enough when he watches you pitch ball games. Needn't show off to him now.'[2]

The "big fellow" Mack called Reuben was George Edward "Rube" Waddell, the 6' 1½" left-handed pitcher of the Athletics. Waddell had helped Connie Mack's team capture the 1905 American League pennant by leading the league in wins and strikeouts, despite the fact he injured his shoulder on September 1 and missed most of the last month of the season. The A's lost the 1905 World Series to John McGraw's New York Giants in five games, all of them shutouts, with three of the Giants' victories coming behind the pitching of the incomparable Christy Mathewson. Philadelphia fans were left to wonder if the outcome might have been different if Waddell had been available to pitch against Mathewson, but it is hard to imagine the Athletics doing any better since they managed to score in only one game in the entire five-game series, and those runs came as the result of Giants' errors. Rumors implying that gamblers had convinced Waddell to be unavailable for the championship series had circulated, but Mack angrily dismissed such rumors, pointing out that Waddell had almost no concept of the value of money.

Waddell was the prototypical left-handed pitcher — tall, strong, fast, and eccentric. Having started his career by pitching five years in the National League, he joined the Athletics as a twenty-five-year-old in 1902, and immediately proceeded to lead the league in strikeouts, a feat he accomplished for six straight years. In the dead ball era where both home runs and strikeouts were much less common than they are a century later, Waddell used his blazing fastball to strike out 349 batters in 1904, 110 more than runner-up Jack Chesbro. Waddell's single-season strikeout total was not exceeded until 1965, when Sandy Koufax, another hard-throwing left-hander, whiffed 382 batters.

Waddell's personal catcher during his tenure with the A's was Ossee Schreckengost, who later in 1906 would drive in the winning run in Coombs' twenty-four-inning masterpiece. "Schreck" would not turn into the dominant player that Waddell became, but he could certainly match his battery-mate in eccentricities. Schreckengost roomed with Waddell when the team was on the road, back in the days when players not only shared the same room, but shared the same bed as well. Schreckengost found Waddell's habit of consuming crackers in bed particularly aggravating, complaining to Connie Mack, "I don't like to sleep dunked in cracker dust."[3] He insisted that a clause be put in Waddell's contract prohibiting him from eating crackers in bed, and Mack acquiesced. In response, Waddell claimed that Schreckengost's usual midnight snack, a rye bread sandwich made with limburger cheese and raw onions, was much more annoying.

Waddell was a "baffling combination of friendliness, irresponsibility, simplicity, insobriety, courage and profligacy."[4] Baseball was his occupation; enjoying himself was his mission in life. When Connie Mack told him that he needed to make a stronger effort to stay out of trouble, Waddell replied, "I can't stay around the hotel all the time. I'd get nervous."[5] His employers found it better to pay him in one dollar bills rather than tens or twenties; the money would appear to last longer, since Waddell rarely looked at the numerals on the bills before handing them over to someone else. Later in his career, while pitching for St. Louis, Waddell was paid by the club to go hunting in the woods during the off-season so he would not engage in more costly activities in the city.

Waddell gained notoriety for such curious activities as chasing after fire engines, playing marbles with youngsters outside the stadium before a game, and missing a game to be the drum major in a parade. He was reported to have saved a person from drowning and rescued two people trapped in a burning building. Once, having been jilted by a romantic interest, Waddell threatened to commit suicide by drowning himself. Chased down to the waterfront by Schreckengost, Waddell jumped off a dock into what he thought was deep water, yet turned out to be mostly muck due to low tide. He rolled around in the muck for some time before Schreckengost and several local stevedores pulled him out.

When considering the life of Rube Waddell, it is always difficult to separate fact from legend. His penchant for pleasure included the enjoyment of alcoholic beverages, not an uncommon pastime for a major league ballplayer, but one in which Waddell excelled. Whether it was his fondness for alcohol and mischief or the lingering effects of his shoulder injury from 1905, Waddell was not the same performer in 1906 as he had been in his previous four seasons, each of which he had attained at least twenty victories. Waddell finished the 1906 season with fifteen victories against seventeen defeats. Throughout the season the *Sporting News* reported that teammates were losing patience with Waddell's erratic, irresponsible behavior.[6]

Entering the month of July, the Athletics were tied for first place with the New York Highlanders and were four games ahead of the eventual pennant winners, the Chicago White Sox. John Coombs, just short of his twenty-fourth birthday, was called upon by Connie Mack to pitch his first major league game on July 5 in Philadelphia against the seventh-place Washington Nationals. Despite his anxiety about being able to pitch at the level demonstrated by Waddell, Coombs gave a credible debut performance, throwing a seven-hit complete-game shutout and beating Washington by a score of 3–0.

He struck out six and walked five, and displayed increasing poise as the game proceeded. The *Washington Post* reported, "Probably no pitcher on his first appearance was given such critical scrutiny as this young giant.... If Coombs can maintain the form he showed today, he will be a most valued addition to Manager Mack's pitching staff."[7]

A week later, on July 12, Coombs was called upon as a pinch-hitter, a role he would fill thirty-six times in his career, compiling a .306 average off the bench. The next day he lost his first game, to Detroit, by a 4–3 score, giving up five walks as the team committed four errors behind him. He started again on July 18, beating St. Louis by a score of 10–5, and getting the first two base hits of his career.

On July 25, Coombs was called into a home game against the White Sox in the first inning in relief of Waddell. Rube had hit one batter and walked three others, then managed to get ejected for arguing with the home plate umpire. Inheriting a one-run deficit and a bases-loaded situation, Coombs, "the icy hearted collegian," calmly worked out of the jam and held the White Sox to five hits the rest of the game.[8] He also struck two singles, the last of which drove in the game-winning run in the seventh inning. The *Chicago Tribune* reported, "For a youngster breaking in, Coombs works with all the skill and confidence of a seasoned veteran."[9]

The *Sporting News* took note of the strong-armed rookie throughout the summer. "There seems no longer any doubt but that Connie Mack has picked up a corking good young pitcher in Coombs. Besides being a pitcher, Coombs is a good all around player. He can cover almost any position, and is a good man at the bat, being quite the hitter and fast on the bases."[10] He was described as comparable to "Chief" Bender, the Athletics star right-handed pitcher, "and promises to soon hold his own with the best of them."[11] Mack was quoted as saying, "Aside from his pitching, Coombs promises to be a future king on the ball field. He is a great ballplayer now. Coombs would make a Cracker Jack fielder, either in the in- or outfield. He is a natural ballplayer, and he is going to be a great batter."[12]

Mack was also impressed with the rookie's assertiveness. At one point during the season, Coombs entered Mack's office to ask the manager about his intentions to use Coombs in the next day's game. When Mack asked him why he needed to know, Coombs reportedly responded, "Well, I thought I would ask you, Mr. Mack, because I intend to go to the theater tonight. Of course, if you were going to use me tomorrow, I shouldn't do anything that would put me out of condition."[13] Mack liked the rookie's nerve and marked him for success. Mack predicted, "He's got the idea that makes for success in baseball or anything else, and some day he will be one of the stars of my pitching staff."[14]

The Philadelphia club that young Coombs had joined in July 1906 was the defending American League champion, staffed with veteran ballplayers, including three pitchers who would eventually be enshrined in the Baseball Hall of Fame: Rube Waddell, Eddie Plank, and Chief Bender.

Like Rube Waddell, Eddie Plank was a dominating left-handed pitcher, although lacking most of Waddell's peculiarities. Like Coombs, Plank came to the Athletics straight from a college campus, having graduated from Gettysburg College. He joined the Athletics in 1901 and spent fourteen seasons with the team, winning more than twenty games in a season seven times during that time span. He was known as a thoughtful, methodical worker on the mound, driving batters to distraction with his constant fidgeting before getting set to deliver a pitch. Coombs considered Plank the best left-handed pitcher he had ever seen, preferring Plank's intelligent, deliberate approach to the game to the raw, explosive talent of Rube Waddell.

The third established pitcher on the Athletics staff was Charles Albert "Chief" Bender. As was common at the time, he was given his nickname because he was of Chippewa Indian descent and had attended the Carlisle Indian School before signing with the Athletics in 1903. Bender's heritage made him the subject of taunts and slurs on the ball field throughout his career, but he refused to be distracted by the verbal attacks, sarcastically referring to the vocal fans and opponents as "foreigners."[15] Bender pitched twelve years for the Athletics, leading the league in winning percentage on three occasions. Mack was selective in his use of Bender, saving him for the important games in which Bender developed a reputation for doing well. Like Coombs, Bender was known for his all-around skills on the diamond; earlier in 1906 he replaced an injured Athletics outfielder early in a game against Boston and proceeded to stroke two home runs, a very rare feat in baseball's dead ball era.

Rounding out the Athletics pitching staff that season was Jimmy Dygert, a second-year pitcher who had appeared in six games in 1905, and Andy Coakley, who had joined the team in 1902 and won eighteen games during the championship season of 1905.

In addition to their deep pitching staff, the A's had some strong hitters, led by ten-year veteran first baseman Harry Davis. Davis led the league with twelve home runs in 1906, the third of four consecutive seasons in which he paced the circuit. He also topped the league in runs batted in for the second consecutive year. Davis's slugging was supported by the hitting of right fielder "Socks" Seybold, who led the team with a .316 batting average and finished fourth in the league with five home runs. Other strong hitting performances were turned in by second baseman Danny Murphy, who batted .301; left fielder "Topsy" Hartsel, who led the league in walks and was second in runs scored; and catcher Ossee Schreckengost, who hit a solid .284. The only glaring weaknesses in the offense were on the left side of the infield, where thirty-six-year-old shortstop Monte Cross hit .200 and third baseman John Knight hit a woeful .194 before being replaced in August by Rube Oldring.

Despite this veteran talent, the Athletics were not able to cling to the first place position they occupied at the start of July. They were still in first-place by the end of July, but did poorly in August, winning nine games while losing eighteen. They were abysmal on the road, winning four while losing twelve, including five straight setbacks to the White Sox. Injuries to the pitching staff were a particular problem. Waddell was sidelined for a period of time with a bruised thumb, although he still managed to pitch in forty-three games for the season, recording eight shutouts. The *Sporting News* was particularly critical of Waddell, explicitly accusing him of excessive drinking and claiming his thumb injury was due to his extra-curricular activities. According to the paper, the team had tired of Waddell's larking about, and players were frustrated with Mack's apparent inability to bring the big left-hander under control.[16] In addition to Waddell's troubles, Bender came down with cholera during the season, and Plank missed almost a third of the season with a variety of ailments.

While the Philadelphia Athletics were struggling, the Chicago White Sox were nearly unbeatable in August, winning twenty-one games while losing only four. During the month they vaulted from fourth place to first in the league, and they held off a serious challenge in September by the New York Highlanders to win the American League pennant. The "Hitless Wonders" had the lowest batting average and slugging average in the league, but they were surprisingly good at manufacturing runs out of their limited opportunities and finished the season scoring more runs than the stronger-hitting Athletics. They were particularly strong on pitching and defense, giving up fewer runs than any other team in the league.

On August 27, Coombs experienced just how tough the White Sox could be. For the first time in his career, he started a game against Ed Walsh, Chicago's ace right-handed pitcher. It was the first of several classic duels between the two "iron man" pitchers. An unrelenting rain had left Philadelphia's Columbia Park in a "truly sad and deplorable plight."[17] There was standing water in the outfield, but the game proceeded nonetheless. Coombs pitched four-hit ball, with two of those hits coming together in the fourth inning, leading to Chicago's sole run. While Coombs' pitching was strong, Walsh was masterful, allowing only one hit and no runs, and striking out nine in only six innings, at which point the umpires mercifully called the game off.

Coombs' twenty-four-inning performance on September 1 looked as if it would portend a change of luck for the Athletics for the month of September, but the team went to New York two days later and lost a doubleheader to the Highlanders. (The Highlanders, who garnered their name by playing at Hilltop Park on the site of what is today Columbia Presbyterian Hospital, would not be officially known as the Yankees until the 1912 season.) This marked the fourth consecutive doubleheader played by the Highlanders and their fourth consecutive sweep. The next day Boston visited New York and was swept in another doubleheader, giving the Highlanders ten consecutive victories in a five-day period and temporary possession of first place in the American League.

The sweep at the hands of New York took the wind out of the Athletics' sails, and the team went on to complete the remainder of the season with a mark of twelve wins and fourteen defeats, leaving them in fourth place, twelve games behind the pennant-winning White Sox. Coombs, however, showed he still had considerable drive. Despite being so weakened from his epic battle against Boston on September 1 that his only form of nourishment for two days was a cup of tea, he took his regular pitching turn against the Washington Nationals just four days later and pitched a complete game, holding them to five singles and beating them by a score of 3–1. Five days later he was again on the mound against Washington, and again beat the Nationals in a complete game, this time limiting his opponents to four hits and winning by a score of 2–1. In a ten-day time span, he had pitched forty-two innings, giving up only three runs on twenty-four hits, while striking out twenty-six batters. A century later, forty-two innings pitched would be considered a good month's worth of work for a pitcher, but Coombs went on to appear in six more games for the Athletics before the end of September.

The month of September also witnessed the arrival of another Athletics rookie, one who would contribute on a grand scale to the team for years to come and ultimately earn a place in the Baseball Hall of Fame. Eddie Collins was at that time getting ready to return to Columbia University for his senior year. He had spent the summer playing in the independent Northern League, the same league that Coombs had pitched in the previous summer. Collins had also come to the attention of Tom Mack, Connie Mack's brother. Connie wanted to see Collins play firsthand, and since the Athletics were no longer in the running for the American League pennant, convinced Collins to play a few games for the Athletics under the assumed name of Eddie Sullivan. Collins' debut was on September 17, when he collected one hit in four trips to the plate against Ed Walsh of the White Sox. Collins played in six games towards the end of the season; his covert identity was subsequently discovered by officials at Columbia, and he was declared ineligible for play during the school's 1907 spring season.

Coombs' final start of the season was on October 2, against Jack Chesbro of the New York Highlanders. Two seasons earlier, Chesbro had won forty-one games for the Highlanders as they battled the Boston Americans for the pennant right down to the last day of the season. In the first game of the pennant-deciding doubleheader, Chesbro uncorked a wild pitch in the ninth inning with a base runner on third to allow the winning run to score, clinching the 1904 pennant for Boston. This disappointing finish could not diminish one of the most remarkable seasons ever turned in a by a major league pitcher. In addition to his forty-one wins, Chesbro pitched forty-eight complete games, including thirty straight to start the season, leading to a staggering total of 454 innings pitched for the campaign.

Chesbro was never again as dominating a pitcher, although he did come into the October 2 game against the Athletics having won twenty-three games for the Highlanders in the 1906 campaign. Despite the fact that Mack fielded a team with a number of substitutes, including Chief Bender in center field, the Athletics beat the Highlanders by a score of 4–3. Coombs held the Highlanders to six hits, all singles.

This was Coombs' tenth and final victory of the season. In eighty-one games as a member of the Athletics, just over half of the season, Coombs had appeared in twenty-six games, winning ten and losing ten, and made a significant contribution to the veteran pitching staff. Along the way he had pitched the longest complete-game victory in the history of the game, a record he will likely hold forever. In a league that batted only .248 for the year, Coombs posted a creditable .239 batting average. The nervous rookie, who during his first warm-ups had questioned his ability to pitch in the big leagues, had shown beyond a doubt that he belonged.

Connie Mack had high hopes for his team in the spring of 1907. His optimism was not shared by the press, as the roster had changed little from the 1906 team that had finished a disappointing fourth in the league. The only notable change was the addition of shortstop Simon Nicholls, who was expected to be a substantial hitting upgrade over Monte Cross. The *Washington Post* picked the Athletics to finish in the second division, citing the team for a lack of hitting strength and weak left side of the infield. The team's only noted strength was its pitching staff, which was considered "excellent when going right ... Mack has several young flingers who may develop into cracks."[18] Jack Coombs, as he was now usually referred to in the press, was looking forward to his first full season in the major leagues, hoping to build on the success of his rookie year. His role was that of the fourth starter on the team, behind the veteran trio of Waddell, Plank and Bender.

The Philadelphia Athletics were scheduled to open their season on April 11 at home against Boston. The Boston team was still in shock over the suicide of manager Chick Stahl during spring training, and Cy Young had been named the temporary manager of the team. As was befitting a seasoned veteran with seventeen years of major league pitching experience, manager Young selected pitcher Young to be his Opening Day starter. Mack had indicated that he would open the season with Eddie Plank unless the weather was going to be wet. The weather was worse than wet; it was wet and cold, with temperatures only in the low 40s.

(In New York, 100 miles to the north of Philadelphia, the Giants' home opener was delayed as the grounds crew cleared six inches of snow from the playing field, piling it in foul ground. They did not have the resources to clear the snow from the stands, and the Giant fans, frustrated with the weather and the home team's poor performance against the Philadelphia Phillies, disrupted the game with a fusillade of snowballs, ultimately forcing the forfeiture of the game.)

Mack decided not to risk the thirty-one-year-old Plank against Boston in such weather, and gave the ball to the younger, stronger Coombs. The maneuver seemed to be another brilliant move on the part of the "Tall Tactician," as Coombs held the Americans to one run through eight innings, carrying a 3–1 lead into the ninth. But in the ninth, Boston scored three runs, two of them on one of the six errors committed by the Athletics that day. Cy Young had removed himself from the game for a pinch-hitter in the top of the ninth, and Jesse Tannehill was brought in to relieve Young. Manager Young had neglected to give Tannehill much notice about his impending pitching duties, and he struggled to warm up in the cold weather. The Athletics took advantage of Tannehill's condition and one of Boston's three errors to tie the score in the bottom of the ninth. Coombs and Tannehill traded zeroes for the next four innings, but in the top of the fourteenth, Coombs finally tired and was batted soundly by Boston, giving up four runs, including a two-run home run to outfielder Buck Freeman. The Athletics went quietly in their half of the inning, giving Boston an 8–4 victory. Under the scoring rules of the day, Young was given the victory for Boston, as Tannehill was deemed to have been ineffective in his relief performance. Coombs took the loss. It is hard to comprehend Mack's thought process, leaving a pitcher in for fourteen innings on Opening Day in cold, damp weather. Perhaps he thought the strapping Coombs on any given day was capable of going another twenty-four innings against Boston, as he had done in beautiful weather the previous September. It would not be the last time Mack's pitching decisions could be called into question that season.

Coombs had two more opportunities to go head-to-head with Young during the 1907 season, and both times he proved victorious. On April 24, in another wet, miserable day with gale-force winds, Coombs pitched a clever

Eleven of the Athletics pose for an informal team picture. Coombs is in the back row, second from the right. Standing next to Coombs at the end of the row is fellow pitcher Chief Bender. Bender went on to win 212 games in his major league career (courtesy Wentworth Family Personal Collection).

game and bested Young by a score of 6–1, helped by a three-run home run off the bat of Harry Davis, who once more led the league in home runs, this time with a grand total of eight. On May 29, Coombs shut out Boston by a score of 4–0, limiting Boston to five hits while striking out seven batters.

At this point in the season, the Athletics were fulfilling the *Washington Post*'s prognostication, faltering in fifth place with a 17–17 record, seven games behind the Chicago White Sox, who were making a bid for a second consecutive pennant. Coombs' record at this juncture was 3–4, and his performance had been inconsistent. In addition to his two strong wins against Cy Young and Boston, he had thrown a two-hitter against Washington, a game for which the American League had neglected to provide any umpires, forcing each team to designate a player as a substitute umpire. The *Washington Post* gave Coombs high praise for his poise on the pitching mound. "The beauty with Coombs' pitching is that he never dishes anything up to the batsmen that he can punish very much. The ball is always over the in or out corner, or just high or low enough to be within the strike territory. To watch him work one would not suspect that this is only his second season in fast company. He works like an old-timer, and, incidentally, has a lot of speed and excellent curves."[19] There were other games, however, where his control was not as sharp as necessary, and hitters were able to handle his pitches.

Coombs appeared to be rounding into form in the middle of June as the Athletics started playing better ball. On June 17, Coombs pitched against Addie Joss, the star pitcher of the second-place Cleveland Naps, who were at the time five games ahead of the fourth-place Athletics. The Naps, later known as the Indians, were named after their premier player, Napoleon Lajoie. The 1907 season was the pinnacle year of Joss' brief career. He won twenty-seven games for Cleveland while losing only eleven. He went on to win another twenty-four games in 1908, including a perfect game at the close of the season. At what should have been the height of his career, he contracted tubercular meningitis in 1910, and subsequently died from the consequences of the infection at the age of thirty-one.

While Joss was at the peak of his form in 1907, Coombs out-pitched him in this game, winning by a score of 4–1. Although he gave up eight hits and five walks, Coombs demonstrated he could "pitch in a pinch," striking out eight batters and stranding eleven Cleveland runners. Five days later, Coombs took the mound against Washington, and this time pitched a masterful shutout. He "was in the finest fettle imaginable," and again showed his greatest skills when runners were on base.[20] He contributed to his own cause by stroking his first major league home run, a long drive to right field that brought exuberant applause from the hometown crowd. Three days later, he was brought in to relieve Waddell in the eighth inning of a close game against Washington, pitching two shutout innings and saving the 3–1 victory for the Athletics.

At this point things were looking good for Coombs and the Athletics, who had climbed into third place, a mere three games behind the league-leading White Sox. That optimism began to unravel on June 27, as Coombs suffered an arm injury in the third inning of a game against Boston, described in varying degrees as a strain, a sprain, or a rupture. The pain was so severe that he was unable to complete pitching to the batter. A reliever was brought in and promptly gave up the hit that drove in the only run of the game, giving Boston a 1–0 victory. The *Sporting News* commented in dire terms on the Athletics' prospects given Coombs' injury.

> The loss of these two games ... are, however, nothing as compared with the loss of that great pitcher, Jack Coombs. Whether Jack is only temporarily hurt remains to be seen, but the Athletics will be minus his services for at least several weeks and that is itself a great loss, as his absence handicaps Mack very much. But should

it turn out that Coombs is permanently disabled what a great loss that would mean to the Athletics. Coombs promised to rate as the greatest pitcher living before another year and no amount of money could have purchased his release from Connie Mack.[21]

Coombs was out of action for nearly seven weeks, during which the Athletics actually moved up in the standings, from third place to first. It is not that Coombs' services were not missed, but Chicago and Cleveland had cooled off a bit, and the Athletics played consistently strong ball.

Lurking right behind the Athletics in the standings in mid–August were the Detroit Tigers, an aggressive, hard-hitting club under the direction of first-year manager Hughie Jennings. Jennings had played shortstop for the Baltimore Orioles in the 1890s, as rowdy an aggregation of ballplayers as ever appeared on a baseball diamond. Led by Ned Hanlon, the Orioles lineup included future Hall of Fame players Willie Keeler, Wilbert Robinson, and John McGraw. Compared to the rest of the Orioles, Jennings was a sweetheart of a guy. But he developed a tougher, more competitive posture while with the Orioles, a team that took no prisoners on a baseball field. That competitiveness is what attracted Jennings to Tigers owner Frank Navin, who had to overcome the objections of American League president Ban Johnson to hire Jennings for the Tigers. Johnson had tried to bring a cleaner, more professional approach to American League baseball, in contrast to the belligerent style practiced in the National League. This aggressive brand of baseball was epitomized by the old Orioles and espoused by John McGraw, then manager of the New York Giants. McGraw had briefly managed in the American League, and during his tenure had so many confrontations with Ban Johnson that the two became bitter enemies. McGraw eagerly jumped back to the National League to take the manager's position with the Giants, and Johnson made his best efforts to make sure that the hoodlum friends of John McGraw stayed out of the American League. Navin persuaded Johnson that Jennings was the only man capable of leading the Tigers to victory, and Johnson reluctantly agreed to the hire, promising to keep Jennings on a short rope.

Jennings did his best to determine just how much Ban Johnson would tolerate. He managed his team from the third base coaching box, and was a constant source of noise and motion while on the field. He would reach down, grab a handful of grass to chew on, raise his foot, clench his fists, and scream "Ee-yah!" at the top of his lungs. Fans around the league found his histrionics very entertaining, but he was an annoyance and distraction to his opponents. In May of 1907 he was accused of inciting a riot over an umpire's decision in Detroit during a game against the Athletics. In July he was briefly suspended for arguing too vociferously with an umpire, a practice that Ban Johnson would not tolerate. He was threatened with suspension again in

August, this time for persisting in the use of a tin whistle while operating in the coach's box.

While Jennings made his best efforts to taunt and distract the opposition, he had the undivided attention of the Tiger ballplayers, taking a team that had finished sixth in 1906 and turning it into a pennant-winner for each of the next three seasons. The Tigers were a strong hitting team, led by Ty Cobb, who in his third major league season hit .350 and won the first of nine consecutive batting titles. Cobb also led the league in runs batted in and stolen bases. Cobb's hitting was complemented by that of Sam Crawford, who led the league in runs scored, and finished second to Cobb in the batting race. As a team, the Tigers led the league in hitting and runs scored, plating more than one hundred more runs than the Athletics tallied.

Coombs' first pitching appearance since his injury in June against Boston occurred in a relief effort versus the Tigers on August 14. He started a game two days later and was pulled from the game after only three ineffective innings. His arm was just not right, and he suffered through a series of starts and relief appearances with little assertiveness to his pitching. In eight appearances between August 14 and September 17, he recorded only one victory against two defeats. After the last defeat at the hands of the Highlanders, Connie Mack decided to shut Coombs down for the rest of the season. At this point, the Athletics were still clinging to a one-game lead over the tenacious Tigers. The Tigers came into Philadelphia for a scheduled three-game set in late September, with the Tigers then leading by half a game. The Tigers beat Eddie Plank in the first game of the series, and, following a rainout, the next two games were scheduled as a doubleheader.

In the first game of the doubleheader, which attracted a huge overflow crowd, Philadelphia jumped off to a three-run lead in the first inning. Jimmy Dygert was pitching for Philadelphia, and he found himself in trouble in the second inning. Detroit had already scored one run, and the bases were filled with only one out when Connie Mack decided that Dygert seemed nervous and a pitching change was in order. Rube Waddell, who had been his usual incorrigible self throughout the summer, was brought in to relieve Dygert. And in typical Waddell fashion, he struck out the first two batters he faced to end the Tigers' threat. The Athletics built their lead to 7–1 by the end of the sixth inning, when Waddell and the Athletics began to unravel. Waddell, backed by some shoddy defense, gave up four runs in the seventh and another run in the eighth. With the Athletics having scored once more, they went into the ninth inning with a two-run lead. While Mack had been quick to remove the young Dygert early in the game, he stuck with Waddell for too long. In the ninth inning, Waddell hung a curveball to Ty Cobb, who promptly deposited the ball in the right field seats to tie the game. It was

Cobb's fifth home run of the season, tying him for second in the league behind Harry Davis, whose total of eight again led the league. Mack was so surprised by Cobb's clutch hit that "he slid off the bench and sprawled out among the bats which were strewn along the ground."[22] He recovered to frantically wave Plank into the game in relief of Waddell. Mack had been counting on Plank to start the second game of the doubleheader, but by this time the damage was done. As it turned out, there would be no second game that day.

The game continued for seventeen innings, ending in a tie on account of darkness. The Athletics thought they had the game won in the fourteenth inning, when Harry Davis hit a long fly ball into the overflow crowd that was ringing the outfield. The Tigers claimed that a Philadelphia policeman, who was at the perimeter of the crowd to keep order, interfered with Sam Crawford's attempt to catch the ball. Silk O'Loughlin, the home plate umpire, at first ignored the protests of the Detroit players, saying that he had seen no interference. But then he conferred with base umpire Tommy Connolly, a common practice a century later, but an unusual practice at that time. Connolly was of the opinion that there had been interference, and O'Loughlin proceeded to call Davis out. The usually mild-mannered Mack became wild with anger, one of the few times in his career that he verbally abused an umpired. The ballpark was in an uproar, and a fight broke out between two players. Once order was restored, the Athletics next batter, Danny Murphy, stroked a long single that would have scored Davis with the game-winning run if interference had not been called. Instead, the game ended in a tie, and Detroit left town clinging to a 1½ game lead, a margin they maintained at the end of the season.

Mack never forgave Silk O'Loughlin for reversing his call, feeling that the decision cost his team the pennant in 1907. He also had finally tired of Waddell, who despite his incredible talent was simply too unreliable to be counted on in a big game. Following the season, Waddell further alienated himself with his teammates on a barnstorming tour, claiming that he had been denied his fair share of the tour revenues while conveniently ignoring his share of the tour expenses. Mack shipped Waddell off to the St. Louis Browns following the end of the season. Waddell went on to win thirty-three games while losing twenty-nine as a member of the Browns over the next three years, finally retiring from baseball in 1910 at the age of thirty-three. Four years later he would die from tuberculosis.

3

A Second Ty Cobb

A winter of hard work back home in Maine and no strain on his pitching arm left Jack Coombs ready and eager for the 1908 season. Coming off their surprisingly strong showing in 1907, the A's were expected to contend for the American League pennant. The pitching staff of Bender, Coombs, Dygert and Plank was considered to be one of the best in the league, and the team's offense, while not as explosive as that of the Tigers, was still deemed capable of scoring enough runs to amply support the fine pitching staff.

Mack again chose New Orleans as the spring training site for his team, a seemingly innocuous choice that wound up having a material impact on the fortunes of Coombs and the team for the season. While Coombs quickly demonstrated in his early spring training pitching appearances that his arm was back in good condition, things unraveled for the team in the middle of March. The warm and damp New Orleans weather led to illnesses for Mack and a number of his players, particularly center fielder Rube Oldring, who was described as having "malarial symptoms."[1] The exact nature of Oldring's illness was not disclosed, but he was so ill as to be sent home from spring training, with little expectation of being available for the season's start. In addition to the loss of Oldring, the Athletics lost the services of right fielder Socks Seybold, who tore ligaments in his leg as a result of sliding into home plate during a pre-season game in New Orleans. Both Seybold and Oldring had been steady contributors to the team's success. Seybold, a seven-year veteran with the Athletics, had a career batting average near .300, and he hit with reasonable power for the times, having led the league in home runs in 1902 with a total of 16. Oldring was entering his third season with the team, having hit a steady .286 in 1907, his first season as a regular outfielder.

Connie Mack had previously released Bris Lord, an experienced fourth outfielder, and now was missing two-thirds of his starting outfield trio, with no experienced substitutes available. Not wanting to start the season with two inexperienced players in the outfield, Mack initially thought of moving second baseman Danny Murphy out to right field, shifting shortstop Simon Nicholls to second, and inserting Eddie Collins, the twenty-year-old out of Columbia University, at Nicholls' position on the left side of the infield. Mack was reluctant to make the switch, questioning Murphy's defensive capabilities for the outfield, and doubting whether the inexperienced Collins would be able to adequately coordinate with Nicholls around the keystone sack. Instead, he decided to move Jack Coombs to right field, given Coombs' hitting, speed and overall athleticism. In Mack's opinion, he was "confident that Coombs has the making of a first-class outfielder."[2] Rube Vickers, a Canadian-born right-handed pitcher who to that point had a career record of two victories against six defeats for three different clubs in three seasons, was slated to take Coombs' spot in the starting rotation.

Horace Fogel, the Philadelphia beat writer covering both the Athletics and the Philadelphia Phillies for the *Sporting News*, led the parade in support of Mack's decision to put Coombs in right field. In the March 26 issue, Fogel wrote, "Manager Mack probably made a wise move when he decided to leave his infield intact and send Jack Coombs to right field in place of Seybold until the latter gets back in the game. Coombs is a corking good ballplayer. He can hit and run and plays well in the outfield."[3] A week later, having observed more of Coombs' play in the outfield, Fogel reported that, "Mack has half made up his mind to make a fielder of Jack, because of his natural ability as a ballplayer."[4] By the end of April, Fogel reported, "The way Coombs is going, and the promise he holds out to develop into a second Cobb, it is unlikely that Mack will take him away from the outfield, so that the fight for a regular place in the outfield will most likely narrow down between Seybold and Oldring."[5] In a little over six weeks, Coombs had grown from being a talented but temporary stand-in for a decimated outfield corps to being considered a rival to Ty Cobb, who in the previous season had won the first of his twelve batting championships and six stolen base crowns. Interestingly, Mack chose to insert Coombs into the daily lineup over Eddie Collins, who would, like Cobb, develop into one of the greatest hitters in the history of the game with a batting average of .333 over a twenty-five-year career with the Athletics and White Sox.

Connie Mack doubtlessly considered Jack Coombs one of his most talented and versatile ballplayers. And he may have indeed considered a permanent switch to the outfield for Coombs, as Coombs did not pitch in a single game until the middle of June. Also, Coombs' demonstrated poise on the diamond had to have been an important consideration in Mack's decision to try

Coombs in the outfield rather than inserting Collins in the lineup and restructuring his infield defensive arrangement. But to consider Coombs the future equal of the young Ty Cobb seemed to be a bit of hyperbole on the part of Horace Fogel.

Prior to becoming a sportswriter, Horace Fogel had briefly managed the New York Giants for forty-four games in 1902 and experimented using future Hall of Fame pitcher Christy Mathewson as a first baseman. As a sportswriter, Horace Fogel was never shy about overstating his opinions. When either Philadelphia team was playing well, he jumped on the bandwagon, predicting the eventual submission of all rivals. And when either team was not playing well, he was quick to identify the players he saw as the culprits; he had been very critical of Rube Waddell's drinking and revelry during the 1906 and 1907 seasons. Fogel's criticism of Waddell was particularly ironic, as fellow sportswriters described Fogel as having "a chronic dry whistle."[6]

Following the 1909 season, Fogel led a group of investors who purchased the Philadelphia Phillies franchise. Believing that Phillies was "too trite" a name for a team, Fogel proposed calling the team the "Live Wires," a name which fortunately never caught on with the fans nor the press.[7]

Overstatement of his views wound up being Fogel's final undoing. Following the 1912 season, he was expelled from the National League by his fellow owners for having publicly accused, with seemingly no basis, the league management, umpires and rival managers of bias and corruption.

If Coombs had any choice in the matter, he would have stayed on the pitching mound. He liked being at center stage for every play as a pitcher, rather than tucked away in right field where the ball only occasionally came his way. However, only Connie Mack had a vote on the subject, and his vote had Coombs starting in right field and batting sixth for the Athletics on Opening Day, a game won by the New York Highlanders by a score of 1–0 in front of an overflow crowd of more than 20,000 people. The game went twelve innings, and Coombs had one single plus a stolen base in five at-bats. He also made six putouts in right field, handling all chances flawlessly. The meager five-hit output of the Athletics batters in the game was an indicator of the offensive futility they exhibited for the entire season. The team batting average for 1908 was thirty-two points lower than the previous season, and total runs scored by the club dropped by nearly 100, the team's worst hitting performance since being founded in 1901. The weak hitting led to a mediocre position in the standings, a sixth-place finish which to that time was the worst result for the franchise in American League competition.

Coombs did his best to rally the team's offense, as was illustrated in the team's first victory of the season, a 4–2 win over Boston. He collected a double and a triple, driving in a run and scoring twice. In a season that ultimately was divided between the outfield and the pitcher's mound, Coombs proved to be one of the Athletics' leading hitters with a .255 batting average and a .355 slugging percentage. While this was nowhere near the level of Ty Cobb, who again led the league with a .320 batting average and .475 slugging percentage, Coombs' performance was well above the league's .239 batting average and .303 slugging percentage. The only teammates who performed better at the plate for the season were Danny Murphy and Eddie Collins. By late May, Mack made a variation on the move he had rejected in spring training, shifting Murphy to the outfield and replacing him with Collins at second base. Both players' performance in 1908 refuted Mack's early hesitation as to their capabilities, and both became mainstays at their new positions for years to come.

Rube Oldring returned to the lineup in mid-May and Socks Seybold returned in early June. The Athletics had finished May in fourth place, but they were a mere one game behind the pace-setting New York Highlanders. When Seybold returned to the lineup, the Athletics proceeded to go into a seven-game losing streak, including three consecutive shutouts. As suddenly as Mack had decided in spring training that Coombs was going to the outfield, he decided he would return the tall right-hander to the pitching corps. While hitting proved to be the Athletics' major weakness throughout the season, the pitching staff was suffering from a variety of ailments in June, leaving Mack in need of additional arms. Plank and Bender were particularly limited throughout the season, with both pitching significantly fewer innings than in 1907, and ultimately posting losing records.

Coombs returned to the mound in a relief appearance on June 11, not having pitched in a major league game since the previous September 17. He started his first game on June 22, winning against Cleveland. By then the Athletics' June swoon had already dropped them to fifth place, ten games behind the league-leading Chicago White Sox. Over the course of the next 2½ months, Mack used Coombs in both starting and relieving roles. Coombs posted a record of two victories against a single defeat going into an August 29 game against the Detroit Tigers. While the Athletics were still floundering in fifth place, the Tigers had surged to the top of the league on the basis of a torrid performance in July, winning twenty-three of twenty-nine games played. For the first time since he was injured against Boston fourteen months earlier, Jack Coombs was about to demonstrate once more that he had the talent to be among the elite pitchers in the game.

From August 29 to September 14, Coombs started six games for the Athletics, winning five. Four of the victories were shutouts — two against the Senators, one against the Tigers, and one against the Highlanders. In addition to his outstanding pitching, Coombs went on a hitting spree to rival that of Ty Cobb, batting .400 with a triple and a home run in six starts and two pinch-hitting appearances. The pinch-hitting appearances both came against the young Walter Johnson, with Coombs stroking a single against "The Big Train" on both occasions. While the Athletics won five of the six games started by Coombs during this period, they won only five of the other fourteen games played. At this point, Mack wrote off the season and decided to experiment with his lineup in anticipation of the 1909 campaign. Even though by mid–September Coombs' pitching record was an excellent 7–1, on the basis of Coombs' recent hot hitting streak, Mack inserted

Coombs (left) and teammate Eddie Plank relax from the rigors of the major league schedule by dressing up in cowboy gear. Plank won 326 games during his eighteen years in the major leagues (courtesy Wentworth Family Personal Collection).

him back in the lineup as the starting centerfielder and cleanup hitter. That shift lasted only a week, and Coombs was once more returned to the starting rotation. Mack rested many of his starters, and with a makeshift lineup behind him, Coombs wound up losing four of his last five starts. Despite this, Coombs finished 1908 as the only Athletics starting pitcher to record a winning record, going 7–5 in eighteen starting assignments and eight relief appearances.

While Mack's lineup experimentation may have hurt Coombs' pitching record in 1908, Mack was also laying the groundwork for the first Athletics dynasty. Eddie Collins finally had the chance to play regularly in 1908. Two rookies were also given some playing time in 1908: Jack Barry debuted on July 13 and Frank Baker debuted on September 21. Collins, Barry and Baker eventually became the second baseman, shortstop, and third baseman, respectively, on the A's teams that won four of five American league pennants from 1910 through 1914. Early in 1909, first baseman Stuffy McInnis made his debut with the Athletics, giving Mack his "$100,000 infield," and giving the Athletics' pitching staff strong defensive backing.

On October 3, Coombs started the second game of a doubleheader against the Boston Red Sox. It was the final Athletics home game of the season. Epitomizing its offensive futility during the 1908 campaign, the team managed only one hit, a single by Coombs in the third inning. It turned out to be the last Athletics base hit in Columbia Park.

Ben Shibe and Connie Mack, co-owners of the Athletics, had for some time longed for a better venue for their baseball team to exhibit its talents to paying customers. Columbia Park had been built for a mere $7,500 to accommodate the Athletics in their inaugural season of 1901. When it first opened, the ballpark had a capacity of 9,500 people, later enlarged to 13,600. Columbia Park was located in an area known as "Brewerytown," and the ballpark smelled heavily of "hops, yeast and beer."[8] Consistent with its minimal construction cost, Columbia Park was a single-deck wooden structure, with a covered grandstand extending from first base to third base. There were no dugouts for the teams; the players sat on exposed benches along each foul line.

The Athletics owners had already purchased a site for a new ballpark prior to the 1908 season, and construction of what was originally known as Shibe Park began in April of 1908. Situated at Lehigh Avenue, between North 20th and North 21st streets, the new ballpark was located in a neighborhood characterized by its wet and marshy ground and known as "Swampoodle." Shibe Park was the first concrete and steel ballpark to be built for a major league franchise, offering the dual advantages of greater capacity and reduced fire hazard in comparison to the wooden structures used to house other major league teams. Its opening capacity was 20,000, and in later years various additions would increase that capacity to more than 33,000. Compared to spartan Columbia Park, Shibe Park was a palace. Its exterior was built in a French Renaissance style, with its most notable feature being a circular dome on the third story over the main entrance, which was used to house Connie Mack's office. Construction costs of the ballpark were in the vicinity of $300,000, and the total investment, including the purchase of the land, was believed to have been in excess of $500,000.

The park opened to wonderful weather on April 12, 1909. The crowd started gathering hours before the gates opened, and 30,162 people paid their way through the turnstiles (25 cents for bleachers, 50 cents for grandstands) to see the structure that was described as "commodious and comfortable."[9] It was estimated that another 5,000 guests, both invited dignitaries and uninvited gatecrashers, found their way inside the facility. The overflow crowd was put behind ropes in the very spacious outfield. The partisan assembly was not disappointed, as the Athletics, behind the solid pitching of Eddie Plank, soundly trounced Boston by an 8–1 score.

The opening of Shibe Park ushered in the first golden era of baseball park construction. Forbes Field in Pittsburgh would open later in 1909, followed by ten more new facilities in both leagues from 1910 through 1915. The only ballparks still in operation from this era are Fenway Park in Boston (opened in 1912) and Wrigley Field in Chicago (opened in 1914).

While the opening of Shibe Park represented a new beginning for baseball, it was also a tragic career-ending day for one of the Athletics' most popular players. Mike "Doc" Powers had been a catcher with the Athletics since the team's founding in 1901, the exception being a brief eleven-game stint with the Highlanders in 1905. Powers had attended both Holy Cross and Notre Dame, and earned his nickname through the attainment of a degree in medicine. Powers was described as a "model man, well liked, educated, self-made, clean, honorable and of high ideals."[10] Never a strong hitter, Powers had sustained his major league career through fine defensive work and his expert handling of pitchers, particularly Eddie Plank. Powers had also been the catcher who handled Jack Coombs' first warm-ups for Connie Mack and had expertly caught every inning of Coombs' twenty-four inning victory over Boston in 1906, throwing out five potential basestealers during the course of the game.

As usual, Powers was Plank's catcher in the Shibe Park inaugural. There are inconsistent accounts as to what happened during the game, with some claiming Powers ran into a wall chasing a foul ball, while others stating he became ill from the effects of too many cheese sandwiches. In either event, Powers experienced severe abdominal pains during the seventh inning of the game, but carried on to see Plank through to the conclusion of his victory. After the game, however, Powers collapsed in the clubhouse and was rushed to the hospital, where he was initially diagnosed as having acute gastritis. His condition deteriorated, and over the course of the next several days, three operations were performed on the catcher, with doctors finding that his intestine had folded in on itself, leading to gangrene and ultimately to peritonitis. Despite all the medical attention he received, the thirty-eight-year-old Powers died on April 26, two weeks after the opening game at Shibe Park.[11]

The Athletics and their fans were in shock. Newspapers estimated that in excess of 10,000 people came to Powers' wake, and thousands more lined the streets of his funeral procession. At the funeral, his pallbearers were Eddie Plank, Harry Davis, Simon Nicholls, Danny Murphy, Jack Coombs and Ira Thomas. Ira Thomas also was a catcher whom Connie Mack had traded for during the previous winter. The tragic death of Mike Powers led to more playing time for Thomas, who would develop a deep friendship with Coombs that lasted long beyond their baseball playing days.

The Athletics were obviously distracted by the illness and death of Mike Powers, and they started off slowly in April, splitting their first ten games and quickly falling 3½ games behind the Tigers. That would be the margin of difference between the two clubs at the end of the season.

Jack Coombs was a mixed contributor to the Athletics in 1909. He looked strong on the mound in pre-season, and the experiment as the "next Ty Cobb" seemed finally at an end. In a pre-season five-game exhibition series against the Philadelphia Phillies, the Athletics won only one game. The victory was accomplished through the pitching and hitting of Coombs. He held the Phillies to only one run, and drove in both Athletics runs in a 2–1 victory. In the early part of the season, it looked as though he had finally regained mastery of his pitching form, as his first three victories were shutouts. One of the shutouts was by a score of 1–0 against Walter Johnson, one of a record twenty-six games that Johnson lost by that score during his career. Coombs was credited for showing significant "grit and backbone," as nine Washington runners were left stranded on the bases.[12] Another shutout came against Ed Walsh, again by a 1–0 score, with this contest going thirteen innings before being decided. But it seemed that for every gem thrown against an opponent's ace pitcher, there were mediocre games where Coombs' pitching was erratic. He finished the year with a record of 12–11 and pitched 206 innings, the most he had thrown in his career to that point.

One significant pitching accomplishment did not show up in Coombs' records for 1909. During the season he started to experiment with a new pitch, which in today's parlance would probably be called a sinkerball. As Connie Mack would later describe it, the pitch "didn't break much" but Coombs mastered the offering "so that he could get it over the plate and break it until it almost reached the ground when the catcher caught it."[13] The sinker, or "drop," would become an important part of Coombs' pitching arsenal in the years to come.

The most noteworthy story in the Athletics season was their ongoing rivalry with the Detroit Tigers, who won their third consecutive American League pennant. The focal point of the rivalry, particularly in 1909, was Ty Cobb, who garnered the Triple Crown by leading the league with a .377 batting average, nine home runs, and 116 runs batted in. Al Stump, Cobb's biographer, wrote, "In numerous ways, Cobb's 1909 season was the most brilliant yet reprehensible any player ever lived through. In that span of time Cobb fixed his reputation both as a very great performer and a deeply flawed human being."[14]

Cobb demonstrated both his superior baseball skills and combative personality in a three-game series in Detroit against the Athletics during late August. Coming off a streak where they had won nine of ten games played, the Athletics had finally overtaken the Tigers and were sitting in first place with a one-game lead. In the first game of the series, Cobb took control of the basepaths in such a decisive way that the pennant race was all but determined at that point. Early in the game, Cobb walked and immediately stole second base. He then took off on an attempted steal of third base. The throw from Athletics catcher Paddy Livingston was accurate but low, leaving third baseman Frank Baker with his arm outstretched to tag the incoming Cobb. Cobb spiked Baker in the arm near the elbow, drawing blood and, more importantly, causing Baker to drop the ball. Cobb went on to score, and the Tigers went on to overcome a four-run deficit to win the game by a score of 7–6.

Baker claimed that Cobb's actions were deliberate, and that if Cobb's spikes had penetrated "just one-eighth of an inch deeper" Baker's career would have been ended.[15] Baker also accused Cobb of challenging Baker to a fight while Baker was on the ground clutching at his injured arm. Cobb protested his innocence, claiming he "never spiked a man deliberately."[16] The usually soft-spoken Connie Mack took his grievance to the press, stating, "Cobb is the greatest ball player in the world, but he is also one of the dirtiest."[17] Mack went on to say, "I am not well enough acquainted with the young man to understand why he should do these things. It looks to me as though he gets up with a grouch and decides to take it out on the players of the opposite team."[18] Detroit manager Hughie Jennings responded to Mack as aggressively as Cobb ran the bases. "Connie wouldn't have said that if he had not been bitterly disappointed by the result of the games which Detroit won by superior gameness," opined Jennings. "Connie's worst trouble is found in the fact that he himself knows his team is still sheltering a bunch of yellow dogs who laid down in the world's series of 1905 and later on to us when it came to a pinch in the pennant race of 1907."[19]

Cobb's aggressiveness had taken the Athletics off their game. Cobb had six hits in eleven at-bats in the series and scored four times. The Tigers swept the three-game series, returning to first place to stay. The Athletics made one more run at Detroit in a September series at home in Philadelphia. With the Baker spiking incident still fresh in the minds of Philadelphia fans, Cobb received numerous death threats before the start of the series. Jennings urged Cobb to sit out the first game of the series for his own welfare, but Cobb was not apprehensive. "It's all a bluff," he told Jennings. "We'll have an overflow crowd no doubt. Get me some cops."[20] Connie Mack arranged for nearly three hundred policemen to be part of the more than 25,000 fans who attended each game. While there were plenty of verbal missives thrown Cobb's way, there were no physical attacks. Detroit was still in first place at the end of the series, and Philadelphia's last good chance to overtake the Tigers had evaporated.

Cobb's altercations were not limited to the playing field in 1909. Early in the season, he claimed that he had been attacked by a group of men while on his way to the ballpark in Detroit, finally driving away his attackers when he pulled out a pistol. Later in the season, he got into a brawl in Cleveland with a hotel detective, slashing the detective with a pocketknife while taking several blows to the head from the detective's nightstick. The detective was hospitalized, and pressed charges against Cobb from his hospital bed. Cobb, bandaged about the head, played a doubleheader the next day, with blood soaking through his bandages as the games wore on.

Cobb was never apologetic about his hard-nosed approach to the game, particularly on the base paths. According to Al Stump, Cobb "wished it to be understood that he simply was one who went at it harder, more recklessly and violently than others when facing a blocked-off bag. If enemies were spiked or had bones broken while interposing themselves between Cobb and his destination, the blame was not with him, but with what he called 'base-hogs.'"[21]

Cobb went through life with a chip on his shoulder, ready to fight over any apparent slight. In a twenty-four year career he hit .367, by far the highest career batting average in baseball history. Until the emergence of Babe Ruth as a slugger with the Yankees in the 1920s, Cobb was the single most dominating hitter in the game; he was respected, feared and hated by all of his opponents, and a number of his teammates as well. The 1909 Tigers won their third consecutive American League pennant, although they again lost the World Series to their National League opponents, as they had done the previous two years. With Cobb only twenty-three years old and surrounded by a strong supporting cast, it was reasonable to expect the "Georgia Peach" would have plenty of additional chances to lead the Tigers to a world championship. It turned out that 1909 would be Cobb's last World Series appearance, as the young Philadelphia Athletics were about to embark on a five-year run of dominance, winning four of the next five American League pennants and three World Series championships. Colby Jack Coombs' strong right arm would play a vital role in the establishment of the Athletics dynasty.

4

"No pitcher ever did more for a manager"

Following the 1909 season, for the first time in his career Jack Coombs joined other members of the Philadelphia Athletics on a barnstorming tour of the West Coast, running from mid–October to early December. Their opposition during the tour included a traveling all-star team, dubbed the "Nationals," as well as local baseball clubs.

The tour was organized by Frank Bancroft, a veteran promoter who had previously managed the Providence Grays and organized the first barnstorming trips to Cuba in the 1880s. The Nationals, managed by Bancroft, included such stars as Larry Doyle, Chief Meyers, and Rube Marquard of the New York Giants, and Walter Johnson of the Washington Senators. A California native, Johnson at the time was approaching twenty-two years of age, and had just completed his third season with the pitiful Washington Senators, who finished in last place, twenty games behind the seventh place St. Louis Browns and an enormous fifty-six games behind the pennant-winning Tigers. Despite being handicapped for much of his career with a weak supporting cast, Johnson won 417 games in the major leagues, second only to Cy Young's 511 victories in the history of the game. This barnstorming tour gave Johnson the exposure and seasoning he needed to hone his talents, and 1910 proved to be both the first winning season and the first of ten consecutive twenty-win seasons for the "Big Train."

Jack Coombs benefited from the tour in similar ways. Without the pressure of a pennant race, and allowed to pitch on a regular basis, he too was able to sharpen his technique and bring his pitching skills to a new level in the 1910 season. Coombs had the opportunity to work on his sinker, and learned how to better manage his strength depending upon the circumstances of the ball game. When not taking his regular turn on the mound during the tour, he played the outfield, knowing with certainty that it was a temporary assignment.

The tour started in Spokane, Washington, and worked its way down the Pacific coast, with stops in Portland, San Francisco and Los Angeles. The Athletics took the better end of the results against their various opponents. While the tour could be considered an artistic and professional success for the participants, it was not a financial success, with receipts just barely covering the players' expenses for the tour.

Coombs was eager to get started in 1910. He signed a contract for the season in January, and it was reported that he had initially declined the Athletics' offer of a raise in pay, feeling that he had not merited an increase based on his level of play in 1909.[1] It is not that Coombs was living a life of luxury that would allow him to turn down a raise; far from it. He knew the value of a dollar, and was certainly not a free spender. He smoked Raleigh cigarettes in large part because of the coupons that came with every pack. He was once teased in the press for having "invested" a nickel in a pouch of tobacco, which he then managed to make last for an entire winter.[2] Jack Coombs believed that a ballplayer's pay should be based on the merits of his performance, and he genuinely felt that his performance in 1909 was not up to his capabilities.

Questions had even been raised about just how dedicated Coombs was to a career in baseball. According to Connie Mack biographer Norman Macht, Coombs' inconsistency in the early part of his career led some unnamed teammates to question whether the young pitcher had sufficient courage to consistently excel.[3] Also, in 1909 it seemed that he was spending much of his spare time on the golf links, an interest he had first developed while a student at Colby. His drives were long and accurate, and he had a deft touch on the putting greens. He was considered to have enough talent to pursue the game professionally. Ben Shibe, owner of the Athletics, supposedly invited Coombs to his home on weekends in the summers just to keep him away from the golf course.

To that point in his 3½ year major league career, Coombs' record stood at thirty-five victories against thirty-five defeats. The twenty-seven-year-old expected more than a .500 record of himself, and was determined to demonstrate to his teammates and the world at large that the glimpses of greatness he had shown so far in his career could be sustained over an entire season. He was at a crossroads in his career, needing to determine whether he would continue with baseball or move on to other pursuits. He had the opportunity to enter the business world through a friendship he had developed with Hyman Pearlstone, a wholesale grocer from Palestine, Texas. Pearlstone was an avid fan of the Athletics and occasional scout, having at times toured with the team on its western road trips, even suiting up to practice with the team. That he would develop a friendship with the loquacious and inquisitive Jack Coombs was practically a given, and Coombs had gone so far as to spend time in Palestine with Pearlstone prior to the start of the 1909 season.

At the time Palestine was a town of approximately 10,000 people, located about 100 miles southeast of Dallas and 150 miles north of Houston. The town was established in the 1840s as the county seat of Anderson County. The railroad ran through the town, helping to build and maintain its commercial base.

Coombs was given the star treatment in Palestine, and was tempted by Pearlstone's offer to join his business ventures. The more alluring temptation, though, was the romantic interest that emerged during his visits to Palestine. Coombs met Mary Elizabeth Russ, who in the words of Coombs' family was a traditional "southern belle." He was smitten. Mary, an only child of a railroad employee, was described in the local press as "one of Palestine's handsomest girls" and a "leading society girl."[4] While the two young lovers talked about their future together, Coombs recommitted himself to pursuing his baseball career.

Entering the 1910 season in good health, having added the "drop" to his arsenal of pitches, and with the prospect of again taking a regular turn in the starting rotation, Coombs was confident he would contribute to the Athletics' success. Connie Mack was also confident entering the season. He predicted early in the season that his 1910 squad would prove to be the best he had ever managed, including the pennant winners of 1902 and 1905.[5] Despite the fact that the reviled Tigers were defending their third consecutive American League pennant, Mack felt that the Athletics' combination of defense, speed, hitting and pitching would carry his team past the more one-dimensional Tigers to the World Series. His prognostication proved very accurate, as the 1910 Athletics finished the season scoring only six fewer runs than Detroit, while giving up 141 fewer runs. The Philadelphia offense led the league in batting average and slugging percentage; the defense led in fewest errors and executed the greatest number of double plays; the pitching staff led in complete games, strikeouts, shutouts, and fewest runs allowed. Over the next five seasons, the Athletics became the most dominant team in baseball.

The Athletics opened the season in Washington with three games against the Senators. Eddie Plank pitched against Walter Johnson, and lost the game by a score of 3–0 as Johnson limited the Athletics to just one hit. The highlight of the day was the "pitching" of William Howard Taft, who became the first United States president to throw out the ceremonial first pitch of the season.

The Athletics played well but did not dominate in the early part of the 1910 season. The Tigers started off quickly, leading the second-place Athletics by a game at the end of April. Philadelphia made a strong run in May, winning twenty while losing just five, but followed that with a mediocre 12–12 record in June. The end of June found the Athletics in first place, one game up on the New York Highlanders, with the Tigers and Red Sox lurking close behind. Coombs had been taking a regular turn as a starter and occasionally appeared in relief, compiling a solid 8–4 record by the end of June. He gave more frequent demonstrations of brilliance, including two-hit and one-hit victories over the White Sox. His hitting prowess earned him another two victories by, leading the Philadelphia attack with three hits and two runs scored in both contests.

On June 20, Coombs was invited back to Colby College to celebrate "Coombs' Day," the first of many honorary celebrations to be held at Waterville for Colby's most famous athlete. Coombs and his teammates from the Class of 1906 were invited back to engage in a game against the 1910 Colby varsity squad. A large crowd of 3,000 people turned out to see Coombs, dressed in his Philadelphia uniform, lead his team to a 3–1 victory. A marching band entertained the crowd, and Dr. J. F. Hill, who had initially convinced Coombs to attend Colby, gave a speech in Coombs' honor. Following the festivities, Coombs boarded a train to New York, where two days later he shut out the Highlanders by a score of 8–0.

At the end of June, the Athletics held a fundraising event at Shibe Park for the benefit of Doc Powers' widow and children. Representatives from the New York, Boston and Washington clubs were on hand to join in the occasion. Between 10,000 and 15,000 fans were in attendance to watch a series of skill contests relating to running, throwing and hitting. Coombs, along with speedy infield teammates Jack Barry, Eddie Collins and Morrie Rath, won the relay base running contest. The skill events were followed by a six-inning game, pitting the Athletics against selected representatives from the other three teams. Nearly $8,000 was raised for Powers' family.

With the pennant race still close at the end of June, Jack Coombs began to raise his performance to an exceptional level, literally carrying his team in July. Bender missed most of the month with a stomach ailment, and Plank's play had again been limited throughout the season due to assorted arm ailments. Connie Mack decided to give the ball to Jack Coombs as often as possible, and Coombs did not let his manager down. Coombs started ten games for Mack in July, consistently pitching on just two days rest. Coombs thrived on the opportunity, as the regular work gave him better command of his sinker. He pitched a complete game in every one of his starts, and his record for the month was ten victories against only one defeat. Five of those victories came by shutouts, and one was in relief. Newspaper accounts frequently highlighted Coombs' ability to "pitch in a pinch," bearing down and becoming more effective when runners were on base. He rarely gave hits in bunches, scattering them "as leaves in a cyclone," and he conserved his strength by adjusting his pitching style to the game situation, focusing his energies when needed rather than trying to overpower every batter.[6]

Coombs' ten wins were nearly half of Philadelphia's twenty-two victories for the month of July. Despite Philadelphia's weakened pitching corps, Coombs' July performance had put some distance between the Athletics and their competitors; they ended the month six games ahead of Boston, and then continued to widen their lead as the season progressed.

Connie Mack realized he had a good thing going with Coombs, and he continued to give him the ball every three days for most of the rest of the season. Colby Jack rose to the challenge by pitching some spectacular baseball. On August 4, Coombs faced Ed Walsh of the White Sox in a game that Coombs later considered the best he pitched in his entire career.

"Big Ed" Walsh was the workhorse of the Chicago White Sox and the American League. Relying on the then-legal spitball as his out pitch, in 1908 he had compiled a league-leading record of 40–15, also leading the league with forty-two complete games and an extraordinary 464 innings, the all-time major league record. While he never led the league in victories again, he continued to pitch an incredible number of innings for the White Sox, averaging fifty-one appearances and 361 innings pitched over the seven years ending in 1912.

Coombs and Walsh had faced each other before, to the dismay of the hitters on both clubs. In Coombs' rookie season, he lost 1–0 to Walsh when Big Ed struck out nine Philadelphia batters in a rain-shortened six-inning game. In 1909, Coombs returned the favor, beating Walsh and the White Sox by a 1–0 score, although it took the Athletics hitters thirteen innings to put a run across the plate. Both of those contests would look like slugfests in comparison to what transpired on August 4, 1910.

The sky was bright and clear, with a temperature in the upper 70s as the two teams took the field, much as it had been back in September of 1906 when Coombs and Harris squared off for their epic contest. Coombs started off well, striking out six Chicago batters in the first three innings. For nine innings, he held the White Sox to just one hit in the second inning while accumulating thirteen strikeouts. Unfortunately for Coombs and the Athletics, they had done little with Walsh's spitball during those nine innings, only once threatening to score when they loaded the bases with one out in the seventh inning. With nothing but zeroes on the scoreboard after nine innings, the game went into extra innings, both teams searching for that elusive run to bring the game to a conclusion. The search continued without success for another seven innings, and might have continued beyond the record set in 1906 had darkness not intervened and forced the umpires to call the game after sixteen innings had been completed.

Reporting for the *Chicago Tribune*, Ring Lardner commented on Coombs' effort in the context of his workload:

> Coombs gave a great exhibition of coming back. Every one who has been following the race knows that this young man has been worked as pitchers seldom are worked. For weeks he has pitched every third day at least, and for a while he was used every other day. In the twelfth and thirteenth rounds yesterday he appeared to weaken. He even seemed to be groggy, and was walking around out there as if he knew not what was expected of him.[7]

But as he had done so many times before, Coombs reached deep into his reservoir of strength and got the job done. With darkness beginning to settle in during the sixteenth inning, he ended his performance with a flourish, striking out the last three Chicago hitters. In sixteen innings, he had struck out eighteen batters, limiting the White Sox to three hits. For the nine-inning stretch starting with the third inning, Coombs had not given up a single hit. Lardner wrote, "Perhaps it was not the best ever played, but don't try to tell anyone that there have been many better.... And don't let us say that Walsh was better than Coombs, or that Coombs was better than Walsh. They were both just about perfect."[8]

In the *Washington Post*, Joe S. Jackson offered this view.

> This seems to be the year in which Jack Coombs, one of the heroes of yesterday's great sixteen-inning battle at Chicago, is due to pick for himself a place in the baseball hall of fame. His work yesterday ... is especially commendable because it comes not as the single striking feat that almost any pitcher accomplishes at some time in a summer or in his career, but as the climax to a season of consistent and brilliant effort. That the Athletics are as far in front as they are is largely due to his efforts.[9]

The game is the longest double shutout in major league history in which both pitchers went the distance. Only four double shutouts have gone longer, and in only two of those games did a pitcher go more innings than both Coombs and Walsh. In 1909, Oren Summers went eighteen innings for Detroit against Washington, and in 1916 Ernie Koob of the St. Louis Browns threw seventeen shutout innings against the Boston Red Sox.

Three days later, Coombs took his regular turn on the mound and shut out the St. Louis Browns, limiting them to five hits while striking out nine. This time the Athletics bats were a bit livelier, providing six runs of support as Coombs won his nineteenth game of the season. Two days later, the *Washington Post* reported that Coombs had "succumbed to a slight attack of pleurisy and his left side is now as stiff as a boiled shirt."[10] It was speculated that he would miss several days, but he took his regular turn on the mound the very next day, beating the Tigers and their ace pitcher, Bill Donovan, by an 8–3 score. Staked to a five-run lead in the first inning, Coombs coasted to his twentieth victory. The *Boston Globe* reported, "Jack Coombs, whom reports said was on his death bed, or something to that effect, appeared in the box as Donovan's opponent, and impressed those who saw the performance that he is still very much alive."[11]

Starting in mid–August, Coombs astoundingly elevated his pitching to an even higher level. He started nine games in a thirty-day time span and won all of them; in none of the games did the opposition score more than one run. The win streak ended on September 21, when Coombs found himself in another pitchers' duel, this time with Harry Fanwell of Cleveland. This game ended in a scoreless tie, called on account of darkness after eleven innings. While his winning streak was at an end, the eleven shutout innings against Cleveland put Coombs at forty-six consecutive innings without a run being scored against him, tying him with Doc White for the major league record for consecutive scoreless innings.

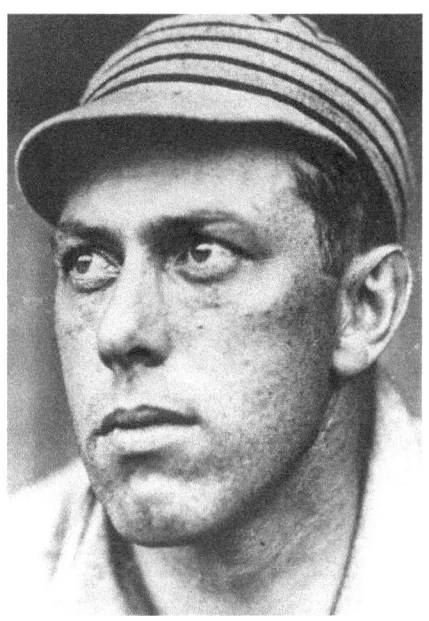

Colby Jack Coombs during the peak of his career with Philadelphia, when he led the major leagues in victories for two consecutive seasons (courtesy National Baseball Hall of Fame Library, Cooperstown, N.Y.).

Coombs' next start was scheduled for the second game of a doubleheader against Chicago on September 25. The Athletics had already clinched the American League pennant, so the games had little meaning. In the first game Eddie Plank drew the assignment against Big Ed Walsh. As usual when Walsh took the mound for the White Sox, runs were hard to come by. Mack sent a pinch-hitter in for Plank in the top of the ninth as the Athletics scored a run to tie the game at 1–1. Rather than send in one of his little-used extra pitchers in a meaningless game, Mack decided to bring Coombs in as an early warm up to his second-game assignment. Coombs went on to pitch six innings of shutout ball, bringing his scoreless streak to fifty-two innings, as the Athletics finally rallied for two runs against Walsh in the top of the fourteenth inning to beat the White Sox by a 3–1 score. The victory was Coombs' thirtieth of the season, the first pitcher in club history to achieve that milestone. Again, rather than use one of his other pitchers, Mack had Coombs go ahead with his regularly scheduled assignment as the starting pitcher in the second game of the doubleheader. Coombs was only able to hold the White Sox scoreless for the first inning of the second game, which Chicago won by a score of 5–2. His scoreless streak had been stopped at fifty-three innings, a major league record at the time.

Coombs made two more appearances before the season concluded. The first was a complete-game victory over Joe Wood of the Red Sox, and the second was a relief appearance against New York, most notable for being the major league debut of catcher Earle Mack, Connie Mack's son. Earle knocked out a single and a triple in his debut. These proved to be the only two hits of his major league career, which was comprised of only five games spread over three seasons. Before the game, the Athletics players presented Connie Mack with a new automobile as a token of their appreciation for the job he had done leading them to the American League pennant.

The Chicago Cubs had also won the National League pennant by a large margin, there by giving the press plenty of time to evaluate the teams' prospects for the upcoming World Series. Writing for the *Chicago Tribune*, Ring Lardner had high praise for Coombs' work during the regular season. "Coombs' performance is one of the wonders of the land. He has worked in turn, out of turn, and every other way, and he has a record that seldom has been approached. And he didn't win games through luck either."[12] The *Washington Post* added, "Coombs has perfect command, remarkable speed, a fine line of sharp curves, can field his position nearly as well as (Chicago pitcher Mordecai) Brown, and with a good head and ample nerve will prove a hard man to find.... When it comes to hitting the Quaker pitchers have all the best of it, Coombs being one of the finest hitting pitchers in the game."[13] Veteran Boston sportswriter Tim Murnane offered his views, writing that Coombs "this season has pitched perhaps the best ball of any boxman in the business. He has great strength and pitches as well at the close of a battle as when he starts out. Furthermore, Coombs is a fine batsman and a clever fielder in his position, and a player that will show in this series."[14] He prophetically concluded his analysis, "I look for Coombs to do the best pitching of the series."[15]

Most experts figured the World Series would be a close one, with the Athletics having superior pitching and defense, while the Cubs were generally acknowledged to have superior hitting and experience. That experience came from having won three straight National League pennants from 1906 to 1908, and beating the Tigers in the 1907 and 1908 World Series. The Cubs' string of pennants had been interrupted by the Pittsburgh Pirates in 1909, despite the fact that Chicago had won 104 games. With essentially the same lineup that had started their run of success in 1906, the Cubs coasted to the 1910 National League pennant, beating the second-place New York Giants by a thirteen-game margin.

The Cubs manager and first baseman was Frank Chance, "The Peerless Leader." Chance had been with the Cubs since 1898, and had become the team's player-manager during the 1905 season. He had spent his first five seasons as a catcher, but in 1902 was switched to first base, where he developed a reputation as a fine defensive fielder. A steady, though not spectacular, hitter, Chance was thirty three years old heading into the 1910 World Series. The 1910 season proved to be his last year as a full-time player, as he played in only forty-five games over the course of the next four seasons. He finished his seventeen-year career with a batting average of .296.

The Cubs' keystone combination consisted of Johnny Evers at second base and Joe Tinker at shortstop. Evers, known as "The Crab" for his contentious disposition, had been with the Cubs since 1902. A slight man at 5' 9" and 125 pounds, he was fearless on a baseball diamond, gamely taking a beating from runners sliding hard into second base. Known for his brains rather than his brawn, it was Evers who in an important September 1908 game in New York had alertly noted that Giants rookie Fred Merkle had headed towards the clubhouse rather than run from first to second base on what appeared to be the game-winning hit. Evers found a baseball (whether it was the actual game ball was forever debated) and touched second base, with umpire Hank O'Day calling Merkle out on the force play. The Giant fans had swarmed the field, thinking their team had won the game, and it became impossible for the contest to continue. While the Giants had protested to O'Day and the league that it was customary for players to not run to the next base on a game-ending hit, Merkle was ruled out; the game was ruled a tie and ordered to be replayed at the end of the season, if necessary. The Cubs and Giants ended the regular season tied for first place, forcing the extra game. The Cubs went on to win the game and the National League pennant. Evers went on to play in eighteen major league seasons, finishing his career with a respectable .270 batting average.

Joe Tinker's easygoing manner was the antithesis of Johnny Evers' irascible personality. Like Evers, Tinker had joined the Cubs in 1902, and the two worked together as the Cubs' keystone combination through the 1912 season. Despite their close working relationship, the two did not get along, and for many years they barely spoke to each other. The same height as Evers, Tinker outweighed the second baseman by fifty pounds. He too was a smooth fielder and a steady but unspectacular hitter, compiling a lifetime batting average of .263 in fifteen major league seasons.

The infield combination of Tinker, Evers and Chance was immortalized in a poem written by New York sportswriter Franklin Pierce Adams, titled "Baseball's Sad Lexicon."

> These are the saddest of possible words,
>   Tinker-to-Evers-to-Chance.
> Trio of Bear Cubs fleeter than birds,
>   Tinker-to-Evers-to-Chance.
> Pricking our gonfalon bubble,
> Making a Giant hit into a double,
> Words that are weighty with nothing but trouble,
>   Tinker-to-Evers-to-Chance.[16]

From this poem an outsized reputation was born. The threesome was no doubt an excellent defensive unit, but they were never an extraordinary double-play combination. In fact, the Cubs never led the league in double plays while the three played together. And while the three were consistent, respectable hitters, none of them ever led the league in any offensive category. Despite this, all three were elected to the Baseball Hall of Fame in 1946.

Harry Steinfeldt was the Cubs' all-but-forgotten third baseman. Traded to the Cubs in 1906, he helped anchor the infield that won four pennants in five years. He was the only one of the four to ever top the league in an offensive category, accumulating 176 hits and eighty-three runs batted during the 1906 season. Steinfeldt finished his career with a .268 batting average, comparable to Evers and Tinker, but never received any serious consideration for the Hall of Fame.

The Cubs pitching staff was led by Mordecai Peter Centennial Brown, more commonly known as "Three Finger" Brown. Brown came by his nickname through a childhood farming accident that resulted in the amputation of one finger and the mangling of another on his right hand. The injury allowed the pitcher to impart unusual spin to a baseball, a skill he put to good use throughout his major league career. Brown won twenty or more games in six consecutive seasons, from 1906 to 1911. In the 1910 season, he led the Cubs with twenty-five victories. Like Coombs, he thrived on work, and was frequently used in relief. He was a big-game pitcher, and engaged in several epic battles with New York Giant ace Christy Mathewson. He won 239 games in his career and was elected to the Baseball Hall of Fame in 1949.

In 1910, Brown was supported by fellow right-handed pitchers Leonard "King" Cole (twenty wins), Harry McIntire (thirteen wins), Ed Reulbach (twelve wins), Orval Overall (twelve wins), and Lew Richie (eleven wins). The pitching staff was handled by Johnny Kling, a fine defensive catcher. The outfield was comprised of Jimmy Sheckard in left field, Solly Hofman in center field, and Frank "Wildfire" Schulte, who led the league with ten home runs, in right field.

The young Athletics were eager to test their talents against the Cubs' experience, but they had to wait to do so. The National League had decided that it would operate in 1910 under a more drawn out schedule than the American League, finishing a week later than the junior circuit. Thus, while the Athletics had finished their schedule on October 6, the World Series did not start until October 17, with the first game scheduled in Philadelphia based on the toss of a coin. To keep his team in shape while waiting for the Cubs to complete their schedule, Connie Mack scheduled a five-game exhibition series for the Athletics against a collection of American League all-stars who were, oddly enough, called the Nationals. The Nationals squad included the likes of Ty Cobb, Tris Speaker, Walter Johnson, and Ed Walsh. The two teams played for five consecutive days, and the Nationals won the first four games before the Athletics squeezed out a victory in the final contest. The press expressed concern about the Athletics' readiness for the Cubs, given their poor showing against the Nationals. Mack, however, was not the least bit concerned. He had accomplished what he had hoped for, which was keeping his players in game shape against quality competition. Mack spread the pitching chores around over the five games, typically using three different pitchers in each game regardless of the circumstances. Coombs pitched three innings in each of the first three games, which were played on three consecutive days, and then took the next few days off in preparation for the Cubs. The one drawback to the series was the loss of Rube Oldring to a leg injury sustained in the first exhibition game, making him unavailable for the World Series.

Johnny Evers was also unavailable to the Cubs, having broken his leg in a game against Cincinnati in early October. He was replaced at second base by Henry "Heinie" Zimmerman.

Mack was deliberately coy regarding his choice of pitchers for the opening game of the series. It was clear that it would be Bender, Coombs, or Plank. The first game of the series was considered significant; the winner of the first game in each of the previous five fall classics had gone on to win the championship. As a result, it was expected that Mack would go with either Plank or Bender since both had the experience of pitching in the 1905 World Series. He even went so far as to have both pitchers warm up before the start of the first game. He decided to go with the right-handed Bender, based in part on his past performance in the 1905 World Series, where he had won the Athletics' only game, and in part because Bender had spent time scouting the Cubs while the regular season was winding down. Mack's choice worked out quite well, with Bender holding the Cubs to a mere three hits, while the Athletics freely hit Orval Overall, snatching the first game by a 4–1 score.

The second game was scheduled for the next day, again in Philadelphia, and this time Mack left no doubt that Jack Coombs, the "Iron Man," would be the Athletics' starting pitcher. He was opposed by the ace of the Cubs staff,

Three Finger Brown, who was one day short of his thirty-fourth birthday. Coombs had last pitched five days earlier, and that for only three innings, a relatively long layoff in comparison to his workload during the summer. The weather was sunny and warm, the kind of weather under which Coombs had pitched some of his most notable games. However, the normally imperturbable Coombs was visibly nervous for his first World Series appearance. He opened the game by walking Jimmy Sheckard on four pitches. After a force out by Schulte, Coombs walked Hofman and gave up a single to Chance. Zimmerman lifted a sacrifice fly to center to score the Cubs' first run. Coombs then controlled the damage by striking out Harry Steinfeldt to end the inning. Coombs had thrown thirty pitches in the inning, spending an inordinate amount of time between pitches, clearly struggling with his command. He settled down as the game progressed, but he never found the rhythm that had characterized his hurling during the season.

In the fifth inning, the Cubs attempted to take advantage of Coombs' jumpiness through the use of the bunt. Brown led off the inning with a bunt that Coombs mishandled, and Brown was safe at first. Sheckard followed with another bunt; Coombs fell as he chased after the ball, leaving runners on first and second. Schulte then bunted towards first to move both runners up a base. With first base open and only one out, Coombs walked Hofman to load the bases. Chance then lifted a soft fly ball to short right field, and Brown tagged up at third to try to score but was easily thrown out by Danny Murphy for an inning-ending double play.

At the end of six innings, the Athletics had a 3–1 lead. Despite the fact that he had already walked five batters and committed two fielding errors, Coombs once again was "pitching in a pinch," retiring batters when needed and keeping the Cubs from scoring. Coombs ran into a bit of trouble in the seventh inning when the Cubs scored another run as Sheckard doubled and was brought home on a single by Chance. In the home half of the seventh, Philadelphia unloaded on Brown. The first four batters in the inning collected base hits, and the Athletics went on to score six runs in the inning, taking a 9–2 lead. The Cubs threatened again in the remaining two innings, but could only put one more runner across, leaving Jack Coombs and the Athletics as 9–3 victors.

While both teams complained about the consistency of umpire Charles Rigler's calls behind the plate, there was no doubt that Coombs had struggled with his control in the game. He walked nine batters, which stood as a World Series record until 1947, when Bill Bevens of the Yankees walked ten batters in his near no-hitter of the Brooklyn Dodgers. Four of Coombs' walks came with first base open, three of them on four straight pitches, so they may have been of the strategic variety to set up force plays, much as he had done as a rookie in his twenty-four–inning outing against Boston. Coombs threw 151 pitches in the game, and 72 of them were balls. In total, the Cubs stranded fourteen base runners. The Chicago newspapers and the Chicago players grumbled about their luck, feeling that they should have beaten Coombs handily. Frank Chance expounded on the subject, "Coombs didn't show up nearly as well as Bender, and I can promise we will give him all the trouble he wants next time he works against us. If we could have hit in the pinches today we would have won hands down, for we would have taken all the fight out of the Athletics. The latter had luck enough to last them the whole season."[17]

Connie Mack disagreed. "Coombs showed wonderful control in practice, but was a bit worried when he started the game wild, but I had much confidence in John and he finally came around. He gave nine passes, but when he did get his curves over the plate the Chicago batters could not damage them."[18] Coombs added, "I felt sure I could beat Chance's men before the game and had perfect control then, but when I walked on the field and took up pitching I felt my control slipping. Never did I lose my head, and when I was in the tight places I worked my head as well as my arm."[19]

New York sportswriter Fred Lieb was attending his first World Series in 1910. Nearly forty years later, in *The Story of the World Series*, he quoted Jack Coombs, who insisted that this game "was one of the worst games he ever pitched." Connie Mack was much more pragmatic: "They didn't score many runs on him, did they?"[20]

Connie Mack was so untroubled by Coombs' wildness in the second game that he decided he would come right back with Coombs as his starter in the next contest, to be played two days later in Chicago. The press was stunned by Mack's choice, expecting him to pitch the veteran Eddie Plank in the game. But Plank had not been in the best of health during the season, and he had lost his two previous World Series starts, back in 1905. Also, Mack did not want to resort to Bender in the third game because Bender generally required three days rest between starts in order to be effective. Coombs had demonstrated all season that he could take the mound as often as called upon and consistently deliver for the club. Years later Connie Mack reminisced with Fred Lieb about Coombs' performance in 1910. "Jack was magnificent that season. No pitcher ever did more for a manager."[21]

Following the Athletics victory on October 19, the two teams spent more than seventeen hours the next day traveling by train between Philadelphia and Chicago. The Athletics' train arrived in Chicago shortly before the Cubs' train, and the Philadelphia players received a surprisingly warm welcome from the Chicago fans that were at the train station awaiting the arrival of the hometown team. The Cubs fans were an enthusiastic lot. In the days preceding television and radio coverage of the World Series, fans were forced to rely principally on newspaper reports to follow the progress of their team on the road. To provide anxious Cubs fans with a more immediate experience, the *Chicago Tribune* set up an electronic scoreboard in Orchestra Hall where 2,500 devotees were able to "see" the games played in Philadelphia. As results were received by telegraph from Philadelphia, the scoreboard operator would light up the display to show the situation on the field, including the positioning of base runners. The audience responded with the same level of noise and fervor as if they were at the ballpark. Thousands more were gathered on the street outside, hearing the results called out by megaphone.

Despite cold, damp weather for the third game, more than 26,000 people showed up at Chicago's West Side Grounds. Among the attendees sitting in reserved seats close to the field was Federal Judge Kenesaw Mountain Landis, who later became commissioner of baseball following the gambling scandal associated with the 1919 World Series. Since the ballpark's capacity was only 16,000, the overflow was handled by putting up temporary barriers in both left and right field. Balls hit into the overflow crowd were ruled doubles.

Pitching for the Cubs was Ed Reulbach, a twenty-seven-year-old right-handed pitcher born in Detroit. In his five previous seasons with the Cubs, Reulbach had been a steady performer, winning no fewer than seventeen games in any campaign, and leading the National League in winning percentage three straight years. Injuries had limited his effectiveness in 1910, during which he won only a dozen games. Reulbach was to this point undefeated in World Series play, and he had thrown a one-hitter in the second game of the 1906 World Series against the White Sox.

Riding the horse that had taken him to the World Series, Mack went with Coombs against Reulbach. Both pitchers struggled in the first two innings, as each team scored once in the first and twice in the second. Coombs had helped his own cause in the second inning by lining a double to right field, driving in shortstop Jack Barry. When Reulbach was presented with the opportunity to bat in the second inning with a runner on third base, Manager Chance decided to lift Reulbach for a pinch-hitter. Initially, the move looked brilliant, as the Cubs went on to score two runs in the inning to tie the game. However, Chance replaced Reulbach with Harry McIntire, who had performed well in five innings of relief pitching in the opening game of the series. McIntire did not last a single inning in this game; the Athletics exploded for five runs in the third inning. The big blow was a three-run home run by Danny Murphy. Frank Chance argued that in his view Murphy's drive had landed in the overflow crowd rather than the permanent seats, and thus should be a ground-rule double. The umpires did not share the same view as Chance, and when his arguments became more demonstrative, he was thrown out of the game, thus becoming the first player to be ejected from a World Series contest.

Coombs settled down after the second inning and showed the winning form that he had displayed during the season. After the second inning, he limited the Cubs to three hits and one walk, coasting to an easy 12–5 victory. In total, he held the Cubs to six hits, three of them by Joe Tinker, and he struck out seven. His pitch count dropped to 120 following the 152 he offered up in the second series game. He was also a force at the plate, contributing a double, two singles, and three runs batted in to Philadelphia's offensive output.

Coombs displays his pitching form during his days with the Philadelphia Athletics. Coombs, Chief Bender and Eddie Plank made up one of the most dominant pitching staffs in the major leagues (courtesy National Baseball Hall of Fame Library, Cooperstown, N.Y.).

While the Cubs had groused about Coombs' luck following his first outing in the series, Chicago center fielder Solly Hofman gave credit where credit was due following the third game.

> Before the series started I was told that Coombs had a great curve ball. I thought I had been steered wrong when I saw him in the game in Philadelphia last Thursday, for it didn't look good to me then. But it certainly was a beautiful curve ball yesterday. He gave a great exhibition from the third inning on, and I don't believe you can blame us for not hitting him hard the way he was going. No ball club in the world could have done any more against his pitching than we did.[22]

Connie Mack concurred. "Coombs pitched great ball after a bad start, and I don't believe any club could have done a thing with him after the second inning."[23] Coombs said he was simply happy to demonstrate that he could "win on my merits."[24]

The two teams were scheduled to play the fourth game the next day, Friday, and if Chicago were to prove victorious, the clubs were to travel by special train to Philadelphia to play the fifth game on Saturday, and back to Chicago for the sixth contest on Sunday. But the dreary weather from the third game turned into a steady rain, forcing the postponement of Friday's game to Saturday. Since Sunday baseball was not yet permitted in Philadelphia, the teams agreed to play the fifth game, if necessary, in Chicago, so as to not lose the opportunity for a Sunday crowd. Mack had no intention of having the series go to a fifth game, and decided to pitch a well-rested Chief Bender against the Cubs King Cole, who won twenty games for Chicago in 1910.

Bender hurled another strong game for the Athletics, but his performance was nearly matched for eight innings by the twenty-four-year-old Cole. At the end of eight innings, the Athletics led by a 3–2 score and seemed on the verge of completing a sweep of the series. Cole was removed for a pinch-hitter in the bottom of the eighth, and Three Finger Brown took the mound for the Cubs in the top of the ninth, holding the Athletics scoreless. Down to their last three outs in the ninth, the Cubs rallied to tie the score on a double by Wildfire Schulte and a clutch triple by Frank Chance. They went on to win the game in the tenth inning on a single by backup catcher Jimmy Archer and a double by Jimmy Sheckard. It was a frustrating loss for Bender and the Athletics, but there was little time to dwell on the frustration with the fifth game scheduled for the next day. Mack decided without hesitation to have Coombs pitch what he hoped would be the final game of the series. Coombs would be pitching with two days rest, plenty of recuperation time compared to what he had endured during the season. According to Joe S. Jackson of the *Washington Post*, "With any other pitcher than Coombs the proposition (of beating the Cubs) would be tougher. But the team has supreme confidence in the Colby boy."[25] Coombs was again opposed by Three Finger Brown, his opponent in the series' second game.

Coombs lobbied Connie Mack to have Jack Lapp be his catcher in the game; Lapp had been the catcher for twenty-two of Coombs' thirty-one wins during the season. The twenty-six-year-old Lapp shared the catching duties with Ira Thomas in 1910, with Lapp considered the better offensive threat and Thomas the stronger defensive backstop. Lapp was impressed with the strength that Coombs brought to his pitching. "Coombs was the strongest man who ever put on a baseball rig," said Lapp. "Coombs could pitch twenty innings, throwing every ball with all his might, and send them over the plate just as fast at the finish as he had at the start of the game, and the afternoon's work didn't even seem to make Jack tired."[26]

Coombs' desire to utilize Lapp was not a negative reflection on his good friend Ira Thomas, who had expertly caught the first four games of the series for the Athletics. Thomas had helped limit the Cubs to two stolen bases in the first four games, which came as a surprise. The Cubs had stolen bases seemingly at will in their previous championship series against the Tigers, recording sixteen steals in the 1907 World Series and fifteen steals in 1908. But Coombs was more comfortable with Lapp behind the plate, and Mack was willing to give his star pitcher all the support he wanted for the game against the Cubs. Not coincidentally, Coombs gave his best performance of the series with his favorite backstop behind the plate.

The largest crowd of the series — 27,374 — turned out for the game. At first, it looked as though they would be treated to a close match, as both Brown and Coombs held the hitters at bay. The Cubs threatened to break the game open in the fourth inning when they loaded the bases with only one out, but Coombs reared back and struck out both Tinker and Archer to end the threat. Coombs' teammates on the bench became so excited when Coombs set down the Cubs that they accidentally knocked Connie Mack off the bench and to the ground. The ever-unflappable Mack simply stood up, brushed the dirt off his clothes and said, "It's all right boys; I have another suit at the hotel."[27] Eddie Collins later referred to Coombs getting out of this jam as the key point in the game. "When Jack fanned Tinker and Archer in rapid succession with a Cub on second and third," said Collins, "and retired them scoreless, the doom of Chance and his men was sealed."[28]

Jack Lapp made a significant contribution to the Athletics' fortunes in the fifth inning, first driving in the go-ahead run in the top of the inning with a single, and then throwing out Wildfire Schulte attempting to steal to end the bottom half of the inning.

Through seven innings, the Athletics held a 2–1 lead. Coombs started things off for the Athletics in the eighth with a sharp single to right. Another single, two doubles, two walks, two stolen bases and one throwing error later, the Athletics had added five runs, putting the game out of reach for the Cubs. Coombs gave up a meaningless run in the bottom of the eighth inning, and the Athletics went on to win the game by a 7–2 score, giving Connie Mack and the Athletics their first world championship. Coombs' teammates swarmed around the mound to congratulate him on his superb effort. In the clubhouse, Mack, in his usual understated manner, offered his thanks. "You were great, John," he said, "simply great."[29]

Joe Jackson of the *Washington Post* was more effusive in his comments on Coombs' performance. "Coombs yesterday demonstrated his right to be classed among the best pitchers of the country," he wrote. "Coombs ... was at his best in the tight places, and was always possessed of the reserve strength to check the opposition when it got where runs looked likely."[30]

Coombs offered this evaluation of his performance for the *Sporting News*. "It is gratifying to me that I was able to win the three games I pitched against the Cubs. I got better as I went along and I never had any doubt about the result of the final game. I knew I was good and I knew the Athletics could hit any kind of pitching. We beat the Cubs fairly and squarely. I would have been happier if we had taken four straight, but I'm happy enough now."[31]

The citizens of Philadelphia were extremely happy. A crowd in excess of 10,000 people met the team upon its arrival at the train station, and thousands more lined the streets to watch the team motorcade proceed to the Bellevue-Stratford hotel for a dinner and testimonial speeches. The usually reticent Mack was so caught up in the emotion of the moment that he gave a half-hour speech, lauding the accomplishments of his players.

With his three victories in a five-game series, Coombs became only the second player to accomplish that feat; Christy Mathewson had done likewise for the Giants in their victory over the Athletics back in 1905. Mathewson's achievement was even more impressive, because all three of his victories were shutouts. While other pitchers have since recorded three victories in a World Series, all of those were accomplished in a series lasting seven games. Coombs and Mathewson remain the only two to have turned the trick in a five-game series. It has been noted that Coombs benefited from a strong hitting attack, with the Athletics setting a World Series record with a .316 team batting average, a mark that would not be broken until 1960 by the New York Yankees. (The Yankees lost that series in seven games despite scoring twice as many runs as the Pittsburgh Pirates.) It was later revealed that a new cork-centered baseball was introduced in the 1910 World Series, and the ball probably contributed to the Athletics' hitting productivity. When the new ball was introduced full-time in the 1911 season, American League batting averages soared from .243 to .273. That Coombs was able to hold a strong-hitting Cubs team to a .240 average during the series, much lower than their .268 regular season average, gives testimony to just how impressive a pitching effort he put forth. Coombs joined the hitting parade for the Athletics, batting .385 with three runs batted in.

The 1910 season was a breakthrough season for Colby Jack Coombs. In addition to being the hero of the World Series, his pitching accomplishments during the regular season were extraordinary. He led all of major league baseball with thirty-one victories. His thirteen shutouts are still an American League record, and he did not earn a victory in two of those games because they ended in scoreless ties. He established a major league record for consecutive scoreless innings. He was among the league leaders in games, complete games, innings pitched and strikeouts. He was particularly effective over the last half of the season, capturing twenty-three of Philadelphia's sixty-four victories after June 30.

Coombs was arguably one of the best defensive pitchers in the league, making only one error in his forty-five games, for a fielding percentage of .990. Of the leading pitchers in the league, he was the only one not to yield a home run to an opposing batter and the only one to shut out every opponent. He did not give up a home run in 353 innings pitched; the only pitcher to top that mark would be Walter Johnson in 1916.[32] Coombs also led the league with four extra-inning victories. Most importantly, when the pitching staff was shorthanded during the dog days of summer, he took the mound every third day, leading the Athletics as they pulled away from the rest of the league.

Connie Mack had good reason to be thankful for Coombs' effort in 1910. Mack and Coombs both had high expectations of continued success in 1911.

5

A Willingness to Work

Winning the 1910 World Series provided the Athletics players with a significant financial benefit. Players had traditionally shared in the receipts from the first four games of the series; in 1910 the players' share was enhanced by substituting the receipts from the fifth game, played on a Sunday, for the least attended of the previous four games. The Athletics received $2,062.74 per player for their efforts, larger than any previous World Series payoff. This was a sizeable sum in those days, when the average American earned an annual salary of $750 and a gallon of milk cost 32 cents. The average major league ballplayer made on the order of $2,500 a year.

Jack Coombs' salary in 1911 was reported to be in the vicinity of $5,000, a substantial raise over his previous year's wage, merited by his outstanding performance in the 1910 season. His salary was likely comparable to that of Plank and Bender, and exceeded on the Athletics only by Eddie Collins, who was reportedly paid the princely sum of $7,000.[1] Coombs gave the appearance of being a holdout, being the last of Connie Mack's veterans to sign with the ball club. But the *Boston Globe* reported that Coombs and Mack were "too good friends to have much trouble over a little thing like a baseball contract."[2] Coombs claimed he had simply been too busy on his farm, and signed at a face-to-face meeting with Mack on his way to spring training.

The farm in question was Maple Hill Farm, which Coombs had purchased from Walter Day in 1909 with the surplus earnings from his first seasons in the major leagues. The 116-acre farm was located on Alewive Road in Kennebunk, within a few miles of where Coombs had grown up. It became the home and source of income for his parents and siblings. Frank Coombs, Jack's father, was particularly appreciative of his oldest son's accomplishments and generosity to the family. He compared Jack's foresight and career path to that taken by his younger brothers. "Those boys there might be in the same good box that John's in if they'd waited. But no! They thought it was more important to earn a dollar than to get an education. Now John worked his way through Colby. He was all for being an analytical chemist. And look where he is now!"[3]

Coombs had a trophy room in the rear of the farmhouse, known simply as "John's den." The large room was filled with sports memorabilia dating back to his time at Freeport High School. The walls were covered with diplomas, pictures and pennants. A ledge went around the perimeter of the walls, filled with trophies, silver plates and various knickknacks relating to his athletic accomplishments.

In late October of 1910, a number of friends and neighbors from town arrived at Coombs home to honor his accomplishments in the previous baseball season. Frank Bonser, a local clothing dealer, was the spokesman for the town. "We feel honored to have you among us," he told Coombs. "To do any one thing superior to your fellows is a great thing and my dear Jack, as a recognition of this achievement we present to you this pitcher, one of sterling metal, with our love and admiration." The silver pitcher was inscribed, "Presented to John Coombs by his fellow townsmen in recognition of his athletic victories in 1910."[4]

Coombs (back row, right) poses with his parents and siblings in Maine (courtesy Wentworth Family Personal Collection).

There would soon be another resident of the farm, at least during the off-season. John Wesley Coombs and Mary Elizabeth Russ decided during the 1910 season to get married, and the nuptials took place on November 29 in a quiet ceremony witnessed by a few friends — including local businessman and Athletics booster Hyman Pearlstone — and relatives at the bride's home in Palestine, Texas. There were a number of other weddings following the 1910 season: Eddie Collins, Eddie Plank, Jack Barry and Connie Mack all became grooms. The forty-seven-year-old Mack was marrying for the second time; his first wife passed away in 1892, after only five years of marriage. Mack had three children from that first marriage, two of whom, Earle and Roy, later took leadership roles in the Athletics organization. Connie Mack's second marriage resulted in five more children.

Immediately after the ceremony, Coombs and his young bride traveled by train for New Orleans, with Havana, Cuba being their ultimate destination. This was a working honeymoon for Coombs, as he was heading to Cuba to join the Athletics on another barnstorming tour. With the exception of Connie Mack, Eddie Collins, and Frank Baker, all of the regulars made the trip, enticed by a guarantee of nearly $600 each plus all expenses paid for the player and his spouse. (Following the World Series, Coombs had been offered a greater amount to appear on the vaudeville circuit, but turned it down given his prior commitment to play in Cuba.) The Athletics were scheduled to play the Detroit Tigers for two games, and then each major league club was to play a pair of five-game series against Cuban teams.

According to Ira Thomas, the Tigers drew larger crowds during the tour because "the Cubans did not like our uniforms nearly so well as those worn by Detroit."[5] The only significant sartorial difference between the two teams was the "pillbox" style cap with horizontal stripes introduced by the Athletics in 1909 when they opened Shibe Park. The caps were admittedly ugly, and were only worn by the Athletics until 1914, the last year of their run of dominance in the American League. The style mercifully disappeared from major league baseball until reintroduced by the Pittsburgh Pirates in 1976 as part of their garish disco-era uniforms.

It seems doubtful that the sophisticated Cuban fans were passing judgment on the teams based on the cut of their uniforms. More likely, the discerning fans recognized a difference in the effort of the two teams. The Tigers, led by Ty Cobb, had been barnstorming in the states following the close of the season, and they showed up in Havana in game condition. Cobb was at his fiery best in these exhibitions, lulling the fans into complacency with lethargic swings in batting practice and then crushing the ball and running the bases with his usual reckless abandon during the game. The Athletics, on the other hand, had been celebrating their World Series victory for six weeks before heading to Cuba, and the effects of the layoff were obvious. With their money and expenses guaranteed, and Connie Mack back in the states, they had little motivation to perform their best. They split their first two games with the Tigers and proceeded to drop six of the ten games played against the local competition.

According to the *Washington Post,* "Coombs, judging by the records and the scores, was the only one to work conscientiously for the games that he was in."[6] Coombs won each of the games he pitched against the Cuban teams and batted .333 for good measure. Umpire Billy Evans, who was in Cuba for the series, claimed that in one game Coombs' pitching had "surpassed anything he had ever seen," as Coombs won despite a weak pitching arm.[7] It appears that in his first start against the Cuban club, Coombs threw the ball with great velocity as his new bride sat in the stands looking on admiringly. Not having pitched in weeks, Coombs found his arm was dead for his next start, preventing him from having anything. Evans described Coombs' approach as he faced the Cuban batters: "On the preceding Thursday he had studied every batter. Now he used that knowledge. He worked the corners, tossed them up high or low, just as the occasion demanded, never giving the batter the kind of ball he relished."[8] While he was touched up for four runs early in the contest, by the end of the game Coombs "had the Cubans eating out of his hand."[9] The Athletics rallied to win the game in ten innings. "I have seen wonderful pitching exhibitions," enthused Evans, "but I am confident I never saw one that could equal that. Coombs didn't have a single thing except nerve and a grand head."[10]

Tiger manager Hughie Jennings predicted that by virtue of having competed in Cuba without any advance preparation, the Athletics would develop sore arms and other debilitating ailments that would hinder them in the 1911 season. Jennings' Tigers roared off to a terrific start in 1911, and by May 17 they had stormed into the lead with a record of 25–5, a solid 8½ games ahead of the second place Chicago White Sox, with the Athletics struggling in fourth place with a 13–13 record. The Tigers' early success was due to a ferocious hitting attack, led as usual by Ty Cobb. The Georgia Peach was on his way to the finest hitting season of his career. He led the league in batting average, with an extraordinary .420, as well as slugging percentage, hits, doubles, triples, runs and runs batted in. In each of these categories he achieved the highest single-season total of his twenty-four-year career. For good measure, he had a forty-game hitting streak during the season. The mediocre play of the Athletics was attributed to cold weather in the Northeast rather than sore arms from the trip to Cuba. The team had left spring training for Philadelphia about two weeks before the scheduled start of the season, with the intent of playing a series of exhibition games against their cross-town rivals, the

Phillies. But the cold weather had limited the playing and practice time of the two teams, undoing the conditioning that had been gained during spring training.

While Cobb was again demonstrating his preeminence as the best hitter in all of baseball, his offensive figures — and that of most American League hitters — seemed to benefit from the introduction on a permanent basis of the new "lively" cork-centered baseball that had been previewed in the 1910 World Series. The American League batting average climbed from .243 in 1910 to .273 in 1911, the largest single year-to-year differential in the history of the league. Not only were batters hitting safely with greater frequency, they were hitting with greater power, as the number of extra-base hits increased by more than 20 percent. All this offensive output led to a 24 percent increase in the number of runs scored in the league. More than thirty American League players finished the season with a batting average higher than .300. While the hitters feasted, the pitchers suffered. As the number of runs scored soared, the number of complete games and shutouts plummeted. Walks increased as well, as pitchers found themselves more frequently trying to nibble the corners with their pitches while runners occupied the bases.

There are conflicting reports as to whether the National League adopted the new ball in 1911 or 1912, as offensive output also increased in the senior circuit in 1911, but not nearly to the extent it had in the American League. By 1912 the National League's offensive output more closely mirrored that of the American League.

The *Washington Post* commented on the effect of the new ball:

> From present indications, as long as the excessively lively ball now in use is employed, any pitcher is likely to get his bumps on any day.... The men who force the batters to hit to their fielders and take a chance on it, are going to have their troubles all season long. The law of averages will assume a certain percentage of balls going safe, if they are hit at all. And the harder the ball is met, the larger the percentage must be. Good pitchers, as well as those not rated so highly, are being flailed in a manner most astounding.... It will be noted that St. Louis, eighth club in the league, has driven both Bender and Coombs off the slab already. And there is no question about the class of this pair. The absurdly lively ball, not lack of form, was the cause of their discomfiture.[11]

Going into that first series against Detroit, Coombs had a record of 3–4. He had pitched brilliantly in some games, including a three-hit victory over Washington, and a tough 2–1 loss against Walter Johnson. But the May 13 game against St. Louis that had been the source of such "discomfiture" for Coombs was a prime example of the league's offensive explosion. After five innings, the Athletics were sitting on a comfortable 14–3 lead. As he would do several times that season when provided with a big lead, Coombs eased up on the mound, following Connie Mack's dictum that a pitcher should "reserve his forces" during the course of the game.[12] St. Louis took advantage of Coombs' easier tosses and scored ten runs in a three-inning span. When the dust had finally settled, the Athletics won by a score of 17–13. The two teams had combined for thirty-two hits, six of them for doubles, two for triples, and a home run.

When the Athletics pulled into Detroit for a four-game series starting May 18, they knew they were going to have to play well if they were going to slow down the Tigers juggernaut. Plank pitched the opening game of the series and was roughed up in a 9–4 defeat. Coombs started the next game, but was accidentally struck in the head in the first inning by a ball thrown at close range by a teammate and forced to retire from the contest. While the Athletics out-hit the Tigers 19 to 8 in the game, they also uncharacteristically made four errors, and the final score showed the Tigers victorious by a 9–8 margin. The Tigers now had a twelve-game lead over the Athletics.

The blow to Coombs' head was not serious enough to keep him from taking the mound again the next day. The A's continued to pound the ball, with Coombs joining in, singling twice in a six-run third inning. After five innings, the Athletics enjoyed a 12–4 lead, and they held on to take the game by a final score of 14–12. Coombs had four hits for the day, including a double, along with a stolen base, three runs scored and two runs batted in. Perhaps thinking all that base running had reduced Coombs' stamina, Mack brought Eddie Plank in to pitch the last two innings, and the left-hander gave up the Tigers' final four runs. An important sidelight of the game was the broken arm suffered by Tiger first baseman Del Gainer, who was batting over .300 at the time, when he was struck by a Coombs' fastball in the first inning. Ty Cobb later claimed that the Tigers "began to go bad" with the loss of Gainer. Although the Tigers' subsequent record does not support Cobb's assertion, Gainer's injury added more fuel to the already-heated rivalry.[13]

The Athletics took the final game of the series by a 6–2 score and left Detroit trailing the Tigers by ten games.

The Athletics were scheduled to play twelve games before meeting the Tigers again in Philadelphia. With Bender injured, Coombs started five of those games, winning four. He continued his winning ways by defeating Detroit on June 7 in the first game of their next series. The Athletics took two out of three from the Tigers and closed the gap between the two clubs to 5½ games. Following the Tiger series, Coombs also won his next three starts, including a masterful one-hit shutout of St. Louis by a score of 1–0. With minimal offensive support from his teammates, he shut down the same team that had touched him for all those runs just a month earlier. By the end of June, Coombs led all American league pitchers with twelve victories, and only Big Ed Walsh had appeared in more games. Six of Coombs' victories had come in the month of June, propelling the Athletics into second place, only one game behind the Tigers.

In the midst of a four-game series in Boston during June, the Athletics had a Sunday off due to the law prohibiting Sunday baseball in Boston. Coombs invited Connie Mack, Harry Davis, Ira Thomas and Eddie Plank to Kennebunk to join him after Saturday's game for a lobster feast at Maple Hill Farm. Throughout his career Coombs would invite teammates and associates, including Athletics owner Ben Shibe, to his home in Maine to enjoy the

Colby Jack loosening up his arm while pitching for the Philadelphia Athletics. Coombs led the Athletics' pitching staff in innings pitched from 1910 to 1912, capturing eighty victories along the way (courtesy Wentworth Family Personal Collection).

pleasures of life on the farm. The camaraderie enjoyed by Coombs and his guests during these visits was not always shared by Coombs' parents, as they were at times uncomfortable in the presence of these distinguished visitors from the big city. This was particularly true when Mack and Shibe were accompanied by their wives, both of whom changed into fancy dinner clothes to the great discomfort of Coombs' mother.[14] Although Nellie Coombs may have at times felt uncomfortable playing hostess to her son's employers, she and her husband were more comfortable at the ballpark as guests of the Athletics when the team came to Boston. Ben Shibe and Connie Mack provided tickets to Frank and Nellie and other family members, who then joined their son and some of his teammates for dinner at a Boston restaurant following the game.

The Northeast was in the midst of a heat wave on Independence Day in 1911. The Athletics were scheduled to play a doubleheader in New York against the Highlanders. With temperatures in excess of 100 degrees, Coombs pitched six innings in the first game before giving way to Bender for the final three. Coombs had three hits at the plate, including a double and two runs scored, as the Athletics won, 7–4. In the second game, the Highlanders jumped on two Athletics pitchers for seven runs in the first inning. The Athletics started to chip away at the lead, and having had all of two hours rest since pitching in the sweltering heat of the first game, Coombs returned to start the sixth inning of the second game. The Athletics eventually tied the score and won the game in the eleventh inning. All Coombs did in the second game was pitch 5⅓ innings of solid relief in the oppressive heat and pick up two walks in his turns at bat. The doubleheader victory temporarily put the Athletics in first place.

The Tigers and Athletics met again in Detroit for another four games, starting on July 11. A lot had happened since the two teams had squared off back in May. At this juncture, the Tigers were again leading the Athletics, but only by 1½ games. Having won 75 percent of the games they had played since their first meeting with the Tigers, the Athletics seemed poised to surpass Detroit in the standings. But Ty Cobb was not about to relinquish the lead without a fight. Before the series began, it was reported both Cobb and teammate Sam Crawford had purchased new pairs of shoes with extra long and particularly sharp spikes. Cobb denied the report, claiming that "neither he nor Crawford would handicap himself with strange running tackle in so important contests."[15] This intimidation factor, along with Eddie Collins' absence from the Philadelphia lineup due to injury, caused the Athletics to play a tentative brand of baseball. Cobb took full advantage of the situation. He banged out seven hits over the four games, including a double and a triple. He ran the bases with his usual aggressiveness by scoring from second on a sacrifice fly, scoring from first on a single, and stealing second, third and home in a single inning. The Athletics were flattened, losing all four games, with Coombs the losing pitcher in the first and fourth contests. The opportunity to catch the Tigers had been wasted, and now Philadelphia trailed Detroit by 5½ games.

Fortunately for the Athletics, their next opponents were the St. Louis Browns, by far the worst team in the American League. Helped by the return of Eddie Collins to the lineup, Philadelphia won the first two games of the series rather handily. However, the Athletics found themselves in a tight battle in the third game. Three Athletics pitchers had been unable to control the weak Browns offense, and the score stood at 6–5 in favor of the Athletics after five innings. Mack turned to Coombs to take over mound duties in the sixth inning. Coombs gave up a single run to the Browns in the seventh inning, and shut them down thereafter. Unfortunately, the usually prolific Athletics offense went quiet at this point, and the game went into extra innings. In the top of the fourteenth inning, Coombs decided to take matters in his own hands through the use of his bat. Batting left-handed against Jack Powell, the Browns' fourth pitcher of the game, Coombs unloaded on Powell's first pitch, driving it deep into the right-field seats for a home run that proved to be the game-winning run.

The Athletics completed the sweep of St. Louis the next day and captured four of their next seven contests before facing Detroit again, this time for five games in Philadelphia. It looked as though the Athletics would return the favor to Detroit, starting the series by sweeping a doubleheader behind the pitching of Bender and Coombs, then exploding for an 11–3 win the next day behind Eddie Plank. The Athletics had climbed to within a half game of the Tigers in the standings, and appeared to have the Tigers on the run. The next day was Sunday, which meant no baseball in Philadelphia. The Tigers took advantage of the off-day to regroup, and proceeded to take the last two games of the series, with the final being a 13–6 thrashing of Coombs. It had to be considered the worst pitching performance of Coombs' career to that point. Detroit drove him from the pitcher's mound in the second inning by picking up nine runs on nine hits, including a home run by Cobb as well as a double and three triples, before Mack mercifully pulled Coombs from the game. The Athletics still trailed the Tigers in the standings, now by 2½ games.

The two teams did not play each other again for another month. The Athletics, realizing they were not going to pass Detroit in head-to-head matches, started beating up on the rest of the American League. Over the next twenty-two games, the Athletics won sixteen, with Plank accounting for five, Bender four and Coombs three. Detroit finally ran out of steam, losing six out of eight to the Red Sox and five out of eight to the Highlanders. As a result, when the two teams met again in Detroit in late August, the Athletics had a 5½ game lead over the Tigers. The Athletics now had a chance to bury the Tigers, but predictably the Tigers were not about to go quietly. They beat Bender by a 4–3 score, but then took a pounding from the Athletics in the next game, losing by a score of 12–3.

Cy Morgan started for the Athletics in the final game of the series, and the Tigers reached him for six runs in five innings. The Athletics kept pecking away at Detroit, eventually tying the score in the top of the ninth. After Detroit went scoreless in its half of the ninth, Mack brought Coombs in to pitch in the tenth inning. Just as he had done six weeks earlier in St. Louis, Coombs stepped up to the plate in the eleventh and this time drove a two-run home run to give the Athletics an 8–6 lead. This blast was a long drive well over Ty Cobb's head in center field. Coombs' home run turned out to be the last home run hit at old Bennett Park, which was replaced the following season by Navin Field. (Navin Field, later known as Briggs Stadium and Tiger Stadium, was used by the Tigers from 1912 until replaced by Comerica Park in 2000.)

Unfortunately for the Athletics, Coombs' batting heroics were not sufficient to secure the victory. In the bottom of the eleventh, the Tigers loaded the bases on a solid single, a bad-hop hit on Bennett Park's notoriously rough infield (only a two-inch layer of dirt covered a cobblestone foundation) that struck Eddie Collins in the nose, and an infield single. Coombs managed to retire Cobb on a short fly, but Wahoo Sam Crawford then smashed a two-out double to clear the bases and win the game for Detroit.

The Athletics were scheduled to play the Tigers one more time that season, a three-game set starting in late September. Rather than risk the pennant at the hands of the Tigers that late in the season, the Athletics went on a tear, winning sixteen of their next nineteen games, to put themselves so far in front that the next series with Detroit did not matter. Coombs was victorious in five of those sixteen games for Philadelphia, giving up a total of only seven runs in the five outings. One of these victories was a 3–1 seven-hitter against Big Ed Walsh and the White Sox, the second time that season Coombs had beaten Walsh by that score. Coombs' next game was a 2–1 victory over St. Louis, despite the fact that he gave up thirteen hits in eleven innings.

When the Athletics again met the Tigers, they had a ten-game advantage with only thirteen games to play. This time, they took two out of three from the Tigers, eliminating their toughest opponents from contention. Coombs pitched in the pennant-clinching game, helping his cause with a double and a single. Frank Baker, who led the American League with eleven home runs, gave a preview of what lay in store for the upcoming World Series, clouting two home runs and two doubles in the 11–5 victory.

The Athletics coasted into the end of the season. Coombs pitched in two games, but was not involved in the decision. The Athletics finished the season with a comfortable 13½-game margin over the Tigers, having trailed them by ten games on May 17. During this time period, they gained twenty-five games on the Tigers, despite losing twelve of the twenty-two games played against Detroit. The Athletics took advantage of every opportunity against St. Louis, beating the Browns in twenty of twenty-two contests, while the Tigers struggled against the Highlanders, losing fifteen of twenty-two. Given how tough the Tigers and Athletics played each other all season long, the margin of victory in the standings did not reflect just how difficult winning this pennant was for the Athletics.

The measure of Coombs' season was also deceptive. He clearly was not as dominating as he had been in 1910, with the most telling statistic being the increase in number of runs allowed, from 74 to 166. Where he had tossed a record thirteen shutouts in 1910, he had only one whitewashing in 1911, and that at the expense of the lowly Browns. The composition of the new baseball clearly impacted the figures of Coombs and every other pitcher, as offensive production was up dramatically throughout the league. Also, the major leagues did not begin to officially compile earned run averages until 1912, so there was little competitive incentive to worry about the number of runs allowed as long as a pitcher's team won the game. Coombs was known to ease up in a game when the Athletics had built a big lead, as exemplified by the game against St. Louis. Nine times during the season the Athletics scored ten or more runs in a game started by Coombs, and he and various relief pitchers allowed the opposition to score on average 6.7 runs in those games, 2.3 runs per game more than were allowed in the other games he started. Following a game in midseason where Coombs coasted to a 16–9 victory over Washington after being up by an 8–2 score after three innings, Joe S. Jackson of the *Washington Post* wrote about the criticisms that had been leveled at Coombs' pitching: "Mr. Mack was on the Athletics bench, and was watching the game himself. If Coombs had not had that lead and could not have stopped the hitting, he (Coombs) would not have gone until more tallies were scored. Also, he might have pitched a tighter game had it been necessary for him to do so. No experienced pitcher works himself to death when he is out in front and knows that he has something in reserve."[16]

The measure of a pitcher in those times was the number of games he won and how often he took the ball for his team. For the second consecutive year, Coombs led all of major league baseball, this time with twenty-eight wins. (Grover Cleveland Alexander, a rookie with the National League Philadelphia Phillies, also recorded twenty-eight victories in 1911.) In the American League, only Ed Walsh appeared in more games and pitched more innings than Coombs. Among Athletics hurlers, Coombs pitched in seven more games and totaled eighty more innings than Eddie Plank, the next highest total on the team. When Connie Mack needed him to take the ball, Coombs was there. In midseason, the *Boston Globe* offered this commentary: "Jack Coombs of the Athletics affords an example of willingness to work that is unusual in these days, when too many pitchers have to hug the bench most of the time. Jack pitched in four games last week. Most pitchers think that one game a week, and two on rare occasion, is as much as they ought to be called upon to pitch."[17]

Coombs also excelled at the plate in 1911, batting .319 with six doubles, a triple and two extra-inning home runs. He drove in twenty-three runs and scored thirty-one in only 141 at-bats, far greater totals than any other pitcher in the league. At that pace, Coombs would have been among the league's offensive leaders over the course of a full season of play. Part of the reason that Coombs enjoyed strong run support in games he pitched was that Coombs' bat was in the lineup.

The Athletics' opponents in the 1911 World Series were the New York Giants. The Giants had a harder time than the Athletics in winning their pennant while shaking off the defending National League champion Chicago Cubs. The Giants finally pulled away from the Cubs in early September, and won the pennant by a margin of 7½ games. This was the first trip to the World Series for the Giants since they had faced the Athletics in 1905, beating Connie Mack's team in a series that ran five games, every one a shutout.

Early in the 1911 season, the grandstands of the Polo Grounds, the Giants' home field, had been destroyed by fire. The Giants were forced to share rickety Hilltop Park with the Highlanders while a new concrete-and-steel structure was built to replace the demolished Polo Grounds. Amazingly, by June 28 sufficient construction progress had been made to allow the Giants to return to their home field. By the end of the season, all construction was complete. Although Giants owner John T. Brush tried to name the new facility Brush Stadium, the traditional Polo Grounds was again used to describe the Giants' home. The horseshoe-shaped double-decked stadium had a seating capacity of 34,000 by the end of the season, the largest in the major leagues. While construction of the new facility had been rapid, the Giants had spared no expense in creating an elegant home for their team. A façade of Italian marble surrounded the upper deck, and decorative iron scrollwork was placed at the end of every aisle. Encircling the top of the upper deck were eagles with outstretched wings, "symbols of the National Game."[18]

Regardless of where they played during the 1911 season, the Giants were a running ball club. They literally stole their way to the National League pennant by swiping a still-unsurpassed major league record 347 bases during the season. The Giants did more than run, also leading the league in batting average and slugging average. Their pitching staff led the league in fewest runs and walks allowed and garnered the most strikeouts.

The on-field leader and icon of this Giants team was Christy Mathewson, the National League's premier pitcher. Tall, handsome, intelligent, and college-educated, "Big Six" demonstrated to the American public that it was not necessary to be a crude ruffian to be a successful major league ballplayer. Born in Factoryville, Pennsylvania, in 1880, Mathewson attended Bucknell University where he starred in football and baseball and served as class president. His first experience as a professional ballplayer was with the Taunton, Massachusetts, club of the New England League. In 1900, the Giants offered $1,500 to the Norfolk club of the Virginia League for the services of the young right-handed pitcher. In 1902, during the mercifully brief tenure of manager Horace Fogel, who later became a Philadelphia sportswriter and owner of the Phillies, the Giants experimented with Mathewson as a first baseman and outfielder. Later in 1902, John McGraw took over the managerial reins of the Giants and wisely restored Mathewson to the pitching mound, where he remained for the rest of his magnificent career.

McGraw's faith in Mathewson's potential as a hurler was rewarded in 1903, as Matty won thirty games, helping to lead the Giants to a surprising second-place finish following their dismal last-place finish of 1902. It was the first of three consecutive thirty-victory seasons and twelve consecutive seasons with at least twenty victories for Mathewson. The right-handed Mathewson's most famous pitch was the "fadeaway," a screwball that broke in towards right-handed batters. "Matty" showed incredible control of all his pitches — fastball, curveball, and fadeaway — to consistently post low walk and high strikeout totals. It was Mathewson who pitched three shutouts over the Athletics in the 1905 World Series.

Mathewson is widely considered as one of the greatest pitchers in the history of major league baseball, having achieved 373 career victories, the third-highest total in the history of the game. In 1936, he was named one of the five original inductees in the Baseball Hall of Fame.

Mathewson had a typically strong season in 1911, winning twenty-six while losing thirteen. He walked only thirty-eight batters in 307 innings pitched. Mathewson was not the only ace pitcher on the Giants' staff in 1911. He was ably supported by Richard "Rube" Marquard, a hard-throwing twenty-two-year-old left-hander from Cleveland, Ohio. Marquard came by his nickname through comparisons with Rube Waddell, the famously eccentric left-hander who had once pitched for the Athletics. Marquard, while a steady performer, did not have the pure raw talent of Waddell. Fortunately for Marquard's career, he also did not display any of Waddell's personal idiosyncrasies.

Marquard had been purchased by the Giants in 1908 for $11,000, a huge sum at the time. In 1909, his first full season with the Giants, Marquard posted a dismal record of 5–13, earning the nickname of "The $11,000 Lemon" in the process. In 1911, Marquard came into his own, winning twenty-four games for the Giants, the first of three straight twenty-victory seasons. In 1912, he established a major league record by winning nineteen consecutive games in a season.

Mathewson and Marquard were capably supported by three other pitchers on the Giants staff. James "Doc" Crandall, a twenty-three-year-old right-hander, won fifteen games, seven of them in relief. Leon "Red" Ames, who had broken in to the big leagues with the Giants in 1903, chipped in with eleven victories. Left-hander George "Hooks" Wiltse had been a consistent winner for the Giants since 1904, and contributed twelve wins to the Giants' cause in 1911.

Two of the more interesting characters on the Giants squad in 1911 were also pitchers. Arthur "Bugs" Raymond claimed that he came by his nickname for having swept a swarm of grasshoppers off the field in the middle of a game. Bugs was twenty-nine years old in 1911 and a veteran of five prior major league seasons, the previous two with the Giants. In 1909 he had won a very credible eighteen games, but he slipped to a 4–11 record in 1910. Raymond's poor performance in 1910 was the result of his alcohol dependency. Seemingly every dime he had went towards an alcoholic beverage, and when he ran out of money he would develop a scheme to get a drink on someone else's tab. McGraw did what he could to help control the demons that possessed the talented but erratic Raymond, including paying for a hospital rehabilitation stint. McGraw finally threw in the towel when Raymond blew a game in relief in 1911 while making some horrific pitches. When McGraw stormed to the mound to remove Raymond from the game, he realized that Raymond had been drinking before entering the contest. It turns out that when Raymond was sent down to the bullpen to warm up, he snuck out of the ballpark, entered a drinking establishment across the street, and traded away for a couple of drinks the baseball he was supposed to use for his warm-up pitches. McGraw released Raymond, who then bounced around as a part-time bartender and part-time semi-professional ballplayer. A year later, he was found in a hotel room dead from a cerebral hemorrhage resulting from a barroom brawl.

Charles Victor "Victory" Faust literally talked his way onto the Giants in 1911. The thirty-year-old native of Kansas was considered "feeble minded," in the parlance of the times. The story goes that in the summer of 1911 a fortune teller told Faust that he would lead the New York Giants to the pennant. So Faust found his way to St. Louis and introduced himself as both a pitcher and catcher to McGraw, and told the Giants manager that he believed he was destined to lead the team to victory, hence his nickname. In his "tryout" for McGraw, the limitations of his talents were painfully obvious, but McGraw and the team enjoyed the intense windmill windup that Faust used to "blaze" his pitches towards the plate. Uninvited, Faust followed the Giants back to New York, where he was adopted as the team's mascot. Before every game, Faust was asked to warm up, because it just might be the day the Giants needed him to replace Mathewson or Marquard on the mound. While Faust was with the team, the Giants started to pull away from the Cubs in the National League race. When the pennant was finally clinched, McGraw acceded to Faust's wishes and let him pitch an inning in a game against Boston and later in a game against Brooklyn. With the tacit assistance of the opposing teams, Faust got through the two appearances while giving up only one run. In the game against Brooklyn, he came to bat and was declared to have been hit by an inside pitch. He promptly "stole" both second and third, and then dashed home on a squeeze bunt.[19]

It was all great fun for the Giants and their fans, and Faust enjoyed every moment of his fame. While McGraw always took care of Faust's monetary needs while he was with the Giants, the two reportedly parted ways over a dispute over compensation. Four years later, Faust died of pulmonary tuberculosis while confined to a mental institution.[20]

Outside of the pitching staff, the Giants were comprised of steady, albeit unspectacular, players. Manager McGraw made a point of saying that there were "no stars on this ball club," adding that Christy Mathewson was "no better than anyone else." [21]

It is not surprising that John McGraw considered his team as one without stars; with any team managed by the "Little Napoleon," he was always the brightest light at the center of the universe. He was one of the best-known figures in baseball, both as a player and as a manager. His fame as a ballplayer came from his years with the Baltimore Orioles of the National League. McGraw played third base for the Orioles from 1892 to 1899, batting higher than .320 in seven of those seasons. The Orioles won the National League pennant from 1894 through 1896, fielding a lineup that included McGraw, Hughie Jennings, Willie Keeler and Wilbert Robinson, all future members of the Baseball Hall of Fame. Managed by Ned Hanlon, himself a future member of the Hall of Fame, the team developed an unparalleled reputation for rowdiness, with McGraw recognized as the leading practitioner. If there was a way of getting an edge on an opponent, legal or illegal, McGraw and his teammates would find it. They perfected the use of the "hit-and-run" play and mastered the "Baltimore chop" by batting down on a pitch into the hard-packed dirt in front of home plate in Baltimore to create a high bouncing ball that allowed fast runners to reach their base while infielders helplessly waited for gravity to return the ball to earth. Playing at a time when there was only one umpire, the Orioles on occasion took a shortcut from first to third base without the requisite visit to second base, knowing that the umpire's attention was directed elsewhere. At third base, McGraw was infamous for hooking his hand in the belt loop of base runners who were getting ready to tag up at third base, delaying their intended sprint to home plate just long enough to allow the Orioles outfielder to get an advantage on the throw to the plate.

If the Orioles could not beat the other team through on-field stratagems, legal or illegal, they believed it was perfectly reasonable to resort to other means, including fisticuffs with opponents and belligerent intimidation of umpires. John Heydler, an umpire in the 1890s and later president of the National League, was not a supporter of the Orioles' brand of baseball. "They were mean, vicious," he told sportswriter Fred Lieb, "ready at any time to maim a rival player or an umpire if it helped their cause. The things they would say to an umpire were unbelievably vile, and they broke the spirits of some fine men. I've seen umpires bathe their feet by the hour after McGraw and others spiked them through their shoes. The club never was a constructive force in the game. The worst of it was, they got by with much of their brow beating and hooliganism."[22] In the philosophy of McGraw and the Orioles, it did not really matter how you won the game, just as long as you won.

The Baltimore Orioles were dropped from the National League in 1900, when the league contracted from twelve to eight franchises. Ban Johnson, the founder of the American League, incorporated a franchise in Baltimore when his circuit commenced operations as a "major league" in 1901. Hoping to take advantage of McGraw's popularity, Baltimore's ownership signed McGraw as the team's player-manager. Joined by former Oriole teammate and business partner Wilbert Robinson, McGraw tried to introduce the Orioles way of playing baseball to the American League. But Ban Johnson was trying to create a family image for his new league that did not include the hooliganism exhibited in the established National League. Johnson and McGraw were constantly at odds with each other, and during the 1902 season, a fed-up McGraw struck a deal with Andrew Freedman, owner of the Giants, to become manager of the team. Having signed with the Giants, McGraw went back to Baltimore and convinced a number of his former players, including pitcher Joe McGinnity and catcher Roger Bresnahan, both future members of the Hall of Fame, to jump to the National League. Since Ban Johnson had established the American League in large measure by raiding the rosters of National League clubs, there was little he could do but seethe over the audacious behavior of McGraw.

McGraw quickly put his stamp on the Giants, and the team emerged as the National League's premier franchise during his thirty-one-year reign as manager and part-owner. The Giants were known as an aggressive team, reflecting the swagger of their manager and their city, but they did not resort to the flagrant rowdy behavior reminiscent of the old Orioles. Some of that tempering of personality can be attributed to Mathewson, who despite being the antithesis of McGraw in so many ways, was treated like a son by McGraw.

Mathewson was a tall, blond-haired, blue-eyed handsome man, an American Adonis. McGraw was short and corpulent (although he had been wiry in his playing days), with piercing brown eyes and a countenance that earned him the nickname "Muggsy," a name that he detested. Mathewson came from a successful, traditional American family, and was well-educated; McGraw's family life had seen the tragic death from illness of his mother and four younger siblings, leaving McGraw little opportunity to pursue higher education. Mathewson epitomized the concept of fair play, stoically accepting whatever results the fates might bring to him and his team, while McGraw was known as a truculent street-fighter, unwilling to acknowledge defeat under any circumstances. Mathewson was considered by many to be cold and aloof to friend and foe alike, whereas McGraw wore his emotions on his sleeve, displaying unwavering loyalty to his friends and fierce enmity to his opponents. The improbable symbiotic relationship between the two contributed immeasurably to the success of the New York Giants franchise in the early 1900s.[23]

The press offered no consensus as to the likely winner of the World Series. The expectation was that it would be a case of the Giants' speed and pitching against the Athletics' hitting and defense. It was readily acknowledged that the Athletics' pitching staff was deeper with three aces in Bender, Coombs and Plank, but there was a prevailing feeling that Mathewson would be invincible while pitching in every other game, just as he had been six years earlier.

Frank Chance, the first baseman and manager of the Cubs, thought the baseball would prove to be a key factor in the series. In his view, the Athletics had been enjoying the benefit of "hitting at a lively ball during this season, and they will run up against a dead one in the games played on the National League grounds.... The Athletics are no better hitters than the Giants. The difference is that they have been facing easier pitching and they have also been batting the lively cork centered ball."[24]

The Giants were entering the series in good health, whereas the Athletics were without the services of first baseman Stuffy McInnis, who had batted a solid .321 in his first season as Philadelphia's regular first baseman. McInnis had been injured in the last series against Detroit, having been hit in the wrist by a pitched ball from Tiger pitcher George Mullin. Despite the protests of innocence from the Tigers, the injury to McInnis appeared to the Athletics to be a retaliatory measure in response to the early-season injury that Tiger first baseman Del Gainer suffered as a result of an inside pitch from Coombs.

Although the two teams had not met in the World Series since 1905, there was an established rivalry between the two managers, with each considered to be the best in his league. Mack and McGraw had managed against each other in 1901, the American League's first season. It was McGraw who had derogatorily termed the Athletics the "White Elephants" of the league, which Mack subsequently adopted as the symbol of his club when the Athletics won their first American League pennant in 1902. McGraw took special delight in beating the Athletics and the American League in the 1905 World Series, seeing the victory as proof positive of the superiority of the National League and vindication for his own abandonment of Baltimore and the American League.

The two teams were scheduled to meet for a series of exhibitions games in the spring of 1906, but the games were cancelled when Christy Mathewson contracted diphtheria. The series was rescheduled for the spring of 1907, and McGraw was at his raucous worst, having to be forcibly removed from the field for protesting an umpire's call in the second game of the series. McGraw then refused to let his team play the next game as long as the offending umpire was on the field, which resulted in a forfeit. The remainder of the series was cancelled, and McGraw went on a rant, directing insults at Tom Shibe, the son of Athletics owner Ben Shibe. Connie Mack never forgave McGraw for his outrageous behavior in the spring of 1907, and the two men were looking forward with understandable emotion to the opportunity to defeat each other in the World Series.

For the second straight year, the National League schedule went longer than the American League slate. The drawn-out schedule was the inspiration of Brooklyn Dodgers owner Charlie Ebbets, who believed attendance would be enhanced by finishing the season on the Columbus Day holiday. Thus for the second consecutive year the Athletics played an exhibition series against an aggregation of American League all-stars while waiting for the Giants to finish out their schedule. In the four exhibition games, Mack again used his pitchers in brief three inning stints to set up his rotation for the Giants. Knowing that Bender needed the longest recovery time of all his pitchers between starts and that McGraw would likely stick with a two-man rotation, Mack's plan was to start the series with Bender against Mathewson, followed by Plank against Marquard in a battle of left-handers, and by Coombs against Mathewson.

The World Series started at the Polo Grounds in New York on Saturday, October 14, before a record crowd of 38,281. With McGraw always looking for a psychological edge, the Giants took the field in solid black uniforms with white lettering, the same uniforms they had worn back in the 1905 World Series when they had shut down the Athletics hitters. Bender and Mathewson faced each other on the mound, just as they had exactly six years before, on October 14, 1905, in the deciding game of the 1905 World Series. By coincidence, both pitchers gave up the same number of base hits as they had six years previously. The outcome was also the same, with the Giants winning the pitcher's duel by a 2–1 score. Bender pitched masterfully, striking out eleven Giants, but Mathewson was just a bit better. The game was Mathewson's fourth consecutive World Series victory, although his shutout record was blemished by giving up a single run to the Athletics in the third inning.

The Athletics bounced back to take the second game in Philadelphia, this time by a score of 3–1. Plank bested Marquard, although Marquard held the Athletics to only four hits. One of those hits came off the bat of Frank Baker, who smashed a two-run home run in the bottom of the sixth inning that provided the Athletics with the winning margin. In a syndicated article published the next day in the *New York Herald* and The *Washington Post*, Christy Mathewson took Marquard to task for having thrown a fastball to Baker at such a crucial time in the game. Mathewson claimed that he found Baker to be a better fastball hitter than expected in the first game of the series. "I told Marquard about that," he wrote, "but he evidently thought that Baker would not be looking for a fast one at that time, and looked to sneak it over. The Athletics' third baseman outguessed Marquard very cleverly, and made the hit that won the game for his club."[25] Mathewson went on to suggest that perhaps the Giants' signs had been picked up by Eddie Collins, who was the runner at second base at the time of Baker's home run. He warned the Athletics that if that were to happen when he pitched in the next game, "some batter is likely to get beaned."[26]

Mathewson's words caused quite a stir. It is difficult to determine how many of those words were attributable to Mathewson and how many were written by his ghostwriter, John Wheeler. (Ray Robinson, Mathewson's biographer, claimed that Matty neither saw nor endorsed what was in the article before it was published.)[27] It was very common for newspapers of the time to hire famous players to "write" feature articles at the World Series. For the 1911 World Series, Ty Cobb, Tris Speaker, Hal Chase, Hughie Jennings and the legendary Cap Anson all had bylined articles offering their views on the quality of play. Some others also took Marquard to task for throwing a fat fastball to Baker, but none of the others were teammates.

The very next day, back in New York, Mathewson received the chance to demonstrate to Marquard and the sporting world just how to pitch to Baker and the rest of the Athletics. He was opposed on the mound by Jack

Coombs. Both pitchers were undefeated in World Series play, meaning someone's perfect mark was about to change.

The weather for the third game was cold, raw and rainy. Despite this, another 37,216 people entered the Polo Grounds to see what turned out to be the best-played game of the series. Coombs showed none of the jitters that plagued him in his first start of the 1910 World Series, retiring the side in order in the first two innings. He was touched up for a run in the third inning on two singles and a groundout. Over the next five innings, the Giants did not get a hit off Coombs. On the other side of the ledger, Mathewson held the Athletics to three harmless singles through the first seven innings. No Philadelphia runner had reached second base to that point, so Mathewson did not have to resort to any bean balls to keep the Athletics from stealing signs. In the eighth inning, Matty entered into some trouble, but the Athletics ran themselves out of an opportunity to tie the game by getting two runners thrown out at home plate.

Going into the top of the ninth inning, the Giants clung to the 1–0 lead. The second batter in the inning was Frank Baker, giving Mathewson the opportunity to deal with the American League's home run champion "in a pinch." Baker handled Mathewson's curveball in the same manner he had handled Marquard's fastball the day before, launching a long home run into the right-field seats. With that swing of the bat, Baker would be forever known as "Home Run" Baker, and Mathewson would no longer be an invincible World Series performer. Coombs set the Giants down in order in the bottom of the ninth inning, sending the game into extra innings.

In the bottom of the tenth, the Giants threatened to score. Center fielder Fred Snodgrass led off the inning for the Giants, and stepped towards Coombs first pitch, getting hit in the shoulder. The umpire ruled that Snodgrass had made a deliberate attempt to be hit, and did not allow him to take first base. Coombs was bothered by Snodgrass' unsportsmanlike behavior, and the two started shouting at each other. Temporarily rattled, Coombs walked Snodgrass, who was then sacrificed to second base. With first baseman Fred Merkle at the plate, Snodgrass tried to steal third when a pitch slipped away from Athletics catcher Jack Lapp. Lapp quickly retrieved the ball and fired it down to Baker at third, well in advance of the oncoming Snodgrass, who launched himself feet first at Baker, tearing Baker's uniform with his spikes. Baker escaped injury while applying the tag, and the Giants lost an opportunity to score. The running Giants had tried to steal five times against Coombs and Lapp, and failed on all five attempts. Baker, who seemed to be a target for aggressive base runners, later said, "Snodgrass spiked me intentionally. He acted like a swell-headed busher."[28]

Philadelphia reached Mathewson for two runs in the top of the eleventh on three hits and an error. The Giants threatened in the bottom of the eleventh when a run scored on an error by Eddie Collins, but Coombs shut the Giants down, walking away with his fourth consecutive World Series victory. He had shown "coolness under fire" in out-pitching the great Mathewson, giving up only three hits while striking out eleven batters.[29]

Coombs received congratulatory telegrams from all over the country for having defeated the great Christy Mathewson, including one from Maine Governor Frederick W. Plaisted. He also received a telegram from his former German professor at Colby College. Not surprisingly, given Coombs' relatively poor grades in German, the telegram was in English.

Ty Cobb (or his ghostwriter) commented on Coombs' performance: "Of Coombs' work, the most notable thing was his confidence and determination. His good arm shot up curves and fast ones for the eleven innings and he held the Giants completely at his mercy. Of his performance, it was not alone head work that made him so effective, but just natural ability."[30] Mathewson (or his ghostwriter) was not nearly as complimentary, claiming that the Giants "have been beating better pitching than Coombs showed all season in the National League."[31] He also placed blame for the defeat on Snodgrass' running, poor umpiring, and the over-anxiousness of the Giants' batters. The "sour grapes" expressed in the article was inconsistent with Mathewson's image as a good sportsman.

The Athletics now had the advantage, not only in games won, but in the pitching match-ups. With the fourth game scheduled the next day in Philadelphia, Mack was able to come back with Bender on three days of rest, whereas McGraw had to decide whether to go with Marquard on only one day of rest, or one of his other pitchers. The weather gods intervened on the Giants' behalf, as heavy rains soaked the Northeast, forcing a week-long postponement of the next game. This gave McGraw the opportunity to come back with a well-rested Mathewson against Bender. Mathewson was no longer a riddle to the Athletics batters, particularly Baker, who struck two doubles against him as Bender and the Athletics beat the Giants by a 4–2 score.

Up three games to one, Mack came back with Coombs the next day in New York against the left-handed Marquard. Coombs was excited to have the opportunity to pitch the potential series-clinching game for the second year in a row, and took the mound with poise and confidence. The Athletics took a three-run lead in the third inning on the strength of a three-run home run by Rube Oldring. Through six innings, Coombs mowed down the Giants, striking out eight while giving up only four hits. In the seventh inning, misfortune struck. Coombs caught his spikes on the pitching rubber and pulled a groin muscle. Coombs looked unsteady on the mound, and aided by an error by Eddie Collins, the Giants pushed one run across the plate. Coombs was in obvious pain as he went back to the dugout, but insisted that he was able to go back out to pitch in the eighth inning. Again, Coombs looked to be in pain as the Giants got a runner to second base with one out, and Mack sent Ira Thomas to the mound to see if Coombs could continue. Coombs assured his good friend that he was able to finish the job, and proceeded to record his ninth strikeout plus a groundout to end the inning.

Deciding with his heart rather than his mind, Mack let Coombs go back out to start the ninth inning, hoping to give the "Iron Man" from Maine the opportunity to wrap up his fifth straight World Series win, an achievement that Coombs and the Athletics had denied to Christy Mathewson in the third game of the series. Unable to push off the mound with any authority, Coombs still managed to get two groundouts sandwiched between a bloop double. Just one out away from winning the World Series, Coombs gave up a double and a single to the next two batters, and suddenly the game was tied.

There was no quit in Jack Coombs. Due to bat in the top of the tenth, he insisted on taking his turn at the plate, perhaps hoping that he could crush an extra-inning home run as he had done twice during the season, thereby making up for the runs he had given up in the ninth. He only managed to hit a swinging bunt, but gamely beat the throw to first. Seeing the obvious pain on Coombs' face, Mack sent in a pinch-runner for his pitcher. The Athletics failed to score in the inning, and in the bottom of the tenth, the Giants managed to score a run against reliever Eddie Plank to take the game and revive the Giants' hopes for the series.

Coombs was taken to a local hospital after the game for treatment. Ira Thomas visited Coombs the next morning, and found Mary Coombs in tears. Whereas Coombs had received numerous congratulatory telegrams after beating the Giants, this time he received only a single telegram. Instead of offering support for his game effort under pain, the disappointed writer had accused Coombs of selling out to the Giants.

For the sixth game, Connie Mack surprised the Giants and chose Chief Bender to pitch on only one day of rest over a well-rested Eddie Plank. Bender had a reputation of being unable to pitch on short rest, but this time Mack's decision to go with his heart instead of his mind paid off. Unable to go with Mathewson or Marquard, McGraw decided to pitch Red Ames, with Hooks Wiltse ready in case Ames faltered. The Athletics hitters jumped on Ames for five runs in four innings, and then walloped Wiltse for eight more runs. Despite five errors by the Athletics, Bender was able to cruise to a 13–2 victory, giving the Athletics their second consecutive World Series victory. Jack Coombs received news of the victory from his hospital bed.

6

Mack's Greatest Team?

The reward to each of the Athletics players for winning the 1911 World Series was $3,654.58, a 77 percent increase over the prior year's winner's share. The increased attendance made possible by the rebuilding of the Polo Grounds provided the players and owners with the larger financial reward. For many of the players, this amount exceeded their earnings for the full season.

While Coombs' compensation for the 1911 season was substantial, he decided to take advantage of his fame and pursue additional avenues of remuneration in the off-season. He started endorsing products in the newspapers, ranging from cigars to sports books for young boys. A great opportunity presented itself in the form of a vaudeville show that featured Coombs and teammates Chief Bender and Cy Morgan. The show was entitled "Learning the Game," featuring the three players and experienced vaudevillians Kathryn and Violet Pearl. The show had been cast during the summer, and the three players had been rehearsing with the Pearl sisters as the opportunity presented itself. Based on his performance against Christy Mathewson in the World Series, Coombs was offered several other vaudeville opportunities as a solo act, but he refused to consider any offers that did not include Bender and Morgan. Similar circumstances had applied following the 1910 World Series, when Coombs turned down some potentially lucrative vaudeville contracts because he had already made the commitment to the barnstorming trip in Cuba.

The act opened in Atlantic City in early November to very favorable reviews. The *Washington Post* declared that the show "was unanimously voted as being the best ever staged by baseball players.... All three players appeared perfectly at ease, their singing and dancing being a credit to even seasoned

Chief Bender, Cy Morgan and Coombs pose in a 1911 publicity photo for their vaudeville show, "Learning the Game" (courtesy National Baseball Hall of Fame Library, Cooperstown, N.Y.).

stage professionals."[1] The story line was trite: one of the Pearl sisters played the part of a baseball neophyte who inherits a team, while the other played the part of the baseball fanatic who, ably assisted by three dashingly handsome ballplayers, shows her sister the way to fame, fortune, and success in the National Pastime. The show also played in New York and Chicago, again to favorable reviews. The only negative experience on the tour came in Chicago, where a package containing furs Coombs had purchased for Mary was stolen.

Following the vaudeville tour, Jack and Mary Coombs wintered in Palestine, Texas, staying with Mary's family. Connie Mack had decided that the 1912 spring training would be held in San Antonio, Texas. Plans for spring training in Texas were almost cancelled, as the Lone Star State was hit with an outbreak of meningitis. Coombs convinced Mack that the outbreak had been generally confined to the Dallas area and that it would be safe to bring the team to San Antonio.

Despite the physical exertion associated with the vaudeville act, Coombs felt that his World Series injury had completely healed, an opinion shared by his physician. He took it easy in spring training, not pitching a full nine innings in any start. He was looking forward to another successful year with the Athletics, who were the overwhelming favorites to win the American League pennant again.

Coombs was given the honor of being the Athletics' opening game pitcher. Opening at home against the Washington Senators, the Athletics celebrated their World Series victory of the previous fall with the raising of the championship banner. Coombs went out and held the Senators hitless into the eighth inning and coasted to a 4–2 win over Walter Johnson. Coombs helped his own cause at the plate, getting two hits in three at-bats against the Big Train.

Five games later, Coombs was again slated to pitch against Washington. He was cruising along with a 4–2 lead in the seventh inning when disaster struck. While facing the leadoff hitter, Coombs "reeled on the rubber, and called for help."[2] As was the case in the 1911 World Series, Coombs had made a faulty stride on the pitching rubber, this time resulting in ligament damage. Mack was already missing the services of Bender, who was suffering from "rheumatism." Coombs' injury significantly depleted the Philadelphia pitching corps. The *Washington Post* offered this view of the Athletics' prospects without Coombs:

> Should Jack Coombs' injury, sustained during yesterday's game at the local ball park, put him out for all or any great part of the season, it may prove to be a severe blow to Connie Mack's pennant hopes. Not that Mack lacks pitchers, but he has none who can work as often as Coombs, or behind whom his team plays with the

same confidence. They get runs for this twirler, and they play with a feeling that they are going to win, which always adds to a team's chance of victory.[3]

Adding to the Athletics' woes, a day later Jack Lapp, Coombs' regular catcher, was taken out of the lineup due to a case of typhoid fever.

Coombs' injury was not as severe as first feared, although he did miss more than three weeks of playing time. While he was out of the lineup, the Athletics posted a record of five wins against nine losses, and quickly sank to fifth place, 8½ games behind the front-running Chicago White Sox. Coombs returned to the lineup on May 14, starting a game against Chicago, but was not yet in form, giving up five runs in five innings of work. He was relieved by a rookie left-handed pitcher by the name of Herb Pennock, who was making his major league debut. Pennock went on to pitch for twenty-two years in the big leagues, spending most of his career with the Red Sox and the Yankees. While pitching for the Yankees, he twice won more than twenty games in a season. He finished his career with a record of 240–162, and captured an additional five games in World Series action without a defeat. Pennock was elected to the Baseball Hall of Fame in 1948.

Coombs' next start, on May 18 against the Tigers, proved to be the easiest victory of his career, courtesy of Ty Cobb's uncontrollable temperament. Three days earlier, in a game against New York, Cobb took offense at verbal taunts tossed his way by a fan named Claude Leukers that questioned the purity of Cobb's Caucasian ancestry. Cobb, deciding to take matters into his own hands, jumped into the stands, found Leukers, and proceeded to pummel him with his fists and his feet. Cobb was followed into the stands by other Tiger players brandishing bats, but the violence was limited to the altercation between Cobb and Leukers, who was reported to be a "cripple," with limited capability of defending himself. It is doubtful whether a fit young man in the prime of life would have been able to defend himself against one of Ty Cobb's violent outbursts. Order was quickly restored, and the umpires ejected Cobb from the game.

American League President Ban Johnson was in attendance at the game, and upon receiving a written report from the umpires following the contest, suspended Cobb indefinitely while the matter was investigated further. Cobb was infuriated with being suspended without having the opportunity to offer any comment in his own defense. He told the press, "Johnson has always believed himself to be infallible. He suspends a man first and investigates afterward. It should be the reverse."[4] His teammates, who generally did not have a close relationship with their star hitter, rallied to Cobb's aid, sending the following telegram to Johnson:

> Feeling Mr. Cobb is being done injustice by your action in suspending him, we the undersigned refuse to play another game after today until such action is adjusted to our satisfaction. He was fully justified in his action, as no one could stand such

personal abuse from any one. We want him reinstated for tomorrow's game, May 18, or there will be no game. If players cannot have protection we must protect ourselves.[5]

Ban Johnson ruled the American League without the benefit of other people's opinions, and quickly reminded Tigers owner Frank Navin that if his team forfeited the game against Philadelphia, the franchise would be hit with a significant fine, variously reported as ranging from $1,000 to $5,000. Navin instructed manager Hughie Jennings to round up a substitute squad for the game. On short notice, Jennings was able to gather enough players, most of whom played for local St. Joseph's College, to field a team. The Athletics proceeded to trounce the ersatz Tigers by a score of 24–2. Coombs pitched three innings, enough to get the win in the days preceding the five-inning rule for starters, before being replaced by Brown and later Pennock. The Tigers starting catcher for the game was forty-eight-year-old Deacon McGuire, a former major league catcher who was then scouting for the Tigers. Another Tiger scout, forty-one-year-old Joe Sugden, played first base. For eight of the other players, this game was the only one they would play in the major leagues. They were paid $10 by the Tigers for their efforts, with the exception of starting pitcher Al Travers, who was paid $50 for surviving without injury the relentless hitting assault by the Athletics.

The Tiger players tried to organize a league-wide strike by contacting players from other teams. Johnson would hear none of this, publicly announcing that "discipline will be preserved, regardless of cost."[6] He met with the striking Tiger players on Sunday, May 19 (there was no game scheduled that day) and let them know in no uncertain terms that if they continued with their refusal to play, he would have them permanently barred from baseball. He postponed the next day's game against Philadelphia to give the players some time to think over their position. Cobb urged his teammates to go back to work, ending the walkout. Completing his investigation, Johnson fined Cobb $50 and suspended him for a total of ten games; the striking players were each fined $100. In an era of management autocracy, there was no appeal process for the players. Later in the season, the players would organize the Ballplayer's Fraternity in an effort to gain representation when dealing with baseball management.

A week later, Coombs started against the Boston Red Sox in their new stadium, Fenway Park. The ballpark famously described by John Updike as "that lyric little bandbox" had many of the unique features that still characterize it today as the facility approaches a century of continuous service. Coombs' opposition on the mound was a young right-handed pitcher — Howard Ellsworth "Smoky Joe" Wood. Coombs, who was not fully recovered from his injury but felt well enough to pitch, was "remarkably steady in the pinches," and held the Boston "Speed Boys" to three hits.[7] The Athletics roughed up Wood for nine hits, including two by Coombs, to come away with an 8–2 victory. It was one of only five defeats that Wood suffered all season.

From May 18 to June 26 Coombs generally pitched in every third game for the Athletics. And as he had in years past, he thrived on the work, winning ten while losing only two during this stretch, including a tight 3–1 victory over Big Ed Walsh of the White Sox. While the Athletics had started slowly as usual, they started to make their move in the standings on the strength of Coombs' pitching. Trailing the first-place White Sox by 9½ games on May 18, they went on a 24–12 run (10–2 with Coombs pitching, 14–10 behind the rest of the staff), and gained 8½ games on Chicago. Despite this, the Athletics found themselves in fourth place, 6½ games behind the Red Sox, who took the lead position by playing even better ball than the Athletics during this stretch.

In late June, Coombs was again invited to Waterville, Maine, for commencement exercises at Colby College. He and his teammates from the 1906 team played a game against Colby's 1912 varsity nine. The game was not taken very seriously; the real attraction was the opportunity to see Colby's most

Coombs, standing on right, receives accolades on Coombs Day at Colby College, June 1912 (courtesy Colby College Special Collections, Waterville, Maine).

famous athlete in person. Maine Governor Plaisted was in attendance, and had issued a proclamation calling for a reduction in railroad rates for the day to allow as many citizens as possible the opportunity to see Colby Jack Coombs in person. A friend from Freeport High School named Thomas Freeman Noyes drove to Waterville to witness the occasion and penned the following poem in honor of the grand occasion.

Seeing Coombs at Waterville[8]

T'was a bright mid-summer morning
In God's country far and near
When two autos sped the roadway
Leaving Pownal in the rear.
Eight of us, a jolly party
Whirling dust o'er every hill
On our way to meet our hero;
Our own John Coombs at Waterville.

First we sing, then shout with laughter;
Hail all people whom we see
Until they turn and gaze with envy
Wondering "who that crowd can be."
But we "josh" them and we "call" them
As joy-parties always will,
For we care not for our sorrows;
We'll soon see Coombs at Waterville.

How we "purr" across the country,
Now glide through a quiet town.
We hail scare-crows by the acre,
Follow roads both up and down.
We see farmers in their gardens
Hoeing crops there with a will,
But we do not stop to converse;
We must see Coombs at Waterville.

When we meet with clever highway,
Open the throttle; how we fly!
There's a blue spot whirling skyward
Then it's good-by, old cap, good-by.
But we heed not such a mishap,
For there's no danger of a spill,
We're bound to trim all high-speed records
To see Jack Coombs at Waterville.

We enter Maine's old "Sleepy Hollow"
Where we stop there to unload.
'Tis a call of nature's secrets;
We all line up beside the road.
Next we know there's a commotion
And round the curve there whirls
A great three-seated auto
Filled with laughing, pretty girls.

Now there's yells and screeching laughter,
Dismay and glee together rolls.
Such a scramble for the auto!
Like woodchucks scooting for their holes.
But who will blame us our misfortunes?
We must all pass "through the mill;"
We go on our way rejoicing;
T'was all for Coombs at Waterville.

Yes, we saw the sights at Colby;
Met our boy-hood friend once more,
Saw him play our national game,
Ten and seven was the score.
Saw him pitch his team to victory,
Strike the batters out with skill.
The same old friend as in our boyhood
Was John Coombs at Waterville.

Yes, t'was a most delightful outing,
That day of days — June twenty-four
When we re-established boyhood friendships;
May it last forever-more.
Eight "Sons of Toil" from Pownal's gardens
Shall e'er remember with a thrill
The day they met their boyhood hero;
Our own Jack Coombs at Waterville.

Coombs was presented with a silver service by Forrest Goodwin, an 1887 graduate of Colby and a former pitcher on the Colby baseball team. Goodwin lauded Coombs' accomplishments:

> A great athlete brings not only honor to himself but honor to all with whom he is connected.... You have climbed through the classes to success, pitching two championship seasons while in college and later pitching your team into the championship of the world. There is no man living that has reputation superior to John

W. Coombs. We rejoice in your success in the past and down to the present time: you have played squarely, fairly and honorably.[9]

Earlier in 1912, *Baseball Magazine* commented on Connie Mack's use of his pitching staff in 1911. The publication claimed that Mack tried to employ his pitchers strategically based upon the strengths and weaknesses of the opposition rather than use his pitchers in a set rotation. Plank was used principally against the Boston Red Sox and St. Louis Browns, who struggled against left-handed pitchers. Bender was used selectively to preserve his strength, and only pitched against the Tigers twice all year. Cy Morgan was used against

Colby Jack Coombs displays the technique that brought him great success to the admiring crowd on Coombs Day at Colby College, June 1912 (courtesy Colby College Special Collections, Waterville, Maine).

the lesser lights of the league—Cleveland, Washington and St. Louis. Harry Krause, another left-hander, was used primarily against the Tigers and Red Sox. Only Coombs, the iron man who thrived on work, pitched regularly, with little consideration of the strengths or weaknesses of the opposition. It was Coombs' ability to take the ball against all opponents that had made him by far the Athletics' leading pitcher in terms of innings pitched and one of the top workhorses in the major leagues.[10]

At the end of June, Mack and the Athletics faced a tough stretch in the schedule, with five games against the surprisingly strong Senators, followed by six games against the Red Sox. The eleven games were played in nine calendar days, including consecutive doubleheaders against Boston. Playing one of his hunches, Mack went away from the pitching formula that had been so successful for the Athletics in 1910 and 1911. Instead of pitching Coombs as often as possible and using his other pitchers based on the situation, he held Coombs out of the series against Washington, intending to set up a match against Smoky Joe Wood in the first game of the series versus Boston. He used five different starters in the series against Washington (Bender, Morgan, Plank, Brown and Houck), and used Coombs in relief of Bender and Plank. Mack's plan seemed at first to work, as the Athletics took four out of five from the Senators and rose from fourth place to second place during that series. Unfortunately, Boston gained ground on the Athletics by taking six straight from New York, including two consecutive doubleheader sweeps. (New York was in the midst of an absolutely miserable seventeen-day stretch where they won only two of twenty-one games played against Boston, Philadelphia and Washington.)

Coombs was slated to be the Athletics starter in the first game of the Boston series, and the Red Sox were expected to counter with Smoky Joe Wood. Boston manager Jake Stahl crossed up Mack, and instead went with Vermont native Ray Collins as his starting pitcher, seemingly conceding the game to Coombs and the Athletics. Surprisingly, Collins pitched "his first really good game of the year," holding the Athletics to two runs on five hits.[11] Well rested, Coombs was out of his rhythm and was not as sharp as he had been over the previous six weeks. In addition, the Athletics' defense was uncharacteristically sloppy behind him, committing five errors, contributing to three Red Sox runs in the fourth inning and four more in the ninth. Mack used five different starting pitchers in the remaining five games of the series, and again had Coombs relieve in two of them. The Red Sox took four of six from the Athletics, increasing their lead over Philadelphia to eight games. Washington, in the meantime, was fattening its record against New York by sweeping a six-game series, vaulting the Senators back into second place, two games ahead of Philadelphia.

The previous season, on July 20, the Athletics trailed the first-place Tigers by 5½ games, yet managed to win the American League pennant by a comfortable margin. Trailing the Red Sox by eight games on July 6, 1912, did not appear to be an insurmountable margin to overcome for a team that had won the World Series the previous two years. But for all intents and purposes, the race was over at this point. The Athletics played well over the remainder of the season, winning 60 percent of their games, but Boston continued its torrid pace, winning 70 percent of its games, ultimately coasting to the American League pennant by a margin of fourteen games over the Senators and fifteen games over the Athletics.

Even though his team did not win the pennant, Mack would later refer to the 1912 Athletics as his "greatest team."[12] In Mack's opinion, "that club had speed, hitting power, pitching skill, and more brains than one ordinarily finds on three clubs; but it didn't win."[13] Mack attributed the failure of the team to win the pennant to overconfidence. Yet the team won ninety games that season, despite the fact that Mack publicly conceded the pennant to the Red Sox on September 1. Ninety victories was more than any third-place American League team had ever won, and would have been sufficient to take the American League pennant in each of the previous two seasons. The real reason the Athletics did not win the American League pennant was that the Boston Red Sox played at a superlative level all season long, winning more games than any team in American League history to that point. It was not until 1927 that an American League team, the Yankees' famed "Murderer's Row" led by Babe Ruth and Lou Gehrig, won more games than the 1912 Red Sox. The Red Sox simply dominated the league from start to finish.

Smoky Joe Wood had a career year for the Red Sox in 1912, winning thirty-four games while losing only five. Coombs and Wood faced each other just once early in 1912, with Coombs contributing two hits to the Athletics' attack and getting the better of Wood by a score of 8–2. Wood tied Walter Johnson for the American League record for consecutive victories with sixteen, including a highly publicized 1–0 victory over Johnson in front of an overflow crowd at Fenway Park. Wood went on to collect three victories, one in relief, in the 1912 World Series, as the Red Sox beat the Giants. Wood injured his pitching hand in spring training of 1913 and was never again able to throw with the tremendous velocity that had led Walter Johnson to exclaim, "There's no man alive who can throw harder than Smoky Joe Wood."[14] Wood remained in the major leagues for another six years as an occasional pitcher and part-time outfielder. He went on to have a distinguished career as the baseball coach at Yale University. He is still mentioned as a potential candidate for membership in the Baseball Hall of Fame, but has never garnered more than token support from the voters.

The 1912 season was characterized by pitching streaks. Johnson's record of sixteen consecutive victories was achieved earlier in the season. Rube Marquard of the Giants started his season with nineteen consecutive victories to set the National League record.

The Athletics' problem — if one could call a ninety-victory season a problem — was that their pitching staff was in transition. Thirty-seven-year-old Eddie Plank had the finest season of his career in 1912, winning twenty-six while losing only six. Coombs garnered twenty-one victories despite making eight fewer starts than in 1911 due to his early-season injury and Mack's mid-season change in pitching strategy. But both of Coombs' vaudeville co-stars had sub-par seasons. Chief Bender captured only thirteen wins, his lowest total since 1908. Cy Morgan, who had won eighteen and fifteen games, respectively, in the preceding two seasons, won only three games in 1912 while losing eight, and was unceremoniously released by Mack in the middle of the season.

Mack decided to try out new pitchers in the Athletics rotation in 1912, particularly in September after conceding the pennant to Boston by stating, "I do not see how any other team in the league is going to head the Red Sox in the race."[15] The bulk of the work went to Carroll "Boardwalk" Brown, who went 13–11, and Byron Houck, who went 14–6, including eight victories in relief. Both pitchers would make more significant contributions to the Athletics in 1913, but would be traded away in 1914 and play minimally thereafter.

Mack also gave brief tryouts to three pitchers who went on to enjoy significant major league careers. The first was Herb Pennock, whose major league debut was noted earlier. Eighteen years old at the time, he saw limited service with the Athletics until 1915, when Mack traded him to the Red Sox. Mack explained how he let a future member of the Baseball Hall of Fame get away. "I thought Herb didn't care whether he played ball or not ... I thought he was indifferent. But I was never so wrong in my life; letting him go when he had all that natural ability was the biggest mistake of my career."[16]

The second pitcher was Leslie Ambrose "Bullet Joe" Bush, who was nineteen years old at the time. Bush only appeared in one game, giving up fourteen hits and four walks in eight innings of work. He went on to pitch seventeen years in the major leagues, primarily for mediocre teams, compiling a career record of 195–183. His best season was 1922, when he won twenty-six games to lead the pennant-winning New York Yankees.

The third rookie pitcher was twenty-three-year-old Stan Coveleski, who appeared in five games for the Athletics. Mack let Coveleski go to Cleveland following the season, and the right-hander developed into the Indians' leading pitcher for nine seasons, winning more than twenty games in four consecutive seasons. He led Cleveland to a World Series victory in 1920 by winning three games against the Brooklyn Dodgers. He compiled a career record of 215–142, and was elected to the Baseball Hall of Fame in 1969.

Following the series against Boston in early July, Coombs went 8–6 over the remainder of the season. He again beat Ed Walsh in a tight battle, this time coming away with a 3–2 victory. It marked the fourth consecutive time that Coombs had beaten Walsh since the two of them had pitched sixteen scoreless innings against each other in the summer of 1910. Walsh captured twenty-seven victories in 1912, good for third in the league behind Wood's thirty-four wins and Walter Johnson's thirty-three wins. Coombs was undefeated in the games he pitched against these three, beating Walsh twice and the other two once.

Coombs' last victory of the season came against the St. Louis Browns. In a mere one hour and twenty-five minutes, Coombs pitched one of his best games of the season, striking out eleven batters while holding the Browns to only five hits, to come away with a 2–1 victory. Little did anybody suspect at the time that this would turn out to be Coombs' last victory for Connie Mack and the Philadelphia Athletics.

7

"Jack Coombs is a sick man"

Based on his performance over the previous three seasons, Jack Coombs was acknowledged as one of the elite pitchers in the major leagues in the early 1910s. For three years he had been the Athletics leading pitcher, which was a significant achievement given the presence of veterans Plank and Bender. Not coincidentally, Coombs' rise to prominence was an important factor in the establishment of the Athletics dynasty. Coombs easily led the team in games, games started, innings pitched and wins from 1910 through 1912. The Athletics won 72 percent of his decisions, compared to 62 percent when other pitchers collected the decision.

Coombs' numbers over these three years were comparable to two of the greatest pitchers of all time — Christy Mathewson and Walter Johnson. As shown in the table below, Coombs' statistics were very similar to that of Mathewson, with both men pitching for the leading team in their respective leagues. Johnson's statistics are somewhat better, particularly when one considers that the Senators were contenders in only one of the three seasons.

Table 1. Pitching Comparison of Coombs, Mathewson and Johnson in 1910, 1911 and 1912

	Games Won	Games Lost	Winning Percentage	Complete Games	Innings Pitched	Shutouts	Runs Allowed per Nine Innings
Coombs	80	31	.721	84	952	15	3.40
Mathewson	76	34	.691	83	935	7	2.97
Johnson	83	42	.664	108	1065	21	2.54

In the table, runs allowed per nine innings are displayed rather than earned run average. Major league baseball did not track earned runs as a pitching statistic until the 1913 season, and historical records of what constituted an earned run prior to 1913 were compiled after the fact. The most prevalent measures of a pitcher at the time were winning percentage and games won, as these were the principal pitching statistics published in the newspapers. It was noted earlier that Coombs' focus was on innings pitched and winning games as opposed to runs allowed, as he would ease up in games where the Athletics had developed a substantial lead. Mathewson at times took the same approach with the Giants, a strategy that made McGraw squirm. Much of the difference in runs allowed between Coombs and Mathewson can be explained by the difference in hitting performance between the American League and National League in 1911, which is attributable to the different types of baseballs used in the leagues.

Coombs, like Mathewson and Johnson, was among the leading hitters in the pitching ranks. Coombs' .266 batting average over the three years was six points higher than the league batting average of .260.

Table 2. **Hitting Comparison of Coombs, Mathewson and Johnson in 1910, 1911 and 1912**

	Batting Average	Doubles	Triples	Home Runs	Runs	RBIs	Walks	Stolen Bases
Coombs	.266	11	1	2	61	45	29	9
Mathewson	.231	11	2	1	35	32	23	5
Johnson	.225	17	8	5	48	47	11	5

With performance statistics at a leading level, plus four victories without a defeat in the World Series, Coombs had become one of the best-known pitchers in baseball. His name appeared more frequently in feature articles in national magazines presenting personal profiles on professional athletes. In March of 1911, *Leslie's Weekly* published an article on "The College Man as a Professional Ball Player," featuring Coombs, Christy Mathewson, Eddie Collins, Doc White of the White Sox, and Jake Stahl of the Red Sox. The article focused on the increasing presence of college graduates in the major league ranks. "Ten years ago the college player was a rarity in major-league circles. To-day there are over half a hundred college players in each of the big leagues."[1] Eddie Collins and Jack Coombs were profiled because "perhaps no two names are better known in the baseball world."[2] Two years later, the same publication featured an article titled "The Path to Baseball Fame," detailing how some of the game's stars had worked on overcoming their limitations to ultimately reach the pinnacle of performance. The article featured Ty Cobb, Jack Coombs, Christy Mathewson, Ed Walsh, Walter Johnson, Nap Lajoie and Eddie Collins.[3]

In July of 1912, *Munsey's Magazine* did a profile titled "Big Leaguers in the Spangles and Out." In addition to Coombs, people profiled included Ty

Cobb, Christy Mathewson, Joe Tinker, Frank Baker, Rube Marquard, Mordecai Brown, Chief Bender, Honus Wagner, Frank Chance, and Connie Mack. Coombs was considered the peer of these future members of the Baseball Hall of Fame.[4]

Following the 1912 season, the Athletics engaged the Philadelphia Phillies in a "city series" while the Red Sox were playing the New York Giants in the World Series. Although the two Philadelphia teams had regularly faced each other in exhibition games prior to the start of a season, it was the first time since 1903 that they had met in a post-season series for the bragging rights of "champion" of the city. Coombs was picked to pitch the first game for the Athletics. While batting in the sixth inning, he was struck behind the ear by an Earl Moore fastball. Coombs was knocked unconscious by the pitch and carried off the field. He regained consciousness in the clubhouse and was able to walk the six blocks to his in-season residence at 2213 Cumberland Street after the game. The Athletics lost the game when their relievers gave up four runs in the late innings, but went on to sweep the remaining games of the series. Despite the fact that the two teams cohabitated in Philadelphia for another forty-two years, it was the last time they would meet in a post-season series.

Wanting to keep his team in shape and focused on baseball, Connie Mack arranged for another barnstorming tour of Cuba, starting in November of 1912. The Athletics gave a much better accounting of themselves than they had two years earlier, taking ten of the twelve games played. Coombs threw a no-hitter in one of the games, and spent some time in right field, where he threw one lackadaisical opposition batter out at first base on a solid hit to the outfield.

Coombs again wintered in Palestine, Texas, with Mary's family. Connie Mack once more arranged for the Athletics to spend spring training in San Antonio. After haggling over contracts with Plank and Bender, Mack prevailed upon the two of them to join Coombs in Texas prior to the start of spring training; Mack wanted to make sure that his starting pitchers were ready for a fast start at the beginning of the season. Coombs signed his 1913 contract in early January, and wrote to Mack that he expected the "season of 1913 will be his best."[5]

Spring training was uneventful for the Athletics. Mack impressed upon his players that if they worked hard, the pennant was theirs for the taking, but they needed to avoid their usual slow start to demonstrate to the rest of the league that they were not a team to be trifled with. Many prognosticators felt that in 1913 the Athletics would again be the team to beat and that the Red Sox success in 1912 was not sustainable.

The Athletics opened the season against the Red Sox in Boston on April

A group of Philadelphia players pose for a picture during spring training. Coombs is in the back row at the far right (courtesy Wentworth Family Personal Collection).

10, a sunny, brisk day. Coombs was given the honor of being the starting pitcher for the Athletics, while Smoky Joe Wood took the mound for Boston. Neither pitcher was at his best, with Coombs being wild and Wood being hit hard by the Athletics. Both pitchers were removed after five innings, with the Athletics leading at the time by a 7–5 score. Philadelphia held on to win by a 10–9 final, with Bender struggling in relief of Coombs and Plank finally coming in to settle things down in the last three innings.

Wood had injured his ankle in spring training, went on to hurt the thumb on his pitching hand in May, and wound up damaging his shoulder later in the season as he altered his pitching motion to compensate for his ailing ankle and hand. He pitched with pain in his shoulder for most of the season and the rest of his career. He won only eleven games and pitched in 145 innings in 1913, one year after winning thirty-four and pitching 344 innings. Wood never regained his dominating fastball, and by 1918 he had given up on pitching. He spent the remainder of his major league career primarily as an outfielder for the Cleveland Indians.

Two days later Mack brought Coombs back to start the next game against the Red Sox. This time he did not last the opening inning, letting four of five batters reach first base. It was obvious that he had little strength to throw the ball with any control or velocity. He looked unsteady on the mound. The Athletics went on to win the game, as Plank again came on in relief to hold the Red Sox in check. Two days later, the Athletics announced that Coombs had been sent to his Philadelphia home with a "severe attack of grip."[6] Mack thought that Coombs would be able to resume pitching in about a week; it turned out that Coombs would not pitch again for the entire 1913 season. What initially was thought to be the flu proved to be a severe attack of typhoid fever.

In the early twenty-first century, typhoid fever is associated with undeveloped countries, where both the incidence of the disease and the resultant mortality rate are quite high. But in the early twentieth century in the United States, typhoid fever was a major health problem, ranking as the eighth leading cause of death in 1900.

Typhoid fever is caused by bacteria of the *Salmonella* family. The *Salmonella Typhi* bacteria are believed to be more than 50,000 years old, and the presence of typhoid fever can be traced back to ancient times. Alexander the Great may have succumbed to typhoid fever, as the bacterium apparently succeeded in accomplishing what the armies of the world had failed to achieve. Typhoid fever may also have been the cause of the demise of the early English settlement at Jamestown, Virginia.

Humans are the only natural host for the bacterium, which is "spread when water or food are contaminated by fecal matter."[7] The most usual means of spreading typhoid fever is through contaminated water, but it can also be spread through food contaminated by the use of fertilizers containing human feces, or through flies carrying the bacterium from human waste to fresh foods.

The bacterium responsible for typhoid fever was first isolated in 1880. A cure for typhoid fever was not developed until the 1940s following the introduction of antibiotics as a means of treating infectious disease. A preventative vaccine now exists to substantially reduce the risk of contamination should a person come in contact with the bacteria. As a result most cases today in the United States are associated with individuals who have traveled abroad without benefit of the vaccine.

While on the decline, typhoid fever was still a common ailment in the early 1900s. At the beginning of the twentieth century, typhoid fever was responsible for approximately 1.8 percent of all deaths in the United States; the rate dropped to approximately 1.0 percent by 1915. The introduction of safe, chemically-treated water supplies and contained sewage treatment systems contributed significantly to the reduction in the incidence of the disease. With the continued introduction of better sanitation infrastructure, the incidence of typhoid fever in the United States was reduced to an insignificant level by the 1950s.[8]

Coombs was one of several members of the baseball world to contract typhoid fever. Teammates Eddie Collins and Jack Lapp had previously contracted the illness, as had other baseball notables, such as Cy Young and John McGraw. Patrick Henry "Cozy" Dolan, who played outfield for several National League teams over a nine-year career, died at the age of thirty-four from typhoid fever following the 1906 season. In one of those strange coincidences in life, Joe Harris, Coombs' pitching opponent in the twenty-four-inning game in 1906, also contracted typhoid fever.

The most notorious incident involving typhoid fever was associated with a person who was a carrier, not a victim.[9] Mary Mallon was an Irish immigrant who worked as a private cook in the New York metropolitan area. At the same time Coombs and Harris were engaged in their epic struggle, Mallon was cooking for the family of Charles Henry Warren at their summer rental home in Oyster Bay, New York. Warren's daughter became sick with typhoid fever, and within a week five other household members became ill. The outbreak was investigated by health officials, including Dr. George Soper, a sanitation engineer. The investigators found no source for the outbreak, but Soper was struck by the possibility that Mary Mallon had been the carrier of the fever. Mallon had been hired by the family just a few weeks before the outbreak, and had quit her job while the investigation was ongoing. Soper traced Mallon's employment history (private cooks were generally placed by an agency) and found earlier outbreaks of typhoid fever in families where Mallon had worked. It was not until March of 1907 that Soper was able to track down Mallon, when typhoid fever broke out at a home on Park Avenue in Manhattan. The family's cook was Mary Mallon.

Soper rightfully concluded that Mallon was an immune carrier of the disease. He surmised that Mallon was unknowingly contaminating the food she was serving with her unwashed hands. Soper finally convinced New York health authorities of his theory, and laboratory tests on stool samples from Mallon found a "pure culture of typhoid."[10] The connection between Mallon and her unknowing victims had been made; her inadequately cleaned hands transferred the typhoid bacteria to the food she was preparing for her employers. Mallon was placed in involuntary isolated confinement in a dreary facility on North Brothers Island in New York's East River.

Mallon's case attracted significant attention in the press, where she was given the moniker of "Typhoid Mary." After two years of confinement, she hired a lawyer in an attempt to earn her freedom. Her lawyer's argument before the court was that Mallon had been involuntarily confined without a warrant or a legal "commitment" and that she had never been charged with a crime. If she indeed was a carrier, a charge which she denied, why was she the only alleged carrier in New York being incarcerated? She lost her case in court, which drew even more attention as the sympathetic press played on the theme of the cruel treatment of the poor, working immigrant woman due to the unfortunate circumstances experienced by her wealthy employers. Even though the New York Department of Health had won the court case, in 1910 Mallon was voluntarily released based on the expectation that she would no longer work as a cook. In a time where employment prospects for single, uneducated women were very limited, expecting Mallon to avoid working as a cook was naïve. For five years, at times using assumed names, Mallon bounced from job to job without major incident. In 1915 there was a major outbreak of typhoid fever at New York's Sloane Hospital for Women; Mary Mallon was one of the cooks. She was again incarcerated on North Brothers Island, this time permanently. She died at the facility twenty-three years later at the age of sixty-one.

It is unknown exactly where and when Coombs contracted typhoid fever. Given the fifteen-day incubation period associated with the illness, it is likely that he became infected while the team was traveling from spring training in Texas to Opening Day in Boston. Areas of the South had been inundated with floodwaters that spring, making it possible that Coombs had come in contact with contaminated water during the trip. After being removed from the second game in Boston, Coombs returned to Philadelphia and was admitted into Northwestern Hospital. The press contained conflicting statements regarding the nature of his illness, ranging from a cold, the flu, ptomaine poisoning, and even a recurrence of his torn groin muscle from the 1911 World Series. Typhoid fever was not mentioned in the press until late in the summer, even though the nature of Coombs' illness was known to friends and family much earlier than that. In early June, Eddie Plank wrote to Coombs' family in Maine and specifically mentioned typhoid fever in his letter.[11]

Coombs, by nature an optimist, was eager to get back to work. By the end of April, he was saying that he would be back on the mound by the end of May. By mid–May, July became his projected return date. On June 10, Coombs told Mack that after a period of recuperation, he expected to be back by August 1, but two weeks later, his projected return had been pushed back to September.

In mid–May, William Phelon of *Baseball Magazine* was skeptical about Coombs' ability to pitch again in 1913.

> Jack Coombs is a sick man, and, they say, may never pitch again. If so, the Athletics will lose a prop of their team, and the game will lose one of the men who showed up like the pitchers of the olden time. Long ago, a pitcher was under the impression that he should be a ballplayer as well as a specialist, and many hurlers

were intensely proud of their batting, their baserunning, their ability to hop into other positions and make good. Coombs was one of the few throw-backs to that glorious day. He could pitch an immense amount of ball without complaining; he could bat and he could play the field in splendid style. It is to be sincerely hoped that he can come back before the season ends — Jack is too good a man and too fine a character to lose.[12]

In late July, the outlook for Coombs' return appeared more promising. Ring Lardner wrote in the *Chicago Tribune*, "Jack Coombs announces that he will be able to pitch Labor Day, so Connie will have a chance to rest Bender and Plank for the world's series. And Jack probably will pitch the balance of the schedule so as to be just right for the big event."[13] The *Sporting News* echoed the outlook for a September return to the lineup. "Jack is an ambitious mortal and his name may be seen in the box score more frequently than we now expect after he once gets back on the firing line."[14]

Coombs had been seriously debilitated by the illness. His weight had dropped from his usual 185 pounds to less than 140 pounds while he was hospitalized. Had he not been a well-conditioned athlete receiving the finest medical attention, it is likely he would have succumbed to the illness. Given his severe weight loss, it bordered on ludicrous to think that he could return to health and pitch again that summer. But Coombs was determined to rejoin the team and help the Athletics to another pennant and a trip to the World Series. He returned to the club on August 4. As he went out on the field, he was "immediately surrounded by his team-mates, who fairly fell over themselves in an effort to be the first to welcome the pitcher back after his long and enforced absence."[15] Acknowledging the seriousness of his illness, Coombs said, "I was a sick man, so sick that more than one doctor gave me up. I was determined to live and get back once again with the boys, and although the fight was a desperate one, I finally succeeded in coming out victor."[16]

Connie Mack was forced to improvise with his pitching while Coombs was out, needing to replace the twenty-eight complete games and 317 innings pitched that Coombs had averaged over the previous three campaigns. His approach was to use his pitchers more often, but for fewer innings. The best example of this new strategy was Chief Bender. In the previous three seasons, Bender had averaged twenty-three appearances, while in 1913 he appeared in forty-eight games, the second-highest total in the league. However, his 236 innings pitched was only a modest increase over the 212 innings he had averaged over the three previous years. Bender appeared in relief on twenty-six occasions in 1913, as Mack avoided relying on his young, inexperienced pitchers to hurl complete games. Six of Bender's twenty-two victories came in relief.

Throughout most of the season, Mack used a five-man rotation, with

Boardwalk Brown, Joe Bush and Byron Houck supporting Bender and Plank. Mid-season acquisition Bob Shawkey was added to the rotation in July. The 1913 Athletics wound up with only sixty-nine complete games, the lowest total in the league, and well below the 107 complete games they had averaged over the previous three years with a healthy Coombs in the rotation.

At the time of Coombs' return to the team in early August, the Athletics had a comfortable 7½ game lead over the second-place Cleveland Naps. Philadelphia had started the season by taking five of six from the defending champion Red Sox, and pulled away from the rest of the league with a fifteen-game winning streak, starting in late May. The Athletics' ferocious offense and stellar defense had more than compensated for the shorthanded pitching staff.

As Coombs rejoined the team, he was targeting to return to the mound in early September, when the team was scheduled to play three doubleheaders in a five-day period. While the team was on the road in late August, Coombs stayed in Philadelphia to work on his conditioning and arm strength. On Monday, September 1, he collapsed at practice, and was rushed to the hospital with a high fever and severe pain in his spine. Typhoid fever can have a deleterious effect beyond the digestive tract, including the spleen, liver and heart. In Coombs' case, the lower spinal area had been weakened, and his doctors decided to immobilize him in a full body cast for an extended period of time. His opportunity to pitch again in 1913 went by the boards, and questions were raised once more as to whether he would ever be able to pitch again.

The Athletics went on to win the American League pennant by a 6½ game margin over the second-place Washington Senators. Walter Johnson had led the Senators that season with an astounding thirty-six victories, a total that has not again been achieved at the major league level. Along the way, Johnson surpassed Coombs' record of fifty-three consecutive shutout innings finishing with a total of fifty-six. The 1913 Athletics outscored the average American League team by over 30 percent, and outscored Cleveland, their nearest competitors, by more than a run per game. Philadelphia had won on the strength of its offense, even more so than it had done while winning the pennant in 1911, when Detroit had a comparable offensive output. Unlike 1911, when the pitching staff also led the league in fewest runs allowed, this time three teams gave up fewer runs than Philadelphia.

Coombs was still confined to a hospital bed for the World Series. The Athletics met the New York Giants in a rematch of the 1911 series. For the games played in Philadelphia, Coombs "listened" to the games via telephone, with Mary at the ballpark relaying the action to him. He was highly animated during these sessions, predicting the action before it took place for the amusement of the attending medical staff. The Athletics dispatched the Giants in

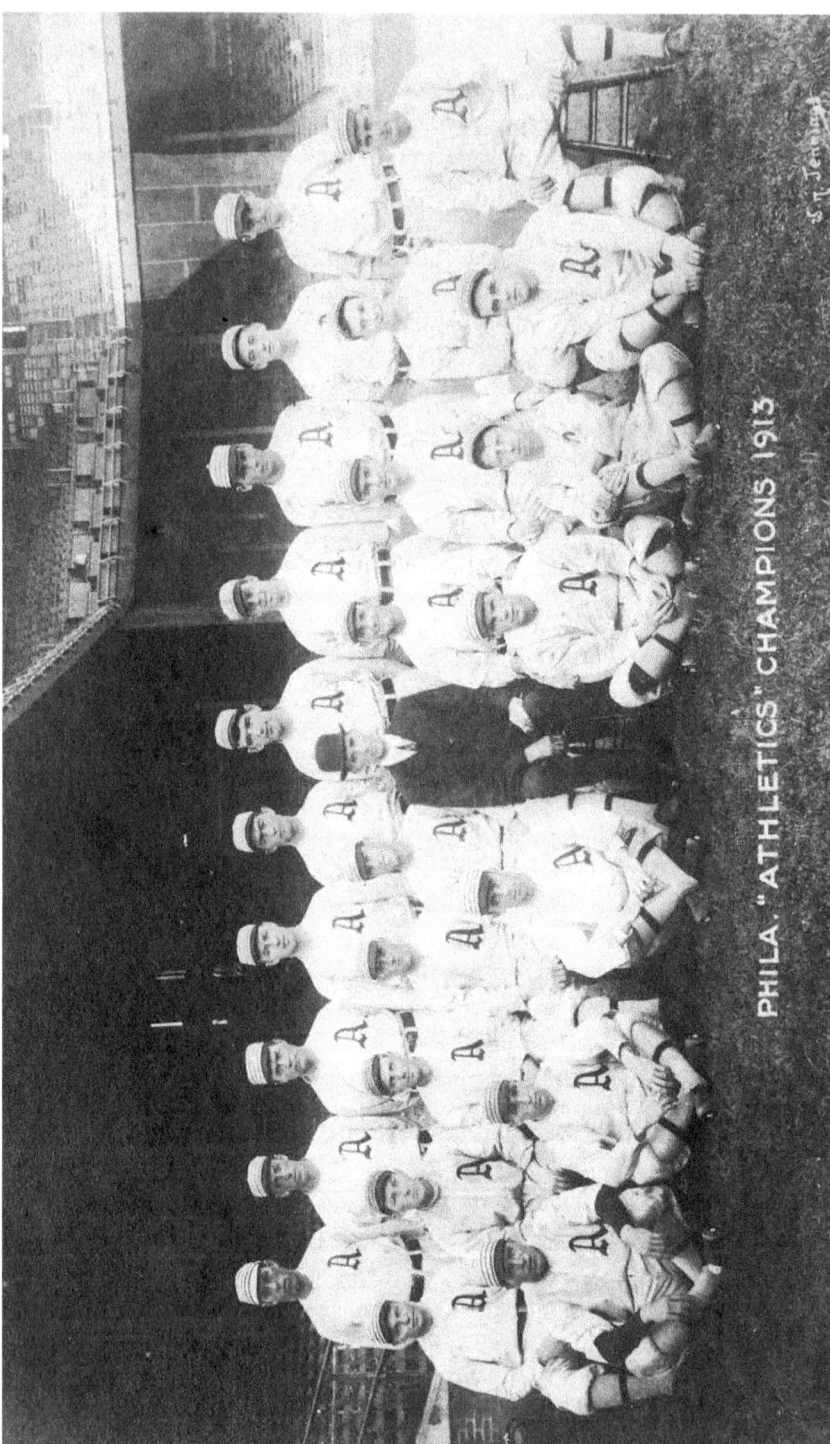

five games, their only defeat coming at the hands of a Christy Mathewson shutout in the second game. A few weeks after the completion of the series, Coombs remained in the hospital, still immobilized in his full body cast. His good friend, catcher Ira Thomas, had remained in Philadelphia with his wife to keep Mary Coombs company during the ordeal. Many of his teammates were in Philadelphia for a celebratory banquet in late October, and afterwards they went to the hospital and filled Coombs' room with flowers while he slept.

A regular visitor to Coombs during his hospitalization was Louis Van Zelst, batboy and mascot for the Athletics. Unlike Charles Victory Faust, who had imposed himself on John McGraw and the Giants, Van Zelst had been "discovered" by Connie Mack late in the 1909 season when Van Zelst was a young teenager. The young man had suffered a debilitating injury when he was ten, leaving him with a hunchback. While attending a game late in 1909, the benevolent Mack offered to let Van Zelst be the team's batboy for the game, which the Athletics won in dramatic fashion. Mack decided that Van Zelst was a good-luck charm, and formally hired the youngster for the 1910 season. Coombs and shortstop Jack Barry were unofficial guardians to Van Zelst, making sure that he stayed out of trouble on the road and regularly attended church services on Sundays. The young man became very devoted to Coombs, and frequently came to the hospital to check on Coombs' condition. Van Zelst was employed by the Athletics from 1910 through 1914, a period during which the Athletics won four pennants and three World Series titles. He died tragically of heart failure in the spring of 1915 at the age of twenty.[17]

Coombs was touched by the treatment he received from Connie Mack and his teammates. Mack kept Coombs on the team payroll throughout the season, and he was awarded a full share of the team's winnings from the World Series. In a time when players had few contractual rights and were readily disposed of when unable to perform, the Athletics' treatment of Coombs was extraordinarily generous.

Coombs was fitted with a back brace and released from the hospital in early December. He went home to Maine later in the month to recuperate and remained optimistic that he would be able to resume his baseball career. "Will I play with the team next year? If God gives me the strength I will.... This rest has done me worlds of good. And let me whisper this softly, I feel that I could clout a ball from here to next week. Next year you watch me.

Opposite: **The 1913 world champion Philadelphia Athletics. Coombs, still showing the physical effects of his bout with typhoid fever, is at the left end of the back row. Standing next to him is left-handed pitcher Eddie Plank (courtesy Wentworth Family Personal Collection).**

Maybe I won't be a five hundred hitter or drive 'Home Run' Baker to the backwoods, but I'll lay you a wager that I will figure in the box score just the same."[18]

His doctors predicted that with adequate rest Coombs should be ready to return to action by June of 1914. Coombs spent an uneventful winter following doctors orders, regaining weight and gradually getting himself back in condition. In March, he and Mary traveled to Palestine, Texas, to be with Mary's family. In May, he was back in Philadelphia to have his back brace removed, and he was given clearance to begin playing baseball.

Connie Mack initially used Coombs as a scout for the team, having him visit various colleges in the Northeast in search of talent. One of his trips was to Colby College, where "his appearance at chapel Monday morning was the signal for a wild ovation, the enthusiasm of which is rarely equaled."[19] After a month of this travel and finding few prospects, Coombs rejoined the team in Detroit in June. At the time, the Athletics were in second place, a game behind the Washington Senators and a half game ahead of the third-place Tigers.

Given the pitching strategy that Connie Mack had adopted in 1913, it would seem at first glance that Coombs could have been worked into the pitching rotation fairly easily, either as a short-inning starter or as a late-inning reliever. But Mack was again employing a different approach with his pitching staff in 1914. In 1910 and 1911, nearly 80 percent of the innings pitched had been handled by four pitchers, with Coombs taking close to 25 percent of the total load in both seasons. In 1912 and 1913, a comparable workload was spread among five pitchers. In 1914, Mack spread most of the work among seven pitchers, all of whom would win at least ten games, but none would win more than seventeen. It was the first time a team would have seven ten-game winners in the twentieth century. The feat was later accomplished by the 1939 New York Yankees and the 1976 Cincinnati Reds. Mack made less use of relief pitching, and the staff complete game total increased from the lowest in the league in 1913 to the second highest in 1914.

Regardless of whether Mack was unwilling to disrupt his rotation by committee or did not believe that Coombs was sufficiently recovered to pitch at a major league level, the fact remains that Coombs was not utilized in a pitching role against major league competition for some time. The first record of Coombs pitching against professional competition in 1914 is in an exhibition game in Syracuse on July 24 when he gave up one run on four hits in five innings, with no apparent strain in his pitching motion. Coombs later claimed he could have easily pitched the entire game. He continued to be used exclusively in exhibition games, and Mack announced in late August that he would not utilize Coombs in a major league game until such time as the Athletics clinched the American League pennant. At that point, the Athletics had bludgeoned their way to a 13½-game lead in the American League, having already outscored every team in major league baseball by more than 100 runs.

Coombs finally pitched in a major league game on September 28, giving up one run on three hits in three innings of work against the St. Louis Browns. Five days later, he pitched five innings against the Washington Senators, giving up three runs on five hits. For a man who had been through a life-threatening illness, leading many to doubt whether he would ever pitch again, Coombs' return to the mound was a tremendous accomplishment. Despite the fact that Coombs was clearly not in the same condition as he was prior to his illness, Mack included him as one of the eight pitchers selected for the Athletics roster in the 1914 World Series.

The Athletics faced the Boston Braves in the 1914 World Series. For a decade, the Braves had been perennial doormats in the National League. On July 4, they found themselves in a customary position, last place, trailing the league-leading Giants by fifteen games. The Giants were seemingly on their way to a record-setting fourth consecutive pennant. Under the fiery leadership of combative manager George Stallings and the diminutive double-play combination of former Cubs second baseman Johnny Evers (5' 9", 125 lbs.) and shortstop Walter "Rabbit" Maranville (5' 5", 155 lbs.), the Braves started a steady, dogged climb in the standings. Stallings relied heavily on a three-man pitching rotation of Dick Rudolph (twenty-six wins), Bill James (twenty-six wins) and Lefty Tyler (sixteen wins), in sharp contrast to Mack's seven-man rotation. By August 1, the Braves had climbed to fourth place, eight games behind the Giants. By September 1, they were in second place, a mere half-game behind the Giants. By the time the season ended, the "Miracle Braves" had won the National League pennant by an astonishing ten games over the Giants. From August 1, at which point they had won only half of their contests, to the end of the season, the Braves went 49–14.

The overconfidence that Connie Mack blamed for the Athletics not winning the pennant in 1912 surfaced again prior to the World Series. Seeking their fourth series championship in five years and the overwhelming favorites to do so, the Athletics did not take the upstart Braves very seriously. With the American League pennant safe in hand in late September, Mack ordered Chief Bender to scout the Braves. Bender instead took the few days to go fishing, telling Mack afterwards that he did not "see any need for scouting that bush league outfit."[20] The "bush league" Braves trounced Bender and the Athletics by a 7–1 score in the first game, and went on to execute the first-ever sweep of a World Series. When Mack pulled Bender from the mound in the first game, he was heard to say, "Pretty good hitting for a bush league outfit."[21]

The interaction between Mack and Bender was symptomatic of the deteriorating relationship between Mack and his star players. Although one could not guess from their performance on the field, the Athletics were a team in turmoil in 1914. The cause of that turmoil was a new rival major league known as the Federal League. The Federal League had claimed major league status for itself in 1914, but was initially not much of a threat to the preeminent position of the American and National leagues. Only a few players of note, such as Cubs shortstop Joe Tinker and Pirates infielder Bill McKechnie, had "jumped" from the established leagues to play in the Federal League in 1914. With new, aggressive leadership in the form of league president Jim Gilmore and some wealthy team owners, the "Feds" made a push to achieve more equal status by heavily recruiting players from the established teams. Danny Murphy, former Athletics outfielder and team captain, was playing for the Brooklyn franchise in the Federal League in 1914. According to Mack, Murphy aggressively recruited his former teammates to join the upstart league, and higher salaries were offered as the incentive for abandoning the Athletics. Faced with losing such star players as Baker and Collins to the rival league, Mack was backed into a corner where he had to tear up existing contracts and offer his players two- or three-year contracts at much higher levels of compensation. Unlike a number of Federal League owners, whose wealth came from interests in oil refineries, bakeries, and restaurants, the Philadelphia Athletics were Mack's sole source of livelihood. As a result, Mack managed his dollars closely, sometimes sharing his accounting ledgers with his star players to demonstrate just how much he could afford to pay them.

Connie Mack was distracted by the Federal League "war" in 1914, and a deep mistrust arose between the manager and his players. To the credit of all involved, it did not evidence itself on the field of play. But Mack expected loyalty to the franchise from his players, and he was not going to be held as an economic hostage by the Federal League.

Shortly after the end of the World Series, Eddie Plank approached Mack and told him that he was seriously considering an offer from the Federal League. Rumors started to circulate in the press that Bender was already under contract to a team in the Federal League. At the same time, the press rather innocuously reported that teammates Bob Shawkey, Herb Pennock and Jack Lapp were going to be Coombs' guests on a three-week moose-hunting trip in the woods of northern Maine.[22] What apparently caught Mack's eye was that Danny Murphy, former Athletics player and current Federal League recruiter and agitator, was joining the four Athletics on the trip.

Mack decided to act, and act precipitously. While Coombs and his friends were roughing it in the Maine woods, Mack announced that he had asked for waivers on the core of his pitching staff: Coombs, Bender and Plank.

Mack's stated intention was to give other American League clubs the opportunity to retain the players in the league by paying them what the players thought they could get in the Federal League. According to Mack, "I am for the American League in victory or defeat, and I am going to keep these players for our league if possible."[23] Mack made it clear in the press that he was confident that each pitcher would perform well for any team that signed them, and he was particularly adamant that Coombs would regain his prior mastery on the mound.

Shortly after being released by the Athletics, Plank and Bender announced that they had signed contracts to pitch with Federal League clubs in 1915. Coombs came back from his hunting trip to learn that he was out of work. Coombs' case was curious, because Mack had carried Coombs on the team payroll for two seasons during his illness and recovery, including shares of the World Series payoffs. Mack had previously told a sportswriter that "he would never release Coombs until he asked to be released."[24] And despite the presence of Danny Murphy on the hunting trip, neither Coombs nor any of his hunting partners were about to sign contracts with the Federal League.

Mack was not through dealing with his star players. In December, he further shocked the baseball world by selling second baseman Eddie Collins to the Chicago White Sox for $50,000 rather than risk losing Collins to the Federal League. He also fell into a prolonged contract dispute with Home Run Baker, resulting in Baker's refusal to play the entire 1915 season for the Athletics. Having lost the services of his three veteran pitchers and half of his "$100,000 infield," Mack's Athletics plunged to the bottom of the American League in 1915, a position they would hold for seven consecutive seasons.

An unknown poet penned the following verse in memory of the four departed Athletic stars.

> Only a gap in a baseball nine—
> A few players missing, so why repine?
> Other heroes will take their place
> And respond to our cheers through the pennant race.
> But Reader, if sentiment is not yet dead,
> You'll brush off a tear and bear your head
> As you see no more in the same old rank,
> Collins and Bender and Coombs and Plank.
>
> Collins and Bender and Coombs and Plank;
> What thrills ye gave us! What joys we drank,
> As bravely as ye fought when the battle was on
> And hurled back the foe with your might brawn.

Year after year we have looked to you
To lead the charge of our flag-winning crew.
Always in the van of the valorous rank
Were Collins and Bender and Coombs and Plank.

Collins and Bender and Coombs and Plank;
Of your best ye gave us; no duty ye shrank.
Yours was the place where the blood grows hot—
Where the less brave trembled, and nerves stretched taut.

But the time comes to all, as it has to you,
When we've got to move on for another crew;
And when our time comes let us hope we'll rank
With Collins and Bender and Coombs and Plank.[25]

In later years, Mack admitted that the heightened emotions associated with the Federal League war had affected him deeply. In 1932, while reminiscing about the 1914 season, he told sportswriter Joe Williams, "I don't know whether you know it or not, but I quit on my team in August." He felt that the distraction of the Federal League led to club morale that was "completely broken." He broke up the team "solely because the boys had shown me that they could not get along together."[26] He later told sportswriter Fred Lieb:

> Even though we won, it was my unhappiest season in baseball. Federal League agents, and one of them was my old player, Danny Murphy, dogged our players all season. In some cases we had to tear up two and three contracts to hold our stars, and I was disgusted and discouraged with the lot of them. Time heals many wounds; the players were trying to get all they could, just as they did in the American League's early days, but I was too close to a bad situation to have much patience with it.[27]

To add insult to injury, the Federal League war may have also clouded Mack's judgment in evaluating prospects. One of the most successful minor league clubs of the time was the Baltimore Orioles of the International League, headed by Jack Dunn. The Federal League had placed a franchise in Baltimore, which caused a significant drop in attendance and financial hardship to Dunn and his team. Looking to raise some money, he offered to sell some of his prospects to major league clubs, including a young, promising left-handed pitcher by the name of George Herman "Babe" Ruth. Mack turned down the offer from Dunn, telling him to sell Ruth to "someone who can give you real money."[28] Ruth was sold to the Boston Red Sox and became a dominating left-handed pitcher, helping to lead the Red Sox to three pennants while Mack's team wallowed in the cellar. The Red Sox subsequently sold Ruth to the New York Yankees, where he went on to become the greatest star in the history of the game.

Mack has been portrayed at times as a parsimonious owner, limiting the compensation of his players for his own benefit.[29] His generous financial treatment of Jack Coombs during 1913 and 1914 shows the fallacy of that portrayal. Earlier in 1914, when former Athletic pitcher Rube Waddell, the hard-drinking, fun-loving left-hander, became seriously ill with tuberculosis and was unable to pay for medical treatment, Mack and the Athletics stepped forward to pay Waddell's medical bills. As noted earlier, Mack's sole source of income was the Athletics, and there were times in his stewardship of the team that he was simply unable to compete financially with some of his well-heeled rivals. At those times, he took the actions that he thought were in the best interests of the franchise. Hindsight may bring into question the wisdom of some of those actions, but Mack tried to treat his players honorably based on his understanding of the facts surrounding the situation. In the case of Jack Coombs, he appears to have wrongfully assumed that Coombs was committed to the Federal League and was assisting Murphy in the raiding of the Athletics roster. Mack decided as a result that he had no choice but to release Coombs, along with Plank and Bender.

The Federal League folded following the 1915 season. Its brief existence had a profound impact on the Athletics franchise and individual players for years to come.

8

"Old Jack Coombs"

The headline of the article in the December 11, 1914 edition of the *Los Angeles Times* read "Jack Coombs is World's Hard Luck Champion." The article did not hold out much promise for the continuation of Coombs' career in baseball. "Jack Coombs is through.... Coombs has taken his place with those who 'used to be.'"[1]

Baseball Magazine was more hopeful for Coombs' revival.

> He is one of the finest and best liked men on the diamond today.... It is the sincere hope of the fans that next season will stage the scene of his come-back, whatever team he may be with. He is a young man as yet, and under the spur of a cleanly lived life there is every chance that one day in the near future he will be the fearless curver of old, shooting his blinding third strike across the rubber with the bases full, and receiving the homage he has so justly earned.[2]

Having made the politically incorrect decision to invite Danny Murphy on his hunting adventure, Coombs found himself out of a job with the Philadelphia Athletics. Unable to pitch for most of the previous two seasons, it would constitute a leap of faith for another club to sign the thirty-two-year-old pitcher to a contract. Coombs considered retiring to his farm in Maine, or working in the wholesale grocery business with Hyman Pearlstone in Texas. He had even briefly flirted with the idea of a political career, making speeches in Maine on behalf of the Progressive Party. But baseball was what he knew and did best, and Coombs was not yet ready to walk away from the game.

Surprisingly, help came from none other than Connie Mack, who wrote a letter of recommendation to Charles Ebbets, owner of the Brooklyn franchise in the National League, giving Mack's view that Coombs' arm was sound. Chief Bender likewise gave a written recommendation to Ebbets. In

January, it was announced that Coombs had been signed by Brooklyn with the expectation that he would pitch and help with the development of the team's young pitching staff. Although offered a guaranteed one-year contract, Coombs insisted on the standard ten-day release clause, giving the team the ability to drop him should he prove unable to pitch once again at a major league level.

The Brooklyn franchise had been struggling for success for a number of years. Charles Hercules Ebbets had been the principal owner of the club since 1905, having risen from ticket-taker to club owner through hard work, dedication, risk-taking and political toughness. The team won back-to-back National League pennants in 1899 and 1900, but had struggled in the second division since 1905. To make matters worse, Brooklyn's neighbors and bitter rivals, the New York Giants, had won four National League pennants and one World Series during this time period. Ebbets steadfastly pursued a course to transition his team from also-rans to contenders. One of the first steps was the opening of Ebbets Field in 1913. Ebbets Field, a cozy ballpark where the rabid Brooklyn fans were in close proximity to the players, became one of the most storied venues in baseball history.

Another important step for Ebbets on the road to respectability was the hiring in 1914 of Wilbert Robinson team manager. "Uncle Robbie," as he was affectionately called by the press, had achieved fame as the steady catcher on the Baltimore Orioles of the 1890s, the hard-nosed aggregation that included Giants manager John McGraw and Tigers manager Hughie Jennings. Robinson had developed a close personal relationship with McGraw, following him first to St. Louis and then to the Baltimore franchise in the infant American League. When McGraw jumped from Baltimore to become manager of the New York Giants, Robinson replaced McGraw as Baltimore's manager for the remainder of the season and then retired from baseball to concentrate on managing the *Diamond Café*, the sports restaurant that he and McGraw co-owned. McGraw coaxed his old friend out of retirement to join the Giants as a coach in 1911, and the Giants went on to capture the first of three consecutive pennants. Following the Giants defeat at the hands of the Athletics in the 1913 World Series, McGraw and Robinson got into a heated argument over the direction of the club, and McGraw fired his old friend. McGraw's loss was Ebbets' gain, as he hired Robinson as Brooklyn's manager for the 1914 season.

Robinson came to the job with a reputation as a strong handler of pitchers from his days as a catcher. Intelligent but coarse, with a propensity for profanity, Robinson was a jovial character, in stark contrast with the bellicose McGraw. Robinson went on to manage Brooklyn for eighteen years, capturing two pennants along the way. He was ultimately elected to the Baseball Hall of Fame.

The Brooklyn club at that time was officially known as the Superbas, a name harkening back to a time when the team was of superior quality. They were also frequently referred to in the press as the Dodgers, in recognition of the citizens of Brooklyn, who were known as "trolley-dodgers" due to the large number of light rail lines that crisscrossed the borough. During Robinson's reign as manager, the team became known as the Robins, in honor of its popular leader. It was not until Robinson's retirement following the 1931 season that the team would be known solely as the Dodgers.

The Brooklyn pitching staff was young and inexperienced, led by twenty-seven-year-old Jeff Pfeffer, who won twenty-three games the previous year in his first full major league season. Three other pitchers, William "Wheezer" Dell, Sherry Smith, and Ed Appleton, had seven innings of major league experience among them. The only veteran pitcher on the staff was George "Nap" Rucker, who was nearing the end of his career after toiling faithfully for mediocre Brooklyn teams over the previous eight seasons. The inexperience of the pitching staff is what made Brooklyn willing to take a chance on Coombs. In the words of sportswriter Frank Graham, "Nobody knew any more about pitching than he did."[3]

The Brooklyn offense was led by first baseman Jake Daubert, a native of Shamokin, Pennsylvania, and the National League batting champion for each of the previous two seasons. Daubert went on to have a fifteen-year career in the major leagues, recording a lifetime batting average of .303.

Complementing Daubert in the hitting department was left fielder Zack Wheat, a steady left-handed hitter who usually batted above .300. A quiet man, Wheat drew most attention with his bat, accumulating 2,884 hits and a .317 batting average in a nineteen-year career. He was elected to the Baseball Hall of Fame in 1959.

There was another future member of the Hall of Fame on the squad — Charles Dillon "Casey" Stengel. He would ultimately achieve fame as the manager of the New York Yankees from 1949 to 1960, guiding the club to ten pennants and seven World Series championships in twelve seasons as the team's skipper. In 1915, the twenty-four-year-old right fielder was entering his fourth season with Brooklyn, having hit .316 the previous season. Over fourteen seasons as a player, Stengel batted a respectable .284 while playing for five National League teams.

Stengel was known for his acerbic wit and outlandish pranks. In 1918, while playing for Pittsburgh at Ebbets Field, he captured a small sparrow and hid the bird inside his cap. When the Brooklyn fans booed him, as they did all opposing ballplayers, he grandly bowed to the stands, tipped his cap, and watched the bird fly away, symbolically "giving the bird" to the fans.

One of the most famous stunts attributed to Stengel took place in spring training of 1915. Brooklyn was training in Daytona, Florida, at the same time that a well-known female pilot, Ruth Law, was taking passengers for flights above the Daytona Beach area in her bi-plane. Air flight was still a novelty at the time, and Charles Ebbets was eager to do a promotion to draw attention to his team. The plan agreed upon was to drop a baseball from the plane and have Wilbert Robinson, manager and former catcher extraordinaire, catch it. Being the only intellectual on the team, Coombs was consulted as to the likely speed of the ball when it would reach Robinson so that the ball could be dropped from a proper altitude. Everything was set for the grand event, with the whole team and reporters gathered on the field to see Robinson perform his stunt. The plane flew a few hundred feet overhead, and the "ball" was dropped. It turned out that the ball was not a baseball, but a grapefruit. Robinson circled under the sphere as he would have done twenty years earlier while playing for the old Orioles. When the grapefruit deflected off Robinson's glove and into his chest, it splattered and knocked him over. Covered with pieces of grapefruit, Robinson thought he was gravely injured and called out, "I'm dead! My chest is split open! I'm covered with blood!"[4] The crowd, realizing what had happened, laughed uproariously at Robinson's expense. Coming to the realization that he was not injured, Robinson's first comment was, "Who done this, Stengel?"[5] Robinson's biographers, Jack Kavanagh and Norman Macht, claim that Stengel had nothing to do with the substitution of the grapefruit for the baseball, but Stengel was at the time considered guilty by reputation.[6]

Coombs looked good in spring training, throwing effortlessly from the mound. He also spent time tutoring the young members of the pitching staff. Grateful for the chance to pitch again after a two-year absence, Coombs told the *Washington Post,* "I would like to remain in major league baseball two or three more years, but whether Father Time will allow me to do so is a question. Although I never received a real fancy salary for my services, yet I have never squandered my earnings, and when the time comes, as it must to all of us in any walk of life, I shall not have to worry over finance."[7] He and Mary found a place to live on Ocean Avenue in Brooklyn and settled in for what they hoped was the resumption of Coombs' career.

The Brooklyn Robins opened their season in New York, losing two out of three to the New York Giants, and then moved on to Boston where they lost four straight to the defending champion Braves. Coombs appeared in relief in the penultimate game against Boston, and "was given a most cordial welcome by the fans, who would be glad to see him 'come back' again."[8] He pitched three innings of scoreless baseball, giving up no hits, but walking four batters. Coombs' continued wildness in relief the next day cost the Robins the final game against the Braves.

Following this rocky beginning to the season, Coombs received his first chance in a starting role on April 30 in a game against the Phillies, played in Philadelphia. It must have been a bittersweet moment for Coombs, taking the mound for the opposition in the city that had given him so much support over nine years. Pitching against Eppa Rixey, a 6' 5" left-hander in his fourth major league season, Coombs pitched a "steady, careful game."[9] He gave up eight hits and six walks, but as he had done so many times in the past with the Athletics, he bore down with runners on base and escaped from tight situations. He had two hits at the plate and pitched a complete game, winning 2–1, with the Phillies' sole run coming in the ninth inning. Coombs' last victory had come thirty-two months earlier, on August 24, 1912. He had been much sharper in that game, recording eleven strikeouts in a 2–1 victory over the St. Louis Browns. While he still had not totally regained his previous form, he had demonstrated to the doubters that he could indeed come back and perform again at a major league level. His Uncle Jesse exclaimed when he heard the news of the game, "Bully for John — that shows that he's not all in by a jug full!"[10]

Now with the Brooklyn Robins, an older, less husky Coombs following his illness and two-year absence from the game demonstrates the fluid motion that made him an effective pitcher (courtesy National Baseball Hall of Fame Library, Cooperstown, N.Y.).

A week later, he again started against the Phillies and Eppa Rixey, this time in Brooklyn. The outcome was another complete-game victory, by a score of 3–2. Beating the Phillies twice was no fluke, as they were a strong club in 1915. They set the tone for their season by starting off with an eight game winning streak. Supported by a fine hitting lineup, their pitching staff was led by Grover Cleveland Alexander, who as a rookie in 1911 had tied Coombs for the most victories in the major leagues. In 1915, "Old

Pete" recorded a season similar to the one Coombs had in 1910, winning thirty-one games, with twelve shutouts and 376 innings pitched. Alexander also won more than thirty games in each of the next two seasons on his way to a lifetime total of 373 victories, tied for third on the all-time victory list with Christy Mathewson. In later years, Alexander suffered from epilepsy and alcohol dependency, but by 1915 he had surpassed the aging Mathewson as the acknowledged ace of the National League. Coombs pitched against Alexander in late June, and the two pitchers turned in a performance similar to the epic battles that Coombs and Big Ed Walsh had previously staged. Coombs tossed a four-hitter against the Phillies that day but tired in the late innings and lost, as Alexander pitched a masterful one-hitter. The entire game was completed in an hour and nine minutes.

Eppa Rixey, whom Coombs had beaten in his first two starts and would beat once more later in the season, had much in common with Coombs. He too had graduated from college with a degree in chemistry, having completed his course of study at the University of Virginia. Like Coombs, he went straight to the major leagues from his college campus, never pitching an inning in the minor leagues. He spent his first four seasons developing his pitching potential, posting a 32–38 record. He went on to pitch twenty-one seasons in the major leagues, compiling a 266–251 record, and was elected to the Baseball Hall of Fame in 1963.

The newspapers were thrilled to see Coombs back. Grantland Rice interviewed Ebbets for the *Boston Globe*. Ebbets said, "Coombs has not only shown better stuff than I believed he still had left, but he is a fine man for a ball club, a good, clean, hard-working citizen, who is a credit to the game."[11] Rice added, "We'd like to see Colby Jack step out and win every game he pitches, that being the type of citizen we have always found him."[12]

After Coombs captured a third consecutive victory, this time a 2–0 whitewashing of the Reds, the *Sporting News* was glowing in its praise.

> Jack Coombs is the real wonder of the season. Make no mistake about it. His comeback to date has no way been a fluke. His three games were won by 2 to 1, 3 to 2, and 2 to 0. Any baseball follower knows what that means. It means that there was not an inning in which Jack could afford to let down and ease the strain. He had to pitch at the very top of his form in every blessed round of the 27. Every game was a grueling, merciless test of Jack's stamina, and he came through with flying colors.[13]

Clearly overstating the extent of Coombs' absence from the game, the "Baseball Bible" went on to add:

> Where in all the history of base ball can a man be found who was totally disabled for four years, a year of which he spent literally on a bed of agony because of spinal trouble, and has then returned to the sport strong enough and fresh

enough to win his first three games of a major league campaign without apparent discomfort? It should further be remembered that — while Jack was in his hey-day when he injured himself on the mound in pitching that World's Series game in Philadelphia in 1911— he was not a spring chicken, but a veteran of several years' standing. His work is a lasting monument to grit, determination and the never-say-die spirit, and credit to the highest ideals of American manhood.[14]

It is a shame that the writer got his facts wrong — Coombs missed two seasons, was injured in New York in 1911, and spent three months in a body cast — but the message was still a valid one. If there had been a Comeback Player of the Year Award at the time, Coombs would have won it easily. He posted a record of 15–10 for the season, second only to Jack Pfeffer on the Robins' pitching staff. He chafed a bit at not starting as often as he had in the past, preferring to go back to the time when he took the mound every third day for Connie Mack. Wilbert Robinson was committed to giving his young pitching staff a chance to develop. Coombs' stamina also was not as great as it had been prior to his illness, as he sometimes lost effectiveness late in a ballgame.

Among the highlights of Coombs' season were two starts against Christy Mathewson and the Giants. After twelve consecutive seasons with twenty or more victories, Mathewson was on the downside of his fabled career. He posted an 8–14 record for the season as the Giants tumbled to last place. Their two meetings in 1915 brought back remembrances of their battle in the 1911 World Series, when Mathewson suffered his first World Series defeat at the hands of Coombs and the Athletics. In 1915, Coombs beat Mathewson and the Giants by scores of 3–0 and 3–2. The *New York Times* recognized the achievement of the two veteran pitchers in their first contest.

> New York got only four hits off of Coombs, and at no time did they have a chance to score. As of old, Coombs was wonderfully effective in the pinches, and several times got out of difficulties by his superb pitching. There may be something more spectacular, more flashy about the twirling of the present-day class of boxmen; but it is a relief to see seasoned veterans like these two work. There is no waste of motion, no delay in posing, no apparent effort or strain. It is the smooth, finished achievement of masters of their craft.[15]

Another highlight of the season came in late August against the St. Louis Cardinals. Pitching in the second game of a doubleheader, Coombs punched out three hits, including a triple, and drove in two runs, including the game-winning run, to lead the Robins to a 3–2 victory. A humorous low point of the season took place on July 6 against Boston. In the fourth inning of the game, Coombs slipped on the mound, fell to the ground in great discomfort, and needed to be carried off the field. There was an immediate fear that Coombs had suffered the same injury to his groin that had occurred in the

1911 World Series. It turned out that when he slipped, he had swallowed the chew of tobacco he had in his mouth, making him nauseous. As he told the *Sporting News*, "I knew that if I attempted to rise I would vomit all over the diamond ... and scare the crowd about the extent of my hurt. For that reason I let them carry me off. When I got out of sight I vomited so much I thought I never would stop."[16]

On September 13, Coombs led Brooklyn to a 6–3 win over the St. Louis Cardinals by collecting three of the Robins' seven hits. He gave up seven hits and seven walks to the Cardinals, but managed to strand eleven baserunners. A rookie by the name of Rogers Hornsby made his first major league start in the game, and Coombs held him hitless in four trips to the plate. Hornsby would not be held hitless by many pitchers over the course of his twenty-three-year career, leading the National League in hitting seven times and topping the .400 mark on three occasions. He finished his career with a .358 batting average, second only to Ty Cobb. Many consider Hornsby to be the greatest right-handed hitter in major league history.

Supported by the pitching of Coombs and its other young hurlers, Brooklyn made a surprisingly strong showing in the National League, winning eighty games on its way to a third-place finish, ten games behind the pennant winning Philadelphia Phillies. It was Brooklyn's strongest showing in fifteen years, and Coombs' contributions to the success of the team, both as a clutch pitcher and sage pitching coach, were widely acknowledged. *Sporting Life* proclaimed, "Coombs is largely responsible for the success of the Dodgers."[17] Brooklyn had started the season in the cellar by losing six of its first seven games, but by the end of August, the Robins were in second place, only three games behind the Phillies. Philadelphia ran away from the pack in September as Brooklyn faded.

While Brooklyn's pitching was surprisingly good in 1915, its offense was surprisingly weak, scoring the second-fewest runs in the league. Zach Wheat had the worst hitting season of his career by far, hitting what was for him a lowly .258. Casey Stengel also suffered at the plate, batting a mere .237 following a .316 mark the prior season. Stengel was reported to be suffering from typhoid fever when he first reported to spring training, and it appears to have taken a physical toll on him throughout the season.

In late August, the Robins picked up Rube Marquard from the Giants. With the Giants floundering in last place, and Marquard coming off a dismal season in 1914 where he lost twenty-two games, McGraw decided to give up on the big left-handed pitcher. The Robins gladly picked up Marquard, believing that he would benefit from being reunited with Wilbert Robinson, who had been a Giants coach while Marquard was winning twenty or more games in three consecutive seasons. Marquard did not make much of a contribution during the stretch drive, but he worked closely with Jack Coombs over the last month of the season. Marquard told the press that he "learned more about pitching just from Jack Coombs during the few weeks he was with the Trolley Dodgers than he did in all the years he was with the Giants."[18]

From his work with Brooklyn in 1915, Coombs developed a reputation as an effective pitching coach. Late in the season, he was offered a three-year contract by Yale to be the university's baseball coach, but turned it down after talking with Ebbets about how he fit in with Brooklyn's plans for 1916 and beyond. Ebbets was enthusiastic about keeping Coombs with the club and offered him a three-year contract to stay with Brooklyn. "Coombs looked good," Ebbets commented after the season, "but I think he will be even better next year."[19] He added this tribute to Coombs' character: "As fine a man and player as I have known in over thirty years in baseball."[20]

Ebbets and Robinson signed more castoffs like Coombs and Marquard for the 1916 season, hoping that by adding some more experienced players to the roster that Brooklyn could improve upon its third-place showing in 1915. Larry Cheney, a tall right-hander who had won twenty or more games for three straight seasons with the Cubs, was traded to Brooklyn late in the 1915 season. Chief Meyers, who had been the Giants regular catcher since 1909, was released by McGraw following the 1915 season and signed with the Robins. Ivy Olson, Cleveland's shortstop who was known more for an argumentative disposition than his baseball skills, was picked up on waivers in the middle of 1915. Third baseman Mike Mowrey was an eleven-year veteran of four major league clubs, most recently with Pittsburgh of the Federal League. Robinson blended the old with the new in 1916 and transformed Brooklyn into a bona fide contender.

The club was enthusiastic from the start of spring training, when pitchers reported to Coombs for the first few weeks at Hot Springs, Arkansas, before joining Robinson and the rest of the team in Florida. Coombs predicted that Brooklyn would be "pennant contenders from the start."[21] The *Sporting News* commented on Coombs' value to the Brooklyn organization: "Coombs is one of the few great pitchers who know why they are great. That is, he not only knows what he throws, but he can make another pitcher understand how he throws it. Besides his ability as a developer of pitchers, he is deeply learned in all the other branches of the pastime, and will be a handy asset in camp."[22] Umpire Billy Evans added his views on Coombs' intellectual contributions, stating "Any one familiar with Jack Coombs was not surprised at his great showing last year, even though he admits his speed does not sizzle as it did five years ago, or his curve break with such a snap. Jack Coombs uses his brain; he makes a study of his game."[23] The *New York Times* added, "There is perhaps no keener baseball mind in the game today than that of Jack Coombs, the former 'Iron Man' of the Athletics. Since he joined the club the pitchers have shown much improvement under his coaching. With Coombs as Manager Robinson's first lieutenant, there is every reason to believe that the Dodgers will prove a stronger club than last year."[24]

The team looked as though it would get off to another slow start, dropping three of its first four games. Coombs and Marquard were blown away by the Boston Braves in Coombs' first start. A week later, Coombs started against the Phillies and former teammate Chief Bender. Bender had spent the previous season pitching for Baltimore of the Federal League. It had not been a happy experience for Bender, as he toiled for a horrible last-place team, accumulating a 4–16 record. Coombs beat Bender and the Phillies with his bat and his arm, stroking a single and a double on his way to a 5–3 victory.

Brooklyn suffered through eight postponements due to rain in the early going, resulting initially in an irregular pitching rotation and a substantial strain on pitching arms later in the season. The team played thirty doubleheaders during the season. Robinson's strategy with his pitching staff was to push his younger pitchers — Pfeffer, Cheney and Smith — and hold Marquard and Coombs in reserve for relief and doubleheaders. Coombs' first relief appearance of the season came against the New York Giants on May 1, when he took over for Nap Rucker in the fourth inning and held the Giants to six hits and two runs the rest of the way in the Dodgers' won 8–5 win. Two days later, he again relieved against the Giants and again picked up the victory as Brooklyn won by a 6–4 score in ten innings. The victory put the Robins in first place, a half-game ahead of the Braves; the Giants, by virtue of a 2–11 start, were in the cellar.

The Giants, coming off a last-place finish in 1915, were rebuilding in 1916. Mathewson appeared in only twelve games for the season before being traded to the Cincinnati in July, giving him an opportunity to manage the Reds. It would prove to be his last season as a pitcher. In May, Mathewson penned an article on the value of pitching in the major leagues that included the following exchange with Jack Coombs regarding the prospects of the Brooklyn pitching staff.

> "We'll have the best pitching staff in the league," Coombs said to me. "We are loaded with consistent left-handers and right-handers. There isn't a poor one in the lot." "Better not get boastful, Jack," I cautioned. "You know pride goes before a fall." "Well. I'll bet you a new hat that I win more games than you do," Coombs came back at me. "I'll take that." I said. So watch out for a real tussle if Coombs and I happen to hook up.[25]

The two big right-handers never did pitch against each other in 1916, and Coombs easily won his bet with Mathewson, earning thirteen victories to Mathewson's four. Coombs wound up winning all three of his career starts against Mathewson: one in the 1911 World Series and two during the 1915 season.

The Robins continued to perch in first place as the season wore on. On June 17, Coombs beat the Cubs in relief by driving in the winning run in the eleventh inning after the previous batter had been intentionally walked to get to Coombs. The Cubs had apparently forgotten about Coombs' hitting prowess, as he had demonstrated with a .385 average in the 1910 World Series against Chicago. The victory gave Brooklyn a three-game lead over the defending champion Phillies.

On July 3, Coombs beat the Giants again, this time a 6–1 complete-game victory. The *New York Times* reported, "Old Jack Coombs tottered out to pitchers' box up at the Polo Grounds yesterday without the aid of crutches and held the Giants to three hits. If Jack were fifteen or twenty years younger, maybe the Giants wouldn't have made any hits at all."[26] Brooklyn still maintained a three-game lead, while the Giants sat in fourth place, 6½ games behind the Robins.

On August 20, Coombs came close to holding an opponent without "any hits at all." He shut out the Cubs in Chicago by a 1–0 score, giving up only one hit and facing the minimum twenty-seven batters. The Chicago fans "were unsparing in their applause for the masterful performance of Coombs."[27] While the newspapers were referring to Coombs as "Old Jack," more often he was demonstrating that there was still some youth left in his strong right arm.

On August 30, the Robins were still in first place, maintaining a three-game lead. They were facing an important five-game series against the Phillies, and Coombs was slated to pitch the first game against Grover Cleveland Alexander. Coombs gave up a home run on the first pitch of the game, which proved to be sufficient offensive support for Alexander, who went on to record his thirtieth victory and fourteenth shutout of the season, winning by a score of 3–0. Alexander's whitewashing of Brooklyn broke Coombs' major league record for shutouts in a season, set in 1910. Ol' Pete went on to notch sixteen shutouts for the season, a record that still stands. Coombs still holds the American League record with the thirteen shutouts he twirled in 1910.

The Robins offense suddenly became anemic against Philadelphia, scoring a total of only five runs in the five games. The Phillies swept the five games, moving into a three-way tie for first place with Brooklyn and Boston. Next up for Brooklyn were the Giants at the Polo Grounds, still in fourth place and trailing the leading triumvirate by 12½ games. Coombs beat the Giants again, scattering ten hits on his way to a 5–2 victory. The *New York Times* again poked fun at Coombs' age. "Old Jack Coombs, who was doing the firing for Brooklyn, was effective in his own slow fashion. Jack can take up more time thinking over what he is going to pitch than a woman can consume making up her mind to step off a street car."[28] The game dragged on for two hours and five minutes.

The Robins split the four games with the Giants and found themselves in second place, 1½ games behind the Phillies. Everybody was anticipating a September dog-fight between Brooklyn, Boston and Philadelphia to see which team would come out on top. Surprisingly, the Giants were to become the dominant story in baseball. McGraw's team had been erratic throughout the season, losing eight straight games in April, winning seventeen straight in May, and losing eleven of twelve in August. Leaving the Robins and Jack "the Giant killer" Coombs behind, the Giants went on a major league-record twenty-six-game winning streak, with all of the games played at home. The Giants played nine doubleheaders during the streak. The streak was finally broken by the Boston Braves in the last game of the homestand. During the streak, the Giants beat Philadelphia four times and Boston three times, helping Brooklyn pull back into first place, clinging to a half-game lead over Philadelphia with four games left to play. Those four games were to be played against the Giants in Brooklyn.

The Giants' improbable run had kept them in the hunt for the pennant, but the loss against Boston that broke the winning streak had mathematically eliminated them from the race. The four remaining games gave the Giants the opportunity to knock Brooklyn out of first, an opportunity against his former friend Wilbert Robinson that McGraw relished. As one might expect, Robinson put Coombs on the mound for the first game against the Giants. For the sixth time that season, Coombs defeated the Giants, twirling a 2–0 shutout. The press described Coombs' effort in heroic terms. "There was no question as to who was the Brooklyn hero. The laurels rest on the shoulders of Colby Jack Coombs. The old Athletic mainstay was there in all his ancient glory. With the pennant possibly hanging in the balance ... Colby Jack was all nerve and iron, and try as they might the glittering Giants could not batter a breach in his defence."[29] The victory gave the Robins a one-game lead.

When the Giants relinquished a lead in the next game against Brooklyn, McGraw seethed, leaving the Giants bench in mid-game and publicly stating that he thought his team was not trying. This brought an outcry from all quarters. The Phillies demanded an investigation, implying that the pennant was being given to Brooklyn, while Robinson and Brooklyn claimed that McGraw's tirade was a jealous attempt to deflect credit from Brooklyn. The Robins took two of the remaining three games against the Giants, while the Braves won three out of four from the Phillies, and the furor over McGraw's outburst eventually died down. For the first time since 1900, Brooklyn was the champion of the National League.

Coombs went 13–8 for Brooklyn in 1916. Uncle Robbie's young staff had carried the lion's share of the load during the season, with Pfeffer leading the team with twenty-five wins. Coombs was used selectively, particularly in those situations where brains were considered just as necessary as brawn to get the job done. He was not the "Iron Man" of his Philadelphia days, but he was again a key contributor as a player and a coach to Brooklyn's success.

Coombs' contributions were recognized in the press as the Robins prepared for the World Series against the Boston Red Sox. According to Hugh Fullerton, "The Dodgers have perhaps the oddest pitching staff in the country, and its hope of beating the Red Sox would lie with three men—Jack Coombs, Big Pfeffer, and Rube Marquard ... I have been back over the records, and if Coombs is, as they claim, as good a pitcher as he was when he won pennants for Mack, he will give the Red Sox a terrific battle, even with the erratic and uncertain support of his panicky team."[30] Christy Mathewson added, "But for ability, gameness and heart, I'll stack Marquard and Coombs against any of them. There is not a better money pitcher in the world than Jack Coombs ... Jack may not be able to do the stunts he did in 1910, when, for the Athletics almost single-handed, he stopped the Cubs, but he'll be able to pitch two of the first six games if the classic runs that far, and do himself justice in each."[31] Tim Murnane of the *Boston Globe* chimed in, "Coombs was considered the shrewdest man Connie Mack had on his staff when the Athletics were the greatest team on earth, and they tell me that Jack Coombs has been a large factor in the success of Brooklyn this season."[32] Finally, Grantland Rice offered his opinion, stating, "Coombs is a smart, courageous pitcher with a world of experience and a lot of stuff left."[33]

The Boston Red Sox were winners of their second consecutive American League pennant. In 1915, their offense had been led by Tris Speaker, one of the premier hitters and defensive center fielders in the history of the game. Speaker had been the Red Sox regular center fielder for seven years, consistently batting well over .300. But the Red Sox were not willing to pay "Spoke" what he thought he was worth and traded him to Cleveland for cash and two players at the start of the 1916 season. Speaker went on to win the batting title with Cleveland that season, breaking Ty Cobb's string of nine consecutive batting championships. In his twenty-two-year career, Speaker achieved a .345 batting average, the fifth highest of all-time. A strong hitter who drove the ball to all corners of the outfield, he holds the major league record with 792 career doubles, and is sixth with 223 career triples.

That the Red Sox were able to win again given the loss of their premier player came as a bit of a surprise. But manager Bill "Rough" Carrigan, a native of Lewiston, Maine, had a balanced ball club. Speaker had been supported in the outfield by Duffy Lewis and Harry Hooper, forming one of the greatest defensive outfield units in all of baseball history. Both men had fine seasons in 1916. Speaker's spot in center field was filled by journeyman outfielder Clarence "Tilly" Walker. The infield, including Coombs' former Athletics teammate Jack Barry, was also a strong defensive unit. Third baseman Larry Gardner, in his ninth season with Boston, was the only regular on the team with a batting average over .300. The strength of the Red Sox was not in their hitting, but in their pitching and defense. While ranking only sixth in the league in runs scored, they led the league in shutouts, fewest runs allowed, and fewest errors. The pitching staff was spearheaded by hard-throwing left-hander Babe Ruth, who led the team with twenty-three victories. Ruth was surrounded by a deep supporting cast consisting of Dutch Leonard (eighteen wins), Carl Mays (eighteen wins), Ernie Shore (sixteen wins) and Rube Foster (fourteen wins). Ruth supported himself with a strong bat, hitting .272 and clouting three home runs. Two seasons later he would start the transition from pitcher to hitter, becoming the most dominant slugger in the history of the game.

Smoky Joe Wood had courageously won fifteen games for the Red Sox in 1915, pitching in pain throughout the entire season. He seemingly retired in 1916, although after sitting out the season, he joined the Cleveland Indians in 1917 and went on to play six seasons primarily as an outfielder.

The Red Sox were strong favorites to win the World Series in 1916 based on the depth and experience of the team. The Sox were such overwhelming favorites that Carrigan had to focus his team on the task at hand. "We'll take them," said Carrigan, "but that means everybody has to play his game. You beat them out there, not in the newspapers."[34] Coombs tried to rally the Robins, telling the *Boston Globe*, "We will be right at their throats all the time. If any one believes Boston is going to ride right over us he is reckoning without men of the stamp of Jake Daubert, Pfeffer, Marquard, and Chief Meyers."[35]

Loyal National Leaguer Christy Mathewson made the case that Brooklyn was going to make a better showing than expected. To Mathewson, Coombs was an important factor for Brooklyn. Matty wrote:

> A pitcher who will go in there and work a good, heady game against Boston will have a better chance of winning than one with a lot of stuff and no bean work. It is my opinion that John Coombs, one of the smartest pitchers ever to mount the mound, will show a game against the Red Sox which will take the clouds away from the eyes of many spectators and put clouds on the lamps of Boston batters. John knows those boys, as I have pointed out before. He showed what he still could do when he shut out the Giants. "Has Coombs got the stuff he used to carry?" I was asked. "Not quite so much stuff in his arm," I replied, "but his head hasn't lost any."[36]

Sportswriter Hugh Fullerton gave a remarkably prescient preview of the series, predicting that the Red Sox would win in five games. He predicted that the sole Brooklyn victory would come in Game Three, with Coombs the victor. "Coombs, as he now pitches, usually is hit freely but not consecutively, and I expect him to record a handy victory by keeping the Boston hits scattered through many innings."[37]

Even Coombs' family had to admit that the odds were against the Robins. His Uncle Jesse wrote in his diary, "I will root for Brooklyn, hoping they will win out handily, but I expect it to be a tough scrap."[38]

The first two games of the series were scheduled in Boston. Instead of using Fenway Park, the Red Sox had arranged to play the games in Boston at Braves Field, which had a much greater seating capacity. Opened in 1915 near the banks of the Charles River, Braves Field was the first stadium to have a seating capacity greater than 40,000. Its outfield was spacious, with a distance to the outfield wall in excess of 400 feet down the left-field line and more than 500 feet in the deepest part of the outfield. The outfield dimensions provided fielders with the challenge of covering an extraordinary amount of territory. Adding to that challenge were the rays of the late-afternoon sun shining directly in the face of the right fielder. The dimensions of the field favored left-handed pitchers, and Coombs had been beaten soundly in his two previous starts at the ballpark in late 1915 and early 1916. Perhaps that is why Wilbert Robinson decided to go with left-handers Rube Marquard and Sherry Smith in the first two games in Boston.

Marquard was opposed by Ernie Shore in the first game. Shore, a 6' 4" right-hander, had come to Boston in 1914 as part of the sale that brought Babe Ruth to the Red Sox. He won nineteen games for Boston in 1915, grabbing another sixteen victories in 1916. Ruth and Shore combined to pitch one of baseball's most unusual games in 1917. Ruth started the game against the Senators and proceeded to walk the first batter on four pitches. Disagreeing with the umpire's calls on each of the pitches, Ruth got into a heated argument and took a swing at the umpire, resulting in his expulsion from the game. Shore was called into the game with little warm-up. The base runner was caught stealing, and Shore went on to retire the next twenty-six batters in succession for a no-hitter. Shore, however, was not nearly as effective against Brooklyn in the first game of the World Series, but he managed to scatter nine hits on his way to a 6–5 victory over the Robins. The game was not as close as it appeared, with Brooklyn scoring four of its runs in the ninth.

While the press predicted that Robinson would pitch Coombs against Ruth in the second game of the series, Uncle Robbie went with left-hander Sherry Smith. The game proved to be a pitchers duel, with Ruth and Boston finally prevailing with a 2–1 victory in the fourteenth inning. The Robins' lone run came on an inside-the-park home run by Hy Myers in the first inning, as Ruth shut Brooklyn down on five hits the rest of the way.

Ruth's complete-game victory remains the longest in the history of the World Series.

While Coombs had not pitched in the first two games, he was involved in both losses as the Robins' third base coach. In the first game, Zach Wheat tripled in the fourth inning to make the score 1–1. With nobody out, George Cutshaw lifted a fly ball to shallow right field. When Boston right fielder Harry Hooper stumbled and fell making the catch, Coombs sent Wheat towards home. Hooper quickly recovered and made a fabulous throw to home plate, getting Wheat for a double play and killing the Brooklyn rally. In the third inning of the second game with Brooklyn holding a 1–0 lead, Brooklyn pitcher Sherry Smith hit a long drive to the right-field fence for what looked like an easy double. Apparently, Smith had not observed Hooper's throwing capabilities the day before. He rounded second and headed towards third despite Coombs' outstretched arms indicating Smith should hold at second. Hooper gunned down Smith by a comfortable margin, again killing another potential Brooklyn rally.

Having failed with his left-hander strategy in the first two games, Robinson went with Coombs for Game Three, choosing the experienced hand that was undefeated in World Series play and bypassing Pfeffer for the third time. The press encouraged Robinson with his choice. According to the *Washington Post*, "Coombs is Manager Robinson's one best bet. Of course, he can take a chance with Jeff Pfeffer, who slabbed a portion of Saturday's combat, but it is generally believed that the Brooklyn leader will send in an older head against the world's champions ... Coombs has been through the grind of these baseball classics and is figured to have an even chance to win his game. Coombs knows how to pitch."[39]

Brooklyn fans were outraged that Charlie Ebbets was charging $5 for grandstand seats in the series, compared to the $3 being charged in Boston. Ebbets' argument was that he needed to charge more per seat if he was to generate the same revenue that had been taken in at the much-larger Braves Field. The fans did not buy Ebbets' economic theory, and there were a number of empty seats when Coombs toed the rubber in cold weather for the third game. He was opposed by Carl Mays, a submarine pitcher who would go down in baseball infamy when he beaned Ray Chapman of the Indians in 1920, resulting in Chapman's death.

Mays was ineffective on this day, and the Robins touched him for four runs by the end of the fifth inning. Through the first five innings, Coombs gave up four singles; three of those runners were subsequently erased on the bases, preventing Boston from threatening to score. He was "in splendid form," and "looked like the Coombs of other days."[40] In the sixth inning he was reached for two runs, the key blow being Harry Hooper's triple. In the seventh, with one out, Larry Gardner hit a long home run for Boston to bring the Red Sox to within a run. Coombs was "game enough and wise enough" to realize he was running out of steam and was unwilling to repeat his experience in Game 5 of the 1911 World Series when he stayed on the mound too long against the Giants after suffering an injury.[41] He motioned to Robinson that it was time to bring in Pfeffer, who retired all eight batters he faced to save the victory.

Coombs was lauded in the press for making the right judgment. "Jack Coombs, already a veteran of two world's series with the Philadelphia Athletics, came in for unstinted praise, both for his splendid twirling in the early innings of the game and later for his self-abrogation in requesting to be relieved when he felt himself slipping and realized that to remain in the box might entail defeat for his teammates."[42] With this victory, Coombs became the third pitcher to achieve five World Series victories, joining Mathewson and Bender. He was the only one of the three to be undefeated in World Series play.

Coombs was pleased with his performance. "Yes, I guess I pitched a pretty good game for an old man. It was cold and I felt it. But at least I knew when I was weakening and had sense enough to get out. I was glad to be of service to the boys. I have been in world's series before and got my share of breaks, but it was a new experience for most of the Brooklyn boys."[43]

The *Sporting News* was unstinting in its praise of Coombs' efforts.

> On the baseball scrolls of the past decade the name of John Wesley Coombs can be found in many places. John went out this afternoon to make new fame for himself. He has known the strain of the Series before, has triumphed before. But he never did himself prouder than today ... Colby Jack loomed out there on the hurling hill like a tower of strength.... He responded nobly to the frenzied appeals of his myriad friends in the stands, and then wished himself out, when he might have remained and had the glory all to himself ... Ancient Jack was the last line of defense as you might say, and Ancient Jack held out long enough to turn the tide of defeat away from the Dodger camp and all things considered that was some honor.[44]

Despite Coombs' inspirational performance, Brooklyn was not able to turn the series around. The veteran Red Sox were simply too strong for the over-matched Robins, and took the next two games easily by scores of 6–2 and 4–1. For the first time in the twentieth century, the cry of "Wait till next year!" was raised by Brooklyn fans.

9

"You can have this glove; I won't need it anymore"

"Next year" was not the experience that Brooklyn baseball fans were hoping for. The year began on the wrong foot long before the players suited up for the start of the season. Despite the team's success in 1916, Charlie Ebbets was faced with another economic challenge. Several of his players were coming off the multi-year contracts they had signed at the height of the "war" with the now-defunct Federal League. Ebbets and a number of other owners wanted to return to pre–Federal League levels of compensation now that the players did not have an alternative option. As a result, Brooklyn players received contracts in the mail representing a reduction in their pay. Seven of those players, including starting outfielders Wheat, Stengel, and Myers, and two starting pitchers, Pfeffer and Smith, became holdouts.

Ebbets did not understand how the players failed to see the economics of the situation from his perspective. He visited some of the players, trying to convince them of the wisdom of his viewpoint, but that strategy backfired. Zack Wheat was suitably self-sufficient on his Missouri farm, and sent Ebbets home without a signed contract. Hy Myers resorted to chicanery to convince Ebbets that he too was financially independent. Myers borrowed prize cattle and horses from neighboring farms to demonstrate to Ebbets that he was no longer reliant upon baseball for a living.

Not surprisingly, Casey Stengel became the most visible and vocal of the holdouts. Stengel had batted a serviceable .279 with eight home runs and fifty-three runs batted in during 1916, but in Ebbets' view he was still not performing at the level of 1914, when he batted .316 with four home runs and sixty runs batted in. Ebbets thought Stengel deserved a significant reduction in pay, from $6,000 to $4,600. Stengel was outraged and responded to Ebbets with an impudent "Dear Charlie" letter, implying that Ebbets must have mistakenly sent Stengel the contract for team handyman Red Hanrahan. Stengel riled the owner further, tweaking Ebbets' nose in the press by recalling Ebbets' unpopular decision to charge high ticket prices during the World Series. "It seems reasonable," declared Casey, "that if he charges such high prices to see his players perform, he should meet the fans halfway by giving them the opportunity to watch high-priced players."[1] Stengel's logic did not impress Ebbets, and Stengel was coaxed back into the fold only when Ebbets agreed to add some bonus provisions to his contract dependent upon Stengel returning to his 1914 performance level.

Ebbets eventually got everybody signed, but not without significant animosity. At times, members of the press felt compelled to intervene between the owner and the players to facilitate resolution. While the 1917 club was essentially the same one that went to the World Series in 1916, the attitude of the players going into the opening of the season was decidedly different.

In addition to the rancor between the owner and the players, there was still a not-so-veiled hostility between the Robins and the Giants. Members of the Brooklyn franchise still fumed over McGraw's accusations of his team's indifferent play in the final series, allowing Brooklyn to win the pennant. Coombs spoke out in the press, comparing the methods of Connie Mack and John McGraw. "When Mack had his old team ... we didn't wrangle with the umpires and swear at the opposing players. I guess we were too businesslike. But that is the way Connie wants his men to play." Coombs added, "Mack's methods are just the antithesis of John McGraw, both in playing the game and in rebuilding a club. McGraw's idea is to buy ball players at any price, then mold them into a machine as quickly as possible and rush on. That method is all right if you have unlimited capital."[2]

The Giants and Robins started the season in different directions, giving a clear indication that 1917 was not likely to be a repeat of 1916. The Giants opened the season by going 13–5, quickly grabbing the National League lead. Brooklyn, on the other hand, dropped thirteen of its first eighteen games, taking up the rear slot early in the pennant race. Two of the Giants' five losses came at the hands of Jack Coombs, giving Coombs ten consecutive victories against McGraw's men since coming to Brooklyn in 1915. The second win was a ten-inning affair in which Coombs performed his usual feat of pitching just well enough to avoid damage, stranding twelve Giant runners on the bases. Coombs "lets them hit to their hearts' content when the bases are vacant, but just let one or two runners get aboard the cushions, and Coombs grasps the batters in the palm of his hand."[3] Grantland Rice wrote that Coombs had the Giants "spellbound and reeling." He added, "The Kennebunk Express has continued to run over the Giants and roll their mangled bodies into the first waiting ditch."[4]

Fortunately for the Giants, and unfortunately for Coombs and the Robins, this mastery of New York came to an end later that season. Brooklyn suffered through listless play and numerous injuries throughout the season. By the Fourth of July a doubleheader against the Giants, Brooklyn was languishing in sixth place, 10½ games behind the Giants. In the second game of the doubleheader, the Giants put Coombs' streak to rest with a vengeance, scoring four runs in the first inning on the way to an easy 8–0 victory.

The only noteworthy accomplishment for the Robins had come a few days earlier, in the form of a Sunday baseball game in Brooklyn. The United States had entered the war in Europe earlier in the year, and Ebbets hit upon an idea to bypass the Sunday blue laws that prohibited professional baseball games. He promoted the event as a fundraiser for the war effort on a Sunday, charging admission for a concert and entertainment, followed by a "free" doubleheader. How much of the proceeds went to charity and how much went to Ebbets to cover expenses was never disclosed, but for the moment at least, Sunday baseball had a foothold in Brooklyn. Coombs pitched that first Sunday game, drawing the assignment against Grover Cleveland Alexander of the Phillies and losing by a score of 6–2. As masterful as Coombs had been over the Giants, he had proven unable to best Alexander, this being his third straight loss against Philadelphia's ace right-hander.

The season proved to be a frustrating one for Coombs. He started only fourteen games, his lowest total in his eleven seasons, including both his rookie half-year and the season where he spent significant time as an outfielder. His nine complete games also represented a career low. He appeared in relief seventeen times. Having thrived on regular work throughout his career, Coombs had trouble adjusting to Robinson's more sporadic use of his pitching talents and his record fell to 7–11.

The entire team slumped in 1917, finishing a dismal seventh, 26½ games behind the pennant-winning Giants. Coombs may not have approved of McGraw's tactics, but the Giants' adroit leader quickly turned the fortunes of his club around. Connie Mack's Athletics, by comparison, finished dead last for the third consecutive time and would continue to do so for four more seasons.

Coombs actively considered other career options. He had helped coach the spring preparation of the Rice University baseball team. He was also rumored to be a managerial candidate for the Pittsburgh Pirates and the St. Louis Cardinals. The *Sporting News* offered this perspective on Coombs' managerial prospects: "Several major magnates are said to be in the market for managers, and it is more than probable that one of them will be wise enough to sign Coombs. We certainly hope so. We hate to see him out of the game."[5] Charlie Ebbets was supportive of Coombs' interest in becoming a manager, going so far as to say that he would appoint Coombs as Brooklyn's manager "without an instant's hesitation" should anything happen to Wilbert Robinson.[6] Shrewd businessman that he was, however, Ebbets was not willing to let Coombs manage another team without getting some compensation in return.

Coombs chats with Brooklyn manager Wilbert Robinson. Coombs played an important role in helping to lead the Brooklyn team, to the 1916 pennant (courtesy National Baseball Hall of Fame Library, Cooperstown, N.Y.).

Having just turned thirty-four, Coombs was becoming a bit long in the tooth for a major league pitcher. In 1911 he had predicted that ten years would be a good career run for any pitcher. His father, on the other hand, had seen no reason at that time why his "stout" son would not keep pitching into his forties, as Cy Young had done. But Coombs was not as strong as he had been prior to his ordeal with typhoid fever, and he was not enjoying himself the way he had throughout most of his career. For the first time since his high school days he was playing on a team with little prospect of contending. Led by clubhouse lawyer Stengel, his Brooklyn teammates seemed to be more focused on competing against owner Ebbets than their on-field opponents. While Coombs had a cordial relationship with Wilbert Robinson, it was not the same type of relationship he had enjoyed with Connie Mack. Robinson was coarse and profane, and while Coombs was certainly capable of communicating in the vernacular of a common ballplayer, as an educated man he preferred to resort to such language solely for effect, not as a matter of course.

While Coombs had never commanded one of the top salaries in baseball, he had nonetheless done well for himself financially, and considered himself fairly compensated. He had also collected more than $13,000 in World Series winnings, surpassed only by former teammates Jack Barry and Eddie Collins to that point in time. While certainly not a rich man, Coombs had accumulated sufficient financial resources, including his farm in Maine, to be able to consider his future with a certain degree of flexibility. He wanted to stay in baseball. He had one year remaining on his contract with Brooklyn, and decided to honor it before seeking alternative employment as a manager or coach.

The Robins decided they would not stick with the same lineup for 1918. Not surprisingly, Stengel was traded in the off-season, sent along with second baseman George Cutshaw to Pittsburgh. Brooklyn received infielder Chuck Ward and pitchers Al Mamaux and Burleigh Grimes in return. Neither Ward nor Mamaux would prove to be of much value to Brooklyn in 1918, as both enlisted in the military. The war in Europe had sufficiently escalated so that the government, needing bodies both in the armed forces and in the manufacturing sector, had issued a "work-or-fight" order to able-bodied men in non-essential industries such as baseball. As a result, three of Brooklyn's young pitchers — Cadore, Smith, and Pfeffer — also enlisted during the season. The only returning pitchers on the Brooklyn staff were the twenty-eight-year-old Marquard, the thirty-two-year-old Cheney and "ancient" Jack Coombs, who at age thirty-five was too old to be subject to service in the military.

Grimes turned out to be the ace of the Brooklyn staff in 1918 as well as eight more seasons. In four of those seasons the rough-and-tumble spitball pitcher won at least twenty games. Nicknamed "Old Stubblebeard" for his refusal to use a razor on the days he was pitching, he was a "snarly and surly" competitor.[7] In total, he spent nineteen years pitching for six different National League teams, winning 270 games while losing 212. He was the last legitimate spitball pitcher in major league baseball, having been allowed to continue to throw the pitch when, in 1920, all pitches that involved the doctoring of the baseball were outlawed. Grimes was elected to the Baseball Hall of Fame in 1964.

Brooklyn's 1918 season began in similar fashion to its 1917 campaign. Brooklyn lost the first nine games it played, six of which were against the Giants, who started their season off on a positive note by winning their first nine games and eighteen of their initial nineteen. The one difference was that Coombs no longer held mastery over the Giants, losing his first two starts against New York in April.

The Robins' offense was anemic in 1918, scoring fewer runs by far than any other team in major league baseball, even though the team boasted the league's leading hitter, Zach Wheat. The team was also weak defensively, placing among the leaders in errors and turning the fewest double plays. The pitching staff showed the effects of this poor support, as only newcomer Grimes posted a winning record. In Coombs' case, this was best illustrated on May 8 against Boston when two defensive misplays in the ninth inning turned a 3–2 lead into a 4–3 defeat. Frustrated but not despondent, Coombs treated his father and uncle to a lobster dinner that evening in an attempt to put the game behind him.

There were few highlights for Coombs or the Robins during the season. Decimated by the loss of so many players to the military, the club struggled to compete. Desperate for outfielders, Brooklyn returned Coombs to the outfield for thirteen games. On May 21, Coombs pitched a masterful six-hit shutout against the Cubs, the eventual National League pennant-winner. According to the *Chicago Tribune*, "It was a battle that called for cunning as much as arm power, and Jack had both. He wasn't in many tight places, but when he was in danger he was master."[8] His performance was even more impressive when one considers that he had been struck on his pitching hand during pre-game batting practice.

The frustrations of a losing season began to emerge in the actions of the team. On June 4, for the only time in his career, Coombs came close to being ejected from a game. Brooklyn and the St. Louis Cardinals were locked in a 1–1 battle at Ebbets Field when Coombs was brought on to relieve in the twelfth inning. During the thirteenth inning, a throwing error, a double, and an intentional walk loaded the bases for the Cardinals with only one out. The next batter hit a hard shot down the third base line, which appeared to be foul to the Brooklyn players and the small gathering of fans in attendance. Veteran umpire Cy Rigler, whose opinion was the only one that mattered, ruled the ball fair. Outfielder Zach Wheat did not bother chasing after the ball, which resulted in the batter and all three runners scoring. An argument ensued on the field with practically the entire Brooklyn team surrounding the umpire. Deciding the umpire could also benefit from their perspective, several fans jumped on to the field to join the discussion. When order was finally restored, two Brooklyn players had been ejected, and the sun was setting. Wilbert Robinson decided that the best strategy to deal with the situation was to stall, hoping the umpires would call the game on account of darkness before the Robins turn at bat, causing the score to revert to 1–1. After several minutes of loitering on the field, the umpires got the players back in position, but Coombs started pitching as if it was batting practice, deliberately lobbing pitches for the Cardinals to hit. The Brooklyn fielders all emulated Zach Wheat and refused to chase after the ball. After three more runs scored, the Cardinals saw through the ruse and decided to stop trying to hit the ball. Although the field was nearly cloaked in darkness at this point, the umpires forced the Robins to complete their turn at bat, resulting in an 8–1 loss.

On the Fourth of July, Coombs defeated the New York Giants almost single-handedly at the Polo Grounds. Brooklyn got off to a 3–0 lead early in the game, but a "luscious assortment of seven errors" by the Robin's defense allowed the Giants to tie the game in the eight inning.[9] With the score tied in the tenth inning, Coombs "plastered" a triple into deep center field and subsequently scored the winning run.[10] It was Coombs' third hit of the game.

The conflict in Europe had increasingly depleted baseball's talent pool as players enlisted in the war effort. The fans, astute judges of talent, noticed the deterioration in the quality of play, and attendance declined significantly. The owners, astute businessmen that they were, saw the number of empty seats and decided to cut the season short, ending the schedule on Labor Day. As the season wound to a close, Coombs had recommitted himself to retiring from active play. He went into his last start on August 30 with a discouraging 8–13 record. That last start was in the Polo Grounds against the New York Giants, the team that he previously dominated "by tossing his glove into the ball yard."[11] Through eight innings the game was a surprisingly crisp affair. Coombs showed his old form, holding the Giants to four scattered hits through eight innings. Unfortunately, the Robins only managed to gather two singles, and the game went into the bottom of the ninth inning as a scoreless tie. The Giants' leadoff batter singled, and when the next batter laid down a sacrifice bunt, Brooklyn's third baseman hurriedly threw the ball over the first baseman's head, putting runners on second and third. Following an intentional walk, "Laughing Larry" Doyle of the Giants stroked a single, driving home the winning run. Frustratingly, one of the Robins infielders cut off the throw to the plate, allowing the winning run to score uncontested.

The game had been played in a mere fifty-six minutes, at that time believed to be the quickest nine-inning game in major league history. As the winning run scored, Coombs stomped off the mound, frustrated both with his defensive support and with his inability to work out of a jam. He flung his glove at the bench and announced to Wilbert Robinson, "You can have this glove; I won't need it anymore."[12]

Shortly after the season ended, with the Robins finishing in fifth place, Coombs officially announced his retirement, stating that he was investing in a wholesale mercantile business in Texas. The *Washington Post* commented, "His passing will be regretted by the fans. Baseball would be better for more players of Coombs' type."[13]

Coombs' retirement from major league baseball did not last long. The Philadelphia Phillies released their manager, Pat Moran, on December 10. A week later, club president William Baker announced that Jack Coombs was going to be the Phillies' new manager for the 1919 season. It was a homecoming for Coombs, returning to the city where he had accomplished so much as a pitcher for the Athletics. Coombs was competing for the loyalty of Philadelphia fans with his old mentor, Connie Mack, whose Athletics were in the midst of a seven-year streak of last-place finishes. At first glance, it appeared as though Coombs had the advantage with the better product, as the Phillies had been dominant in the National League, winning the pennant in 1915 and finishing second the following two seasons. But the Phillies placed a disappointing sixth in 1918, leading to Moran's dismissal. Moran had been at the team's helm for the Phillies' success from 1915 through 1917, and knowledgeable baseball men realized that a decline in talent, not Moran's leadership, was the reason for the team's drop in the standings. Moran went on to prove his managerial skills as manager of the Cincinnati Reds, guiding them to the National League pennant in 1919.

The biggest factor contributing to the Phillies' decline in 1918 was the loss of Grover Cleveland Alexander. "Aleck" had been designated as draft-eligible for the military prior to the start of the season. William Baker decided to lay off the risk on his star pitcher's ability to survive military service, trading him and catcher Bill Killefer to the Chicago Cubs prior to the start of the season for two players and cash. The Cubs were eager to take the risk since Alexander had won ninety-four games over the previous three seasons for the Phillies. Alexander was called into the military during 1918, and later suffered from the stress of significant military action, returning from his one-year term of service both an epileptic and alcoholic. Never again was he as dominant as he had been with the Phillies, where he won 180 games while leading the league in victories in five of seven seasons. He would be a steady winner for the Cubs and Cardinals, surpassing twenty victories three more times, eventually finishing his career with 373 wins, tied with Christy Mathewson for third on the all-time victory list.

While Alexander's pitching prowess was diminished by his military service, the Phillies' pitching prowess was virtually eliminated by the departure of the big right-hander. Eppa Rixey, the number two pitcher on the Phillies' staff, also served in the war in 1918 and came back to post two dismal years, going 6–12 in 1919 and 11–22 in 1920. There was little other pitching talent on the club, and Baker hired Coombs with the expectation that he would help mold this rag-tag collection of arms into a major league staff. Baker also had a financial motivation for replacing Moran with Coombs, trading Moran's $9,000 salary for the $7,000 he paid for Coombs' services.

The *Washington Post* noted, "Jack Coombs has lots of nerve tackling the job of running the Phils. His friends wish him well."[14] The *Sporting News* was more direct: "Jack's best efforts are doomed to failure. To tell the blunt truth he will be licked before he starts. Any painter who wishes to produce a study on a canvas of a morgue should visit the Philadelphia National League Park some hot day in August."[15] The paper later offered this view of the task facing Coombs: "Coombs is one of the grandest characters baseball has ever known and it is distinctly deplorable that he is going to have his managerial baptism under such unfavorable conditions."[16]

The negative press focused on the Phillies' ownership, not Jack Coombs. The following poem, written from the perspective of the city of Philadelphia, demonstrates the esteem that Coombs had earned during his career.

Jack Coombs — As a Pitcher

It seems but yesterday, Old Top,
You pitched for us with steady nerve.
But now your fast one's lost its hop;
No more they fear your speeding curve.
But yesterday strong men would quail,
Opposing teams were grouching glooms,
As harmless you made each dread flail,
And on the peak we saw — John Coombs.

But yesterday — a few short years
Along the trail, a slender gap —
The words that drew our loudest cheers
Were: "For the Athletics, Coombs and Lapp."
Now Time has called, your powers wane,
We call on you as from the Tombs;

We want you back with us again
To lead us from the dark — John Coombs.

But yesterday your arm was strong,
But stronger yet your brain and skill.
We need you now to lead us, John.
And bring new triumphs back to Phil.
The sun shines through, the clouds roll back,
As from the mists your image looms.
As you responded when with Mack
Now hearken to our call — Jack Coombs.

But yesterday — a day is all
That mortal keeps without the vale.
Tomorrow Time's inexorable call
Will start us on the downward trail.
We toil awhile, perhaps gain fame,
Then skid down to the silent tombs.
Then let us hope we've played our game
As well as you have yours — Jack Coombs.[17]

By January, Coombs already had an indication of the Herculean challenge he was facing. The cost-conscious Baker had expressed concern about the expense associated with traveling to spring training, directing Coombs to find a training site in the more-proximate North Carolina. Baker then complicated matters further by engineering a trade with the St. Louis Cardinals without benefit of input from his new manager.

In spring training Coombs made it very clear that he intended to limit himself to managing and not succumb to the temptation to return to the diamond as an active player. He demonstrated in a spring intra-squad game, however, that he was still capable of competing by coming off the bench as a pinch hitter with the bases loaded and sending all the runners home with a long triple. While Coombs tried to "inculcate inside baseball" to the Phillies during spring training, the team was given little prospect of making a favorable showing once the season opened; they were simply lacking talent in too many areas. Many prognosticators picked the team to finish last.[18]

The Phillies opened their season at home against the Giants in a game that unfortunately proved typical for the season. The team scored a healthy seven runs against the Giants, but the pitching staff surrendered ten runs. The Giants offense was aided by three Philadelphia errors. Nine days later the Giants hosted the Phillies for New York's home opener and pounded Philadelphia's pitchers for fourteen runs. Four days later, Coombs returned to Brooklyn for the first time, with the Robins' management giving Coombs a silver tea set while his former teammates presented him with a hunting rifle. With such displays of generosity all around them, the Phillies players decided to make a gift of the game to Brooklyn, squandering a seven-run lead on the way to an 11–9 defeat.

Despite such dismal outings, on May 27 the Phillies found themselves in fourth place with an 11–10 record, 5½ games behind the league-leading Giants. The team's fortunes quickly turned as the offense cooled while the pitching staff continued to give up runs in large quantities. The team also suffered through injuries to a number of key players. Following a thirteen-game losing streak in June, Philadelphia found itself in seventh place, a mere half game ahead of the cellar-dwelling Braves. On June 26, the *Sporting News* opined, "It is significant that there isn't the slightest disposition here to pillory Jack Coombs for the wholesale losses on the recent trip."[19] Apparently, the newspaper had not spoken with team president William Baker, who at this point was embarrassed that ex-manager Pat Moran was guiding an underdog Cincinnati team to the top of the National League while the Phillies were sinking lower in the standings.

Following the *Sporting News'* statement of support, the Phillies went on another thirteen-game losing skid, firmly taking control of the lowest spot in the standings. After the game on July 8, Baker announced to the press that Coombs had resigned as the Philadelphia manager. Coombs told the press that he had been told by Baker that "his services were no longer needed."[20] It quickly became apparent that Coombs and Baker had been at odds with each other over the direction of the club, and that Coombs had particularly grown tired of Baker's penny-pinching ways.

"I did everything that could be done with the material at my disposal," Coombs told the press. "There are weak spots in the club, and I made suggestions for their strengthening, not one of which was acted upon. I have no complaint to make as to Mr. Baker's decision that he wanted another manager, but I object to his passing the buck to me as the cause of his team's failure."[21]

Coombs went on to illustrate the source of the differences between owner and manager.

> We were in fine shape at the start of the season, but on our last Western trip we spent over $28 just for tape to fix up spike wounds and other injuries. Now I understand Mr. Baker has ruled that the players must buy their own tape. Whitted, Sicking and Meusel have been playing games with injuries that would have kept them on the bench with any other team in the League. We didn't have substitutes to take their places, and I had no way of getting any new players.[22]

The Philadelphia players were quite upset when word of Coombs' dismissal reached them. They threatened to go on strike, and prior to their next game took the field and started batting and throwing baseballs into the stands in a spiteful waste of Baker's money.

For the most part, the press was supportive of Coombs. The *Washington Post* reported, "It is a pity that a player who has done so much to make the game popular should retire before a real try-out as a manager because of an owner whose attitude has worked great injury to the sport in Philadelphia."[23] On the other hand, the editorial staff of the *Sporting News* criticized Coombs for using as an "alibi" Baker's refusal to make certain trades that Coombs had lined up, which Coombs felt made him "look like a boob in the eyes of other managers."[24] The editorial did admit, however, that it was Baker who was generally considered "a boob" in baseball circles.

The public exchange of words between Coombs and Baker became worse when Baker threatened to renege on his agreement to pay Coombs' salary for the remainder of the season. Coombs in turn threatened to sue. When Coombs returned to Philadelphia for a dinner in his honor given by the Philadelphia players, he and Baker resolved their financial differences and their dispute disappeared from the press.

Baker named thirty-eight-year-old Philadelphia outfielder Clifford Carlton "Gavvy" Cravath as the team's new manager. Cravath had been with the Phillies since 1912, and had won the league home run title in five of the previous six seasons by stroking the ball to the opposite field and taking advantage of Baker Bowl's short right-field dimensions. Over the course of his career, more than 75 percent of Cravath's home runs were hit at home. His twenty-four home runs in 1915 established the twentieth century major league season record until Babe Ruth decided to forsake pitching for hitting in 1919, slugging twenty-nine home runs in the process. (Ruth also supplanted Cravath as the all-time home run king when he reached a career total of 120 in 1921. Ruth went on to hit 714 home runs in his career.) Despite playing in only eighty-three games in 1919, Cravath again led the league in round-trippers, this time with a total of twelve.

When Baker introduced Cravath as his new manager, he proclaimed, "Cravath is my manager as long as he lives."[25] Cravath lived to the ripe of old age of eighty-two, but he was replaced as the Phillies' manager following the 1920 season. The Phillies remained in last place in 1919 following Coombs' dismissal and trailed the field again in 1920. Pitching was the team's downfall in 1919, as the staff gave up 699 runs, nearly a run per game worse than the next highest total in the league.

Baker continued as the Phillies' owner until his death in 1930. During the 1920s, he employed the services of six different managers. His teams finished last six times during that decade and gave up more runs than every other National League club in each of those ten seasons. In hindsight, Baker's decision to trade away the remarkable pitching talents of Grover Cleveland Alexander following the 1917 campaign proved to be as devastating to the franchise's fortunes as Boston owner Harry Frazee's decision to trade Babe Ruth to the Yankees following the 1919 season. In the thirty years following the loss of Alexander, the Phillies placed no higher than fourth and finished eighth in sixteen of those seasons. The Phillies did not win another pennant until 1950, and did not win their first — and to this point only — World Series until 1980. Perhaps Ol' Pete cast as strong a curse on the Phillies franchise as Babe Ruth was alleged to have placed on the Red Sox.

Coombs again returned to his business interests in Texas following his dismissal from Philadelphia. But major league baseball came calling once more, this time in the form of Frank Navin, owner of the Detroit Tigers. Navin hired Coombs in December to be the Tigers' pitching coach for the 1920 season. Detroit was still under the leadership of Hughie Jennings, who in 1919 had just completed his thirteenth season as the Tigers' manager. The Tiger lineup was still led by the ferocious Ty Cobb, who in 1919 won his twelfth, and final, batting title with a .384 batting average. The Tigers were not the dominating team they had been when Jennings led them to three consecutive from pennants 1907–1909, but they did finish a respectable fourth in 1919, eight games behind the pennant-winning Chicago White Sox. Pitching and defense were considered in need of improvement, as the Tigers gave up more runs than any team in the league other than the woeful Philadelphia Athletics.

The *Sporting News* applauded the hiring of Coombs by the Tigers. "Coombs got credit for giving Brooklyn the staff of moundsmen that hurled the Dodgers to their lone pennant, and Coombs, one of the brainiest men that ever hurled for Connie Mack, should be able to do something with the Tiger flingers."[26] Those "flingers" had been led by George "Hooks" Dauss in 1919, as he posted a career-best record of 21–9. Dauss spent all fifteen of his major league seasons with the Tigers, three times winning more than twenty games in a season. Following Dauss on the pitching staff was Howard Ehmke, a twenty-five-year-old right-hander who went 17–10 in 1919. Ehmke also went on to pitch fifteen seasons in the big leagues for four different clubs. He achieved fame in the 1929 World Series as Connie Mack's surprise first-game starter against the Chicago Cubs, striking out a then-record thirteen batters on his way to a 3–1 victory. The Tigers' starting staff was rounded out by little Bernie Boland (14–16) and former Red Sox left-hander Dutch Leonard (14–13). Despite an experienced staff, Detroit's leadership was focused on bringing in fresh arms for the purpose of developing a young and reliable pitching corps. Three rookies, Jim Roberts, Claude Jonnard, and Ernest Allen, were brought to spring training to see if they had the potential to help the club.

There were high hopes that Coombs could help develop a more dependable Detroit Tigers pitching staff. In spring training, the *Sporting News* implied that Coombs was already making a difference. "The recruit pitchers have absolute confidence in him," the newspaper reported. "Coombs has a way with these raw rookies; he does not try to bully them but, being of the Connie Mack school which puts human understanding and persuasion by kindly methods above all else, Jack makes a practice of what Connie Mack preached."[27]

The big difference between Connie Mack with the Athletics and Jack Coombs with the Tigers was that Mack had intelligent and talented men like Coombs, Bender, and Plank pitching for him. Those three related well to Mack's "kindly" style. While the Tigers staff related to Coombs quite well, they simply lacked the skills to raise their level of performance. Making matters more difficult, the American League went through another offensive explosion in 1920. Led by Babe Ruth's unheard of total of fifty-four home runs, total runs scored in the league increased by over 25 percent.

The Tigers got off to a dismal start, losing their first thirteen games. They were never in contention from that point forward, finishing the season a disappointing seventh, trailed only by Connie Mack's Philadelphia Athletics. The team's one-dimensional nature was cited as the reason for its poor showing. "The Tigers' chief (and one might say their sole) asset is hitting. The Tigers must hit to win. Their fielding is only fair and in spots the defense is weak indeed. Their pitching, except on rare occasions, is mediocre. Their base running is weak to an extreme and as far as intellect is concerned the team absolutely cannot class."[28] The Tigers did not hit with their usual aplomb in 1920. They were the only team to post a drop in batting average relative to the previous season, and scored the third fewest runs in the league.

By the end of June, the pitching staff was already tired and battered. On June 30, in a game against Chicago, the Tigers were trailing 12–0 after four innings. Instead of sending another raw arm out to be mauled by the White Sox, Coombs lugged his thirty-seven-year-old body out to the mound. He had not pitched a major league game in twenty-one months. He did respectably well, giving up five hits and two runs in five innings pitched. Coombs received a loud ovation from the appreciative Tiger fans.

One of the newspaper accounts of the game noted that by pitching in the game, Coombs was taking a financial risk since his life insurance would not pay should he die from injuries sustained while pitching professional baseball. The article went on to note that "baseball, while not being very dangerous, kills more people annually than does the terrible football."[29] Ironically, just seven weeks later, Cleveland Indians star shortstop Ray Chapman was killed when a pitch delivered by the Yankees' Carl Mays struck him in the head. No major league player has died from on-field injuries since Chapman.

Coombs pitched once more on July 18, again in relief in a lopsided game. This time, Colby Jack Coombs hung up his glove for good.

10

The Coombsmen

Hughie Jennings resigned as the Tigers' manager following the 1920 season. During the season, rumors had circulated that Coombs might be in line to be the Tigers' next manager. However, Coombs had no interest in dealing with the hot-tempered Ty Cobb, a man he later described as both "intense" and "crazed," so he packed up and went home to Texas following the season.[1] Cobb was named the Tigers' player-manager for 1921, a position he held for six seasons.

Baseball was going through upheaval during 1920. The "Black Sox" betting scandal from the 1919 World Series had broken during the 1920 season, and major league owners had been split into warring factions for a few years. To many it was apparent that the ruling triumvirate of the old National Commission was no longer capable of running the game to the satisfaction of the owners, players and paying customers. Various alternative governing structures were considered, and Charlie Ebbets of the Dodgers went so far as to suggest that the players should have a representative on the "board of control." His recommendation was that "Jack Coombs or Christy Mathewson would fill the bill."[2]

Given the public perception of the ineffectiveness of baseball's governing structure in the "Black Sox" scandal, the baseball owners decided that a committee of any sort, no matter how well constructed, was not in their immediate best interests. Instead, they chose the route of appointing a dictator, Federal Judge Kenesaw Mountain Landis, as an omnipotent commissioner. Landis ruled the game with a somewhat arbitrary iron fist until his death in 1944.

Coombs was by this time a bit frustrated with major league baseball. His experiences over the past four seasons with three different losing teams did not leave him hungering for another major league job. More than anything, Coombs wanted to be associated with an organization that had winning potential.

Close friend and former Philadelphia teammate Ira Thomas provided Coombs with an opportunity to stay involved with baseball, albeit at the collegiate level. Thomas was the baseball coach at Williams College, but was seeking to walk away from his contract due to conflicts with his other business interests, and suggested Coombs as his replacement.

Williams College, located in the northwestern corner of Massachusetts, was a small liberal arts college, considered along with Amherst and Wesleyan as one of the "Little Ivys," in contrast with the larger premier educational institutions, such as Harvard, Princeton, and Yale. Unlike Colby College, Coombs' alma mater, the student population was comprised solely of men. Williams had participated in the very first intercollegiate baseball game, played under the "Massachusetts rules" against traditional rival Amherst College on July 1, 1859, losing by a score of 73–32. Each team brought its own ball to the game and fielded thirteen players. The game went twenty-six innings, as it had been agreed that the first team to score sixty-five runs would be declared the winner.[3]

Handicapped by its small size and cold weather, the Williams team had not been particularly competitive in the years prior to Coombs' arrival. Given his frustrations over the past four years with losing franchises, it was surprising that Coombs agreed to take the position as Williams' baseball coach. But Coombs liked a challenge, and he very much wanted to stay involved with the game of baseball. For the next four years, he would leave his winter home in Texas and arrive in Massachusetts in early February to start getting the team in shape for the upcoming season.

The team showed progress under Coombs' tutelage, improving from a 5–13 record in 1921 to an 11–6 record by 1923. The highlight of the 1923 season was a victory against the Harvard varsity, the first win for Williams over Harvard in the previous fifteen years. It was also the first time that Coombs was associated with a school that beat Harvard, having lost to the Crimson three times while pitching for Colby. The victory was considered such an achievement that it was reported in the *New York Times*. "Practically the entire student body" welcomed the victorious players back to the campus for a midnight celebration, including "the largest bonfire in the history of the college."[4]

While at Williams, Coombs made a point of sharing with his players as much major league experience as possible. In 1922 he invited Chief Bender to help him in spring training, followed by Eddie Plank in 1923.

The team's fortunes slipped a bit in 1924, as its record fell to 7–8, although they did win the "Little Three" title against Amherst and Wesleyan.

Coombs was presented with the opportunity to move to a more competitive baseball program in 1925 when he was hired as the pitching coach at Princeton. He joined fifty-six-year-old Bill "Boileryard" Clarke, who was the team's head coach. Clarke had spent thirteen seasons in the major leagues as a catcher and first baseman, including a six-year stretch with the Baltimore Orioles of John McGraw, Hughie Jennings and Wilbert Robinson. Clarke was in the second of three different terms as Princeton's baseball coach; his complete tenure totaled forty-six seasons.

Coombs and Clarke spent three seasons together coaching Princeton. When Clarke left the Tigers following the 1927 season, Coombs decided to move on as well. Having worked for four different employers over the previous nine years, he was looking for something a little more permanent. He finally found what he was looking for at Duke University.

Duke University is located in Durham, North Carolina, established in 1924 and built upon what had previously been known as Trinity College. The university was founded on the financial bequest of James B. Duke, whose family wealth came principally from the tobacco and electric power industries. The Duke family had been benefactors of Trinity College since 1890. With ties to the Methodist Church, Trinity College had much in common with Coombs' alma mater, Colby College, as small, regional, co-educational liberal arts schools with religious affiliations. In funding the new institution, James B. Duke spoke of his vision that the university would become "a place of real leadership in the educational world," going beyond its regional focus to become a national university achieving excellence in both research and education.[5]

While the financial backing for Duke University came from the Duke Endowment, the leadership and vision to transform money into a major university rested with William Preston Few. Few had been the president of Trinity College since 1910; for a number of years he had as his goal the creation of a prominent university. Starting with the $40 million endowment from James B. Duke, he set about building "the most harmonious, imposing, and altogether beautiful educational plant in America."[6] Creating an educational institution with a national reputation was not just a function of physical plant, and Few went about hiring educational leaders for both the existing undergraduate and proposed graduate level programs of the university. Few's vision encompassed athletics as well, and one of the first steps down that path was the hiring of John Wesley Coombs as baseball coach in 1928. The university went a step further in 1931 with the hiring of Wallace Wade as football coach and athletic director.

From Coombs' perspective, there were several advantages associated with the Duke University program. First, the weather in North Carolina provided an opportunity for a baseball team to play a more extensive schedule than was available to cold-weather northern schools, such as Colby and Williams. Coombs was a firm believer that college players, particularly pitchers, needed more playing time if they were to have an opportunity to advance to the professional ranks. Second, Duke was in close proximity to other major colleges — Davidson, North Carolina, North Carolina State and Wake Forest — affording the team quality opponents within easy travel distances. Third, as an institution that was in essence building itself anew, Duke University was able to provide excellent facilities for its athletic teams. By 1931, Duke had built the ballpark that would ultimately be known as Coombs Field, along with several practice diamonds. Fourth, and perhaps most importantly, the administration of the university actively supported the advancement of its athletic programs.

The support of the administration was exemplified by the personal relationship between William Preston Few and John Wesley Coombs. Despite the extensive time commitment associated with building the infrastructure of the University, Few took a personal interest in the baseball team. Coombs publicly addressed Few as "Prexy," and invited the school president to umpire practice games. Few "took his umpiring chore seriously," and used his walking cane to make marks in the dirt to keep track of balls and strikes.[7] Few was also the umpire for the spirited annual student-faculty games, where "all students who intend to pass the spring semester's work" were encouraged to show up and "pull for the faculty."[8]

The one drawback that Coombs faced was the lack of financial support afforded potential recruits for the baseball program. While scholarship money was tight throughout the economic depression of the 1930s, there was at least some financial support for the football program, but none for the baseball program. Coombs found a benefactor for some of his baseball recruits in his old mentor and manager, Connie Mack. In a much more lax environment for collegiate athletics than exists today under the auspices of the National Collegiate Athletic Association, Mack helped pay the educational costs for some of the more talented Duke prospects, with no expectations of the student-athlete beyond placing him in the good hands of Coach Coombs. Mack even sent his own son, Connie Mack Jr., to play for Coombs at Duke. The younger Mack, even taller and skinnier than his father, was more suited for basketball than baseball and never did develop as a baseball prospect.

The Duke University team that Coombs took over for the 1929 season had gone 29–28 over the previous three seasons, improving each year. The team was led by slick-fielding shortstop Billy Werber, a good hitter with exceptional speed on the basepaths. Werber was supported by four other players who were considered good enough to be major league prospects.

In his first season as coach, Coombs established the tone that marked his entire tenure at Duke. The team was regularly coached in the fundamentals, with significant preparation time in the classroom as well as on the playing field. Practices were regimented by an old alarm clock that Coombs carried with him, with precise amounts of time allocated to various activities. Coombs demanded his teams be well prepared and to know what was expected of them in every situation they might face on the field. He governed his team in much the manner that Connie Mack had directed the old Athletics. He relied on leadership rather than intimidation, showing his charges that the game should be played intelligently. He treated his players as men, motivating them with wit spiced with the occasional sarcastic jab. A naturally intelligent lot to begin with, the Duke players responded by going 13–5 in Coombs' inaugural season. For the first time in school history, dating back to 1889, they captured the North Carolina state championship. They also took the Southern Conference championship for the first time in any inter-collegiate sport. Despite losing Werber and a number of other players to graduation, the team improved to 17–5 the following year, again taking the state championship.

Throughout the 1930s, Duke University fielded a highly competitive baseball team, winning most of its games and regularly sending a number of players on to professional baseball. Duke's athletic teams were given the nickname "Blue Devils" in honor of a well-known French fighting unit from the First World War. The baseball team, however, in recognition of the influence of their coach and leader, became known as "the Coombsmen," much as the Philadelphia Athletics had been popularly known as the Mackmen. By the late 1930s, the Duke ballpark was already known as Coombs Field, long before the university officially designated it as such.

Starting in 1937, the team went on a phenomenal three-year run with a record of 62–7, including a twenty-five game winning streak and capturing the state title and Southern Conference title all three years. In 1938, Coombs arranged an exhibition game against Connie Mack's Athletics to be played at the Duke campus. Five former Duke players were on the Athletics roster at the time, and it was expected that they would start at the four infield positions and catcher against their alma mater. The game was well promoted, and a crowd in excess of 5,000 was anticipated, but the game had to be cancelled due to rain. The game was re-scheduled to take place in 1939, and this time the weather held up, attracting a crowd in excess of 4,000 people, including baseball Commissioner Landis. The Duke alumni, a.k.a. the Philadelphia Athletics, demolished the Duke varsity by a score of 19–2. Despite the lopsided score, the campus was thrilled at the mere presence of Connie Mack and his team. In the days before television, when major league teams resided only in cities in the Northeast and Midwest, the appearance of the Athletics at Duke was the first and perhaps only opportunity for most in attendance to see major league ballplayers in action.

In 1939, Coombs invited Colby College to play a game in Durham, the first game ever between the two schools. Colby also had a competitive team during the 1930s, having won or shared the Maine state championship in five of the previous seven seasons. After two innings, Colby led Duke by a score of 6–1. Setting aside the common courtesies of a gracious host, the Duke varsity then proceeded to pummel the Colby pitching staff, ultimately winning the game by a score of 26–8. Prior to the contest, Colby's athletic director presented Coombs with a Colby varsity sweater, honoring Coombs as "the most famous athlete in the history of Colby College."[9]

Duke's three-year run of domination concluded in dramatic fashion in 1939 when senior Eric Tipton hit a 445-foot, game-winning grand slam home run in the ninth inning of the team's final game against North Carolina, making Duke the state's first-ever undefeated champion.

Duke's championship reign was interrupted by Wake Forest over the next few years, as future Yankee left-handed pitcher Tommy Byrne dominated league play. By 1943, athletic competition at Duke and all colleges was curtailed by the loss of eligible young men to military service in World War II. While Duke was still able to field a team, due to travel restrictions its schedule from 1943 to 1945 was limited to the "Ration League," comprised of Duke, North Carolina, North Carolina State and the Navy Pre-Flight School stationed at Chapel Hill, North Carolina. The Navy team was comprised of a number of major league ball players in training for their military assignments, including Ted Williams, Harry Craft, Johnny Pesky and Johnny Sain.

It was not until 1947 that college baseball in general and Duke in particular was able to resume the semblance of a normal schedule. The Southern Conference resumed play, including in its membership sixteen teams located in the states of Virginia, North Carolina, and South Carolina. Duke finished third, qualifying for an invitation to a post-season tournament, which was turned down since the event took place during the summer and not all of the Duke players were available.

The Duke baseball team was competitively weak over the next three seasons, posting a losing record in two of the seasons. The 1950 season was particularly disappointing, since expectations had been high for the team. Star infielder Dick Groat had been declared academically ineligible prior to the season, and the team struggled without its expected offensive leader.

When Groat rejoined the squad for the 1951 season, the team's fortunes improved dramatically. Groat went on to become a first-team All-American, leading the team to a 17–8 record and its fourth Southern Conference championship with Coombs as coach. The team was invited to participate in the NCAA national championship tournament, but again turned down the invitation. Two star players were ineligible for the tournament and Coombs and a number of other players had other commitments.

The 1952 season was Coombs' twenty-fourth and final season as Duke's baseball coach. The university had a rule requiring the retirement of all employees after the academic year in which they reached their sixty-ninth birthday. Despite a cigarette-smoking habit and the normal advances of age, such as kidney stones and decaying teeth, Coombs was still in good physical condition, having worked on the field with his team on a regular basis. His only acknowledgement of age during his tenure as the team's coach was that he no longer donned a uniform or appeared in the coaching box during a game, instead wearing a three-piece suit and hat on the bench, just as Connie Mack had done with the Athletics. Coombs was not pleased with his forced retirement and tried to no avail to get an exception to the rule. After all, friend and mentor Connie Mack had continued managing at the major league level until the age of eighty-seven. But Mack had the decided advantage of being the principal owner of the team, able to make his own rules regarding retirement. Resigned to his fate, Coombs focused his energies on the team.

Led by Groat's .381 batting average with forty-five runs batted in, coming in only 147 at-bats, the Duke team rolled to a 31–7 record. They were again Southern Conference champions, and this time Coombs made sure in advance that everyone was available for post-season NCAA tournament play. The team took the District 3 championship by beating Tennessee, Rollins and Florida in a span of twelve hours. This earned them an invitation to the national championship in Omaha, Nebraska, for the eight-team double-elimination tournament. Duke won the first game handily, beating Oregon State by an 18–7 mark, but then lost by a 12–7 score to Penn State. For the first time all season the team uncharacteristically lost its composure, committing three errors, giving up the lead three times, and nearly getting goaded into an altercation when a Penn State runner ran out of the basepaths to take a shot at the Duke catcher. The loss to Penn State still rankled the team the next day, as Duke was eliminated by Western Michigan by a 5–1 score.

With that defeat, the baseball career of John Wesley Coombs was finally at an end. In twenty-four years as the baseball coach at Duke, Coombs' teams had accumulated a record of 381 victories against 171 defeats, with three ties. The team's winning percentage was .689, an astounding record of dominance over such an extended period of time.

Declining the offer of a retirement celebration by declaring himself a loyal soldier who would simply "fade away," he vowed that he would now spend his time catching "all the catfish in Texas."[10]

Dick Groat, the shortstop on Coombs' last championship team, was probably the best of the many players that Coombs sent to the big leagues. Groat went straight from the Duke University campus to the Pittsburgh Pirates, immediately stepping in as the Pirates' starting shortstop. Following two years in the military, Groat returned to spend eight years with the Pirates, playing opposite slick-fielding second baseman Bill Mazeroski to form a fine double-play combination. Groat was a good bat-handler and particularly adept at the hit-and-run. In 1960 he led the National League with a .325 batting average as the Pirates won their first World Series championship since 1925. He was named the National League's Most Valuable Player for both his offensive and defensive efforts in 1960. He was subsequently traded by the Pirates to the Cardinals, where he helped lead St. Louis to the World Series championship in 1964. Groat wound up playing fourteen seasons in the major leagues, was named to the All-Star team five times, and attained a very respectable career batting average of .286.

Groat attended Duke University through an athletic scholarship for basketball, not baseball. And he was good enough on the court to be named an All-American in that sport, one of the rare athletes to be selected as an All-American in two sports. Groat had been recruited to play sports at a number of colleges, yet chose Duke for two reasons. First, he perceived that the university was not only interested in turning out good athletic teams, and as a result he would get a quality education that would benefit him well beyond his athletic career. Second, despite the fact that he was offered a basketball scholarship, he was attracted to Duke because Jack Coombs was the baseball coach. He had been influenced by an article in *Sport Magazine* in 1948, titled "They Play Big League Baseball at Duke." Both his high school coach and his father saw Coombs as a positive role model for a young athlete, an expectation that Groat later claimed Coombs fulfilled many times over. "It was never difficult to go out and play baseball," Groat wrote in his autobiography, "not when you're going out under the eyes of Jack Coombs."[11]

The first ballplayer that Coombs sent to the big leagues was Bill Werber, who was a senior at Duke during Coombs' first year as the team's coach. An All-American in both basketball and baseball, Werber was a hustling third baseman blessed with tremendous speed on the basepaths. Before Coombs' arrival, the New York Yankees had shown an interest in Werber and helped pay for his education at Duke.

When Werber joined the Yankees following his graduation from Duke, the team had future Hall of Fame member Joe Sewell at third base. The Yankees traded Werber to the Boston Red Sox in 1933, and he established himself as one of the best baserunners in the league, twice leading the circuit in steals. He was then traded from the Red Sox to the Athletics, where in 1937 he achieved career highs in batting average and runs batted in while again leading the league in steals. A contract dispute with Connie Mack led to Werber's sale to the Cincinnati Reds following the 1938 season. Although slowed by a chronic foot injury, Werber was the catalyst the Reds needed to help capture their first National League pennant in twenty years. They repeated in 1940 and went on to take the World Series in a seven-game duel with the Detroit Tigers. Werber was the Reds' leading hitter in the series. Werber spent a total of eleven seasons in the major leagues, compiling a lifetime batting average of .271.

Coombs also coached his nephew, Raymond Franklin "Bobby" Coombs, at Duke from 1931 to 1933, where the young man starred in football and basketball in addition to baseball. Bobby Coombs was a hard-throwing right-handed pitcher. He bore little physical resemblance to his Uncle John, standing 5' 9" tall, and weighing only 160 pounds. Despite his slight build, Bobby had been a dominating pitcher at Exeter Academy and Duke. He finished his collegiate career with a flourish, tossing three consecutive shutouts. Upon graduation, he was signed by Connie Mack and the A's.

Bobby Coombs' first appearance in a major league game was in relief against the Washington Senators, the first team his uncle had faced back in 1906. Bobby Coombs did not fare as well, giving up a run in the tenth inning. He was spared the loss, however, when the skies opened up, pouring rain onto the field. This forced the cancellation of play before the Athletics could take their turn at bat, and the score reverted back to the tie that existed at the end of nine innings. Bobby made his first official appearance the next day, again appearing in relief, this time against the Yankees. The Athletics were winning 14–9 on the strength of three home runs by Jimmie Foxx when young Coombs entered the game in the ninth inning to face Babe Ruth. Ruth welcomed Bobby Coombs to the major leagues with a tremendous home run to right field that reached the rooftops across the street from Shibe Park. Coombs settled down and retired the next three batters, including Lou Gehrig and Tony Lazzeri.

Unfortunately for Bobby Coombs, his first game against the Yankees proved to be the highlight of his major league career. Mack kept using him in relief throughout the summer. Later in the season, Bobby Coombs reportedly made the mistake of going to Mack and complaining of a tired arm, something that his uncle, "Iron Man" John Coombs, would have never done. Mack decided to give the rookie some rest by sending him to the minor leagues, where he toiled for the next nine years. He was brought back to the major leagues in 1943 by the New York Giants and released after that season. In his major league career, Bobby Coombs appeared in thirty games, all in relief, compiling a record of 0–2.

10. The Coombsmen

Raymond "Bobby" Coombs practices under the watchful eye of his Uncle John at Duke University in the early 1930s (courtesy National Baseball Hall of Fame Library, Cooperstown, N.Y.).

The story of how Eric Tipton, whose walk-off grand slam home run in his final collegiate at-bat clinched Duke's 1939 state championship, came to Duke University is indicative of the reputation that Coombs had as a mentor and teacher. Tipton, a native of Petersburg, Virginia, was an outstanding high school football player, who was heavily recruited by a number of universities to play football. He chose Duke, not because of the football scholarship offered by coach and athletic director Wallace Wade, but because of the presence of Jack Coombs. Tipton claimed that baseball was his first love and that a position in the major leagues was most probable if he spent four years under the tutelage of Coombs. Tipton did make it to the big leagues, spending parts of three seasons with the Athletics before signing with Cincinnati in 1942. Ineligible for military service due to two perforated eardrums, Tipton had four decent seasons with the Reds, finishing his career with a .270 batting average. And he did play a little football at Duke, becoming a three-time All-American while leading the Blue Devils to their only Rose Bowl appearance, in 1938.

Ace Parker was another football star who went to Duke University because of Jack Coombs. "I skipped out of Virginia Poly, the school I probably should have gone to, because I knew Duke had Jack Coombs as its baseball coach," Parker told sportswriter Bob Considine. "Sure, I might have had football in the back of my skull, but baseball was the important thing. I wanted the kind of coaching I knew Coombs could give me."[12] Parker made it to the major leagues as an infielder with the Athletics, but lasted only two seasons, recording a mediocre .179 batting average. He found that major league pitching was much tougher to hit than college-level pitching. Parker, who had been named an All-American football player at Duke, had a much more successful career as a professional football player. He played for the old Brooklyn Dodgers of the National Football League and was named the league's Most Valuable Player in 1940. His career was interrupted by a three-year term of service in the military, but his accomplishments on the gridiron were sufficient to get him elected to the Pro Football Hall of Fame in 1972.

Some other Duke players who made the big leagues included Wayne Ambler, who spent three years as an infielder with the Athletics; Lawrence "Crash" Davis, who also spent three years as an infielder for the Athletics and whose colorful name was used for the lead character in the movie *Bull Durham*; Chubby Dean, who pitched and played first base in seven seasons with the Athletics and the Indians; Bill McCahan, who spent four years pitching for the Athletics and threw a no-hitter against the Senators during his rookie season; and Ron Northey, who spent twelve years in the majors with five different teams, hitting nine pinch-hit home runs, three of them with the bases loaded. More than twenty of Coombs' players made it to the big leagues.

One of the best pitchers that Coombs coached while at Duke did not make it to the major leagues. George Barley, a hard-throwing right-hander from Lynbrook, New York, went 24–2 for Duke from 1935 through 1937. Signed by the Yankees and sent to their Newark, New Jersey, farm team, Barley never reached his potential and gave up on his career after only a few seasons in the minors.

In later years Coombs offered his observations as to what constituted the fundamentals of good coaching. The first duty of a coach, according to Coombs, was to be realistic in terms of expectations and fair in dealing with his players. "It is to be expected that young players in every ball game will make misplays and errors of judgment, and the coach must not then be tempted to make unjust criticism or sarcastic remarks.... Gentle words, though sometimes spoken sternly, do young players far more good than any verbal abuse."[13]

The second duty of a good coach was to instruct the players on what to do in anticipation of various game situations rather than second-guess them after the fact. Physical errors were to be expected as part of the game, but there should be less tolerance of mental errors, as players should be prepared to execute their roles. Also, "give credit when credit is due," and learn from your mistakes.[14] The Duke University baseball squad was so well prepared that players like Bill Werber later commented that as a young player in the major leagues, he felt he was better schooled in the fundamentals than many experienced players.

Harkening back to simpler times, Coombs believed another important duty of a coach was to teach his players to dress properly for a game, both in terms of safety and physical appearance. He wanted his players to look and act like ballplayers.

Coombs was a firm believer in a regimented practice schedule, with specific routines to be covered in specific time periods. This was particularly important for the college-level player, thereby allowing sufficient time for the athlete to pursue his studies. Coombs' practices were governed by the alarm clock that he brought to the field, and when the alarm sounded for a change in activities or the end of practice, everyone on the field took note. Knowing how much that old clock governed Coombs' behavior, his players would occasionally reset the clock when their coach was pre-occupied with other tasks, thus allowing themselves some extra time on the field to pursue a favorite activity.

An important part of Coombs' practice regimen was the use of intrasquad games. As mentioned previously, in his early years at the university he solicited the services of Duke's President Few to umpire these games, giving the players the opportunity to show off their skills in front of the administration. The games were more than competitions; they were teaching opportunities, with Coombs running on to the field at various points to demonstrate how a certain play should be made. And each team batted for three consecutive innings before the side was changed, allowing greater concentration on offensive and defensive skills.

Coombs believed that signals should be kept simple, basically instructing batters when to swing away and runners to steal. If the players knew their roles in various situations—and Coombs' players were drilled in the fundamentals of their roles—they would recognize how to execute in accordance with the basic signals. In addition to knowing their roles, Coombs' players were expected to know the rules, and a portion of his practices was devoted to demonstrating how specific rules applied in various situations.

Finally, and perhaps most importantly in Coombs' view, a duty of a good baseball coach was to give his players responsibility and confidence. "The coach must have responsibility in himself to inspire confidence in his players. Each player should be made to feel that the success of the team rests directly on him. I have found that a player does his best playing when responsibility is placed upon him."[15]

Coombs' players thrived under his system. The players knew that he was an advocate for their success on and off the field; he was always available to counsel them on any matter, not just baseball. Dick Groat related that Coombs talked to him about his course of studies, trying to prepare him for life after baseball before his professional career had even begun. There were times when Coombs' counseling might be contrary to the player's aspirations. Bob Wolff, who became a very successful baseball broadcaster, related that during his time at Duke, Coach Coombs advised him to "stick to broadcasting." Coombs' reasoning was "I've never seen an arm or a pair of legs outlast a voice."[16] Coombs advice worked well for Wolff, as he spent nearly twenty years broadcasting for the Washington Senators and Minnesota Twins. In 1995, he received the Baseball Hall of Fame's Ford C. Frick Award, honoring broadcasters for major contributions to baseball.

While Coombs lectured to audiences that a good coach should not resort to "unjust criticism or sarcastic remarks," he was very adept at using sarcasm to make a point with his players during practice. He avoided the destructive, belittling approach of a John McGraw, and instead emulated Connie Mack, whose every word to his players was delivered with an anticipated effect. One of the more common stories told about Coombs related to an outfielder who misplayed a few fly balls in an intra-squad game. The next day at practice, Coombs gave the player surplus catching equipment to allow him to protect himself from balls struck in his direction. The outfielder did much better in the next intra-squad game. But when another outfielder struggled with fly balls hit his way, the first young man loudly called time, walked across the field, and ceremoniously transferred the catching equipment to the other outfielder. The players also knew they could toss jibes back at their coach. One Duke pitcher was struggling with his control during another intra-squad game and grew tired of Coombs' admonitions to bear down and concentrate. When he finally retired the side, the pitcher stormed back to the dugout and loudly asked all his teammates if any of them recalled which former pitcher owned the record for walks allowed in a World Series game.

Sarcasm aside, the Duke players looked up to Coombs. Crash Davis considered Coombs "the next greatest influence in my life after my father," describing Coombs as a "great teacher" and a "great listener." Regardless of the issue, Davis said, "When I had a problem I would go see Coach Jack."[17] Dick Groat in his autobiography related how Coombs took an active interest in his life, not just his baseball career. "My whole point is that Jack Coombs cared," wrote Groat. "He cared more than just the fact I was Duke's shortstop."[18] Bill Werber described Coombs as "a great coach and a great man. He helped me immeasurably."[19]

In a letter written in 1945, Charles E. Jordan, secretary of Duke University, summed up the respect the Duke players had for their coach. "His firm faith in baseball rightly taught and rightly played as a great contributing agency for character development in young men has undoubtedly been his constant strength in his handling of the many young men he has had as his players here. He wins their confidence and their esteem. They believe in him and love him."[20]

11

Professor Coombs

John and Mary Coombs were childless, a fact they had not given much note of during Coombs' busy major league baseball career. But Coombs would later tell family members, "Not having children is not so bad when you are young; you feel it when you are older."[1] While at Duke, he made up for the lack of progeny by "adopting" the entire student body as his own. He and Mary lived in an apartment in one of the dorms on campus, not far from the athletic facilities. It served as an open meeting place for any student, not just the athletes, who wanted to gather after the evening meal for a lively discussion on just about any subject. When the topic was baseball, as it frequently was, Coombs captivated his audience with stories from his major league days. In a deep, sonorous voice, Coombs regaled his audience with tales of the greats of the game, such as Mack, Collins, Mathewson, McGraw, and Cobb. During the storytelling, Mary would sit to the side and embroider. Coombs' participation in the discussion ended promptly at 9:00 every evening, as he announced to all gathered that he was heading to bed. His guests were free to stay and continue the discussion without him, but he was unfailing in his adherence to a regular schedule.

Coombs' insistence on regular habits became legendary on the Duke campus. Every day he arrived at the university post office at 10:00 A.M. At 10:45 he arrived in the student center for a "bull session" that ended promptly at 11:55 when his wife arrived for their 12:00 lunch. If Coombs showed any indication to linger, Mary would admonish, "Hush John," so that Coombs' audience could get to their next appointments on time.[2] Coombs and his wife were frequently seen together on campus, although as they went from one building to another, Coombs and his eager, long strides invariably outdistanced his wife. Once, on an icy day, Mary slipped and tumbled to the ground

Mary and John Coombs (courtesy Wentworth Family Personal Collection).

before Coombs could turn to arrest her fall. Making the best of the situation, Coombs turned and in an exaggerated motion spread his arms in imitation of an umpire's "safe" signal while calling out, "Nice slide, Mary!"[3]

Coombs' social interactions were not limited to the students. In addition to his close relationship with President Few, Coombs developed strong friendships with faculty in the fields of religion, law, history, political science, medicine, and economics. He was a frequent guest lecturer in economics classes. And his relationship with Dr. Lenox Barker of the medical school, whom Coombs first met when Barker was a medical student, became so close that Coombs insisted that Barker be on the bench with him for all of Duke's home games in case one of his players became injured.

The *Duke Alumni Register* reported that "Coach Jack Coombs can claim the distinction of being perhaps the most popular man on the Duke campus. Seen everywhere, he always has a friendly word for everybody."[4] He became renowned as a "story telling pied piper" on the Duke campus, attracting a crowd wherever he went.[5]

While at Duke, Coombs developed and taught an academic course on baseball. Attendance was required for all varsity baseball players, but the course was open to any student. It was not an easy course, with Coombs giving out few As. Students were expected to learn the rules of the game and the proper plays to make in game situations. Quizzes, exams and papers were all a part of the course, with the students regularly challenged to demonstrate that they knew the intricacies of the game.

Coombs believed that schools at both the secondary and collegiate level should be offering a course on baseball, as football was, in his opinion, getting a disproportionate amount of attention at educational institutions. To facilitate that end, Coombs wrote a textbook based on his course at Duke University. In the preface of the book, Coombs offered his reason for writing. "Many young men have not had an opportunity to study baseball under experienced guides who know how the game should be played. It is especially for the purpose of helping them to play the game with a greater degree of proficiency that I have prepared the data in this book. I have tried to keep all personal feelings from its contents and to present facts which years of experience have taught me."[6]

The book, titled *Baseball: Individual Play and Team Strategy*, was first published in 1937. It proved to be so successful that three editions were ultimately published, the last being issued in 1951. A Spanish language edition was also published, and copies were sold as far away as Japan.

Promotional materials for the book were targeted at high school and college coaches. "Why not increase your popularity with the entire student body by conducting a separate course for all students not on the baseball squad? In addition to arousing tremendous interest in the national game and putting the whole school solidly behind the baseball team, such a course may uncover for you potential stars who have never tried to make the team."[7] Whether the book helped uncover academics with latent baseball talent was never documented, but the publishers claimed that the book was widely used in more than 150 educational institutions. No less an expert than Connie Mack endorsed the book. "It would be slighting the value of this work to infer that its usefulness is limited to a young boy in a school or on a semi-pro field who wants to get ahead in the national sport. There is not a player in the major leagues, not even the most famous star, who would not be better for reading it."[8]

The book reads very much like a typical textbook from the middle part of the twentieth century, dominated by text in small type, with some black and white pictures and simple diagrams. At the close of each chapter is a short-answer quiz on the material covered. The first nine chapters are devoted to the defensive aspects of the game, covering the roles and responsibilities of each position. Chapters ten through twelve focus on the offense — batting, running and structuring a batting order. Emulating the approach Coombs used in Duke's practices, two chapters present a "mythical" ball game, whereby the reader can see the application of the lessons in the context of a "real" ball game. Additional chapters are dedicated to the subjects of scoring a game, managing a team's logistics, coaching, and the treatment of injuries. In typical Coombs fashion, the text is analytical and comprehensive, and developed without aid of a ghostwriter.

The book, more than three hundred pages in length, is exceptionally thorough and well written in straightforward language. Some standard tenets of baseball strategy are offered. Infielders, for example, are advised in potential double-play situations that "the first out must always be made sure before the second out at first base is attempted."[9] Instruction is also offered on how *not* to play the game. Harkening back to the confrontations between Ty Cobb and the Athletics infielders, base runners are admonished, "Any deliberate attempt on the part of a runner to spike or injure his opponent will never be tolerated. It is never necessary or justifiable."[10] The occasional philosophical statement makes its way into the text, as infielders are told to contemplate the fact that "[W]henever a defensive player takes a step to complete a play, a base runner is also taking a step to complete his objective."[11] Long before baseball strategy was being subjected to statistical analysis, Coombs used common-sense observation to describe the desired qualities of a leadoff hitter.

> The first or lead-off batsman is not necessarily a small, short man ... but he must be a good "waiter," a player sound and quick in his judgment of all pitched balls. The duty of the first batsman is to reach first base if possible, no matter by what means.... It is unsound judgment to play a heavy hitter in the lead-off position, because, after the game is under way, the players coming to bat before the lead-off man are always those who get on the bases the fewest number of times.[12]

Finally, there is the occasional instruction that appears comic in light of contemporary practice. "I have seen so many permanent injuries caused by athletes wearing jewelry on the athletic fields that I have established this rule, in my coaching work, that a player wearing any jewelry is not allowed on the playing field over which I have authority."[13]

A major component of the success of Coombs' book and his course was the emphasis placed on the questions that students were expected to answer. Copies of his final examinations found their way into newspapers, the *Sporting News*, and even *Life* magazine. Some questions could be so obvious as to be considered tricky, such as "What is the first rule of base running?" The answer: "Never miss a base."[14] Others concentrated on the physical mechanics of playing the game correctly. "What should outfielders and infielders always remember in regard to the first throw of a relay?" The answer: "First throw of the relay is the long one, second one the accurate one. Infielders should never go out too far or they will make the relay inaccurate."[15] Often questions revolved around game situations where the student was challenged to know the rules. For example: "Two on, none out. The batter bunts and pops up. The umpire shouts 'Infield fly, the batter is out.' The pitcher drops the ball. The base runners advance. The umpire sends them back. Are there any discrepancies here?"[16] The student was expected to respond that the umpire made two mistakes on the play as an infield fly should not have been called on a bunt and runners are allowed to advance at their own risk in the case of an infield fly.

Coombs at Duke University wearing the Colby College sweater presented to him by the Colby baseball team in 1939 (courtesy Colby College Special Collections, Waterville, Maine).

Coombs' efforts at educating young people on the proper way to play baseball were not limited to the classroom or the textbook. Along with good friend and former teammate Ira Thomas, Coombs conducted baseball clinics around the country, particularly in the Philadelphia area. The clinics were sponsored by a cereal company (Kellogg) and an oil company (Atlantic Richfield). In Philadelphia there were summers where thousands of boys were involved in the clinics, hearing lectures from Coombs and getting to play in numerous leagues around the city. As always, Coombs' message focused on playing the game properly and the value of pursuing one's education.

Coombs also frequently gave speeches at schools, with his talks focused on what a young man needed in order to be a success in life, regardless of his chosen career. His themes were centered on responsibility, hard work, character, the importance of mastering mathematics and English, and the value of a college education. Coombs had earlier expounded on his philosophy regarding education in a letter he wrote in 1917 to the graduating class of his former high school in Freeport, Maine.

> There may be a young man in your class who has the ambition of being a ball player, desirous to devote his future to the professional game. I hope there is for I do not know of any profession which is as clean, wholesome, free from all vicious thoughts, and full of things elevating and honorable as that of baseball. But first, from a business standpoint I advise him to consider his education as an asset no one can take from him; and secondly, the National game. A college course will better fit a man for his future work than all his traveling and associations put together. There are opportunities for every man of ability and the training at the higher institutions will help him to make a success in after life.[17]

He added, "I have advised a large number of young men to go to college before starting their career as ball players. The young student will receive a better chance to advance, a better opportunity to be taught and a better opportunity to study the game from a scientific standpoint than he would have should he go into some of our minor leagues expecting to work up in his profession."[18]

Clinics and educational presentations were not limited to youngsters. For example, in 1952, Coombs had the opportunity to join other coaches and umpires in conducting a clinic for military personnel serving in Germany. Wherever there was an opportunity to promote the game of baseball, Colby Jack Coombs could be counted on to be there.

While Coombs devoted his efforts to baseball throughout the year, he always set aside time to pursue his hobbies, hunting and fishing. From the time he was a young man at Colby College, Coombs had owned a rifle and loved the thrill of the hunt. Maintaining homes in both Maine and Texas, he annually availed himself of the opportunity to explore the wilderness areas of both states. During his major league career, following each season he gathered a group of teammates and colleagues and headed up to the northern reaches of Maine for a few weeks of hunting. Novice hunters were surprised to learn just how much hard work was involved in hunting, and developed a greater appreciation of Coombs' strength when he would single handedly shoulder a canoe over a portage. Through years of experience Coombs became so familiar with the Maine woods that he was considered as knowledgeable as a professional guide. His expertise included an ability to cook up a delicious meal for his famished colleagues. According to friends, the only drawback to hunting with Jack Coombs was his legendary snoring, which at times frightened unsuspecting newcomers into believing that bears were outside their tents.

Hunting was understandably a hazardous hobby, even for an experienced woodsman such as Coombs. Following his dismissal as the Phillies manager in 1919, he was accidentally shot in the leg while hunting with friends in Texas. In 1936, while climbing over a barrier in the woods, the barrel of the gun he was carrying burst, mangling one of the fingers on his left hand, resulting in its amputation. Despite these mishaps, hunting was an activity that Coombs pursued with vigor throughout his life.

In his later years at Duke, he would have fun with some of his educated but naïve colleagues at the university by describing the prey that he would be pursuing on his next hunting trip in Texas. Particular favorites were the "dingle-feddus" and the "pie-eyed wabble-nix." According to Coombs, both birds were difficult to hunt because of their unique characteristics. The dingle-feddus had "wind bags on its feet to blow its track away" while the wabble-nix deceived you by appearing to move towards you "when in reality it is going away." Every year upon returning to the Duke campus Coombs would report that he had come close to capturing his quarry, one year claiming that the hoarseness he was experiencing was because "he had gotten a dingle-feddus feather in his throat."[19]

Following the close of each collegiate baseball season, Coombs headed north to his farm at Kennebunk to spend the summer with his family. His nephews looked forward with delight to Uncle John's visits. In particular, during the economic uncertainty of the Great Depression, his visits lent an air of security to all around him. Clam bakes for twenty or more people, including the family and invited guests, were a popular summer activity, with Coombs in charge of all the food preparation. Typical feasts included steamed clams, lobster, sweet corn, string beans, potatoes, apple pie, cheese and coffee. Most days, in the morning and after dinner, Coombs would drive into town in his Chrysler, and any children who happened to be about were expected to join him for the ride. Quiet time was spent with family members playing cribbage or pinochle. The time in Maine was not all leisure, as Coombs regularly worked the farm with family members, joining in the harvesting of apples and hay, feeding the animals, chopping wood, and repairing buildings.

During the 1920s Coombs organized and managed a summer baseball team that was comprised of local collegiate players. The team played other nearby communities and Coombs' celebrity helped to draw crowds. He rarely pitched, preferring instead to play right field and enjoy once more the thrill of swinging a bat against live competition. Coombs' nephew Bobby joined the team while he still was in high school, playing opposite his uncle in left field. The catcher on these teams was the son of a prominent Kennebunkport resident by the name of George Herbert Walker. Coombs developed a good relationship with the Walker family, visiting them at their splendid home on the peninsula known as Walker's Point. George Herbert Walker was an avid golfer and responsible for the creation of the Walker Cup, the biannual golf tournament staged between American and British/Irish amateur golfers. He also became both grandfather and great-grandfather to future presidents of the United States.

While Coombs was understandably proud of his accomplishments as a major league pitcher and college baseball coach, he was particularly proud to be a graduate of Colby College. Having been one of the first players to go directly from the college ranks to the major leagues, Coombs felt that his academic training was an integral part of his preparation for his major league career. Coombs was such a keen observer of the action on a field that he developed a reputation for being able to steal signals. It was a source of distraction for Christy Mathewson and the New York Giants in the 1911 World Series, so much so that the Giants were constantly changing signs and going through extraordinary efforts to conceal their communication. It was not the signs that Coombs was stealing; he was such a keen observer of the opposing pitchers that he was able to identify the next pitch by the pitcher's slightest movements on the mound. He was so adept at this that he was occasionally referred to as "Wireless Jack."[20]

Coombs made an effort to attend every Colby class reunion. He gathered with his former teammates and classmates for stories and laughs, enjoying the camaraderie so much that he would forget about his watch and stay up long into the night. He maintained regular communications with the leadership of Colby's administration, and was on occasion chosen by the administration to represent the college at the inauguration of a new president at other universities. To Colby Jack Coombs it was perfectly natural for a former major league ballplayer and college baseball coach to appear on the dais surrounded by leading academicians and administrators at a university function.

On the occasion of the fortieth reunion of Colby's class of 1906, the college decided to honor Coombs. Seeking input from the administration at Duke University, the following letter of recommendation was received from Charles E. Jordan, secretary of Duke University.

> Mr. John W. Coombs has been our coach of baseball since September, 1929. He has been remarkably successful in that capacity. By that statement I mean to imply more than the training of good baseball teams throughout the years. His firm faith in baseball rightly taught and rightly played as a great contributing agency for character development in young men has undoubtedly been his constant strength in his handling of the many young men he has had as his players here. He wins their confidence and esteem. They believe in him and love him. As

a consequence, they have always played the game as gentlemen. While they play hard to win, they always keep in mind the coach's instruction and example; they represent the school and conduct themselves accordingly. The Coach is quite a figure both in the memory of those long out of college and also in the respect and affection of those on the campus. He is also well-known by many members of the Faculty and citizens of the community and is held in high respect by them. He is in demand for talks on baseball and has served in the capacity of representative of the great game in summer gatherings of boys who want and need such aid as comes from baseball well taught by an outstanding representative of the great sport. There are few men who know the game as he does and probably fewer who have achieved such success of the finest kind in teaching it to young men. The game is fortunate to have such a character as its interpreter and friend.[21]

Colby decided to honor Coombs with an honorary master of arts degree at the 1946 commencement. Colby President Seelye Bixler conferred the degree with the following testimonial:

John Wesley Coombs, pitcher with the Dodgers, the Tigers, and with the Athletics in the days of their glory, coach at Williams and Princeton, and now for many years at Duke, author of a text on baseball that bids fair to become a classic, idol of the nation's youth and exemplar of the highest ideals of sportsmanship, your college takes advantage of your fortieth reunion to honor you in the best Greek tradition as a consistent winner in the stadium of life.[22]

Five years later, Colby decided to once again honor Coombs. This time the school dedicated a new baseball field in his name. The dedication plaque at Coombs Field read as follows: "John Wesley Coombs — major league pitcher, college coach, and author, he has inspired countless young ballplayers to face life with a determination to succeed and with high standards of character and sportsmanship."[23] Coombs was thrilled with the honor. He told the audience at the dedication, "It is my wish that this field shall be but another testimony for the value of college athletics. I hope that all young men who play upon it will be inspired to live the lives of clean, honest, true-blue athletes. I trust that it will be an influence to the betterment of the game I love so dearly around which are conditions of good health, physical vigor and sound ethical principles." He concluded his remarks by saying, "Men and women of Colby, I am glad I am one of you. I accept the honor which you have given me with unusual joy."[24]

Duke University also celebrated the career of Jack Coombs, despite Coombs' protestations that he simply wanted to "fade away" at his retirement. On the occasion of his team's last home game at Duke on May 12, 1952, Billy Werber, the first man that Coombs sent to the major leagues, organized a tribute to his former coach. Coombs was presented with a leather-bound book filled with testimonials from former players, friends and colleagues, including Connie Mack. Mack's observations were as follows.

I have long felt that Jack Coombs is certainly deserving of a place in Baseball's Hall of Fame.

Although he was one of my former great pitchers, it is not so much for his ability as a player that I feel that Jack belongs with baseball's immortals. He has contributed much more to our great national pastime by devoting a lifetime to teaching the game to others.

Jack's contributions to baseball have been surpassed by few. In his long years of coaching at Duke University he has produced many great stars. Through his work with the Connie Mack Baseball School he has reached thousands of youngsters all over the country. His books have been used by baseball men everywhere.

I have known Jack for many years and have seen the great influence he has had in developing strength of character in the youth of America.

I hope that I can live to see the day when Jack Coombs is elected to the Hall of Fame.[25]

At the NCAA tournament that year, Coombs was honored for his years of outstanding service to college baseball and presented with a painted portrait. *Life* magazine ran a story on Coombs' retirement in June, containing one of the coach's difficult final examinations from his course.

For the most part, Coombs remained in Palestine with Mary and her family following his retirement. There was plenty to keep him busy there, as he had several business interests, including directorships of the East Texas National Bank and the Ezell Mercantile Company. There was also plenty of opportunity for hunting and fishing, as Coombs vowed that he was going to use retirement to "catch all the catfish" in Texas. While he was still a robust individual, Mary's health had been failing for a number of years, and Coombs devoted significant time to her care. She particularly suffered from vision problems, which limited their ability to travel together. The *Sporting News* encouraged major league teams to make use of Coombs' knowledge of the game, concluding, "Such men come along too seldom and the game should not overlook the opportunity to avail itself of John Wesley Coombs' services."[26] But with the exception of some scouting assignments for Connie Mack, Coombs had little further association with professional baseball after his retirement.

Coombs was periodically mentioned as a potential candidate for the Baseball Hall of Fame. He received one or two votes for the hall in elections held in 1937, 1938, 1946, 1948 and 1951. At the time of his retirement from Duke in 1952, the only teammates from the great Athletics team of 1910–1912 who had already been elected to the hall were Eddie Collins and Ed Plank. Collins' career had spanned twenty-five years with the Athletics and White Sox, where as one of the dominant offensive forces in the game he had collected more than 3,300 hits and a career batting average of .333. Plank had spent seventeen seasons on the pitcher's mound, totaling 326 wins, which at the time made him the winningest left-handed pitcher in major league history.

A special committee, called the Committee on Veterans, was established by the Hall of Fame in the 1950s to consider as potential candidates those former players who at that point had been retired from major league baseball for at least thirty years. The committee was headed by J. G. Taylor Spink, the noted publisher of the *Sporting News*. The committee met every other year, and was only permitted to elect two players to the hall. The committee elected Coombs' former Athletic teammates Chief Bender and Home Run Baker to the Hall of Fame in 1953 and 1955, respectively.

Coombs was hopeful that he might receive consideration for the hall in the 1957 election. However, the committee instead chose former Tigers outfielder Sam Crawford and former Cubs, Red Sox and Yankee manager Joe McCarthy. In response to a letter from a fan following the announcement of the election results in February of 1957, Coombs was gracious.

> I had hoped that the committee would give me the honor of joining the other baseball men in The Hall of Fame. However, they made a grand selection in giving Crawford and McCarthy that honor. I shall live in hopes that I can join that group in 1959 when the men who make the selection will again meet. If the honor is going to come to me I hope that I will be alive when it comes, for to me it would not be a pleasurable honor to enjoy after I am six feet under the sod.[27]

Six weeks after writing that letter, Coombs walked from his home in Palestine into town to get some donuts. He felt ill on the way home, and immediately went to his room to lie down. Within hours he was dead, the victim of a heart attack at the age of seventy-four.

Coombs' passing was mourned by the many people with whom he had come in contact during his lifetime. Ace Parker, Coombs' former student at Duke and the man who replaced him as the school's baseball coach, wrote, "There will never be another one like him. He was an inspiration to all who knew him, whether a lowly freshman or member of the faculty."[28] Eddie Cameron, athletic director at Duke, described Coombs as "one of the great sports personalities of all time."[29] Ellsworth Millett, Colby College's alumni secretary, wrote to Mary Coombs, "Our hearts are heavy today, for we share your grief. Jack Coombs was a great athlete, but he was more than that. He was a wonderful man. None of us who knew him failed to respond to the friendliness and the essential goodness of his character. The world is richer because he lived and many people mourn his passing.... His name will always be cherished here as one of the greatest of Colby's sons."[30] Sportswriter and author Frederick Lieb described him simply as "one of the greatest right-handers of all time."[31]

In a radio interview with sportscaster Ernie Harwell in 1941, when asked to offer his life philosophy, Coombs responded, "Those ideals and aims which one desires in life can be obtained only through self-sacrifice, firm determination and much courage."³² In a 1943 interview with Frederick Lieb of the *Sporting News*, Coombs said, "There is much in life if a man lives and does all things above-board. I hope I have lived that kind of life at all times."³³ Unselfish, determined, courageous, always above-board — John Wesley Coombs had lived his life demonstrating an abundance of each of these qualities.

Epilogue: "The times have certainly changed"

John Wesley Coombs graduated from Colby College in 1906. One hundred years later, although its student population has increased ten fold, Colby is still a relatively small, highly regarded liberal arts institution. The student population is still approximately half female, but no longer is that considered a potential drawback to the recruitment of male students. The campus is no longer located in downtown Waterville, Maine, having been moved in the late 1940s to its current scenic location on Mayflower Hill on the outskirts of Waterville. Dr. J. F. Hill, who recruited Coombs to Colby, played a key role in the early discussions regarding the relocation of the campus.

The baseball field that was dedicated in Coombs' name in 1951 is well maintained, although the plaque honoring Coombs is no longer at the field. The field was refurbished in 2001, including new dugouts, sprinkler system and drainage.

Befitting a small institution that promotes academics over athletics, Colby currently competes at the Division III level in inter-collegiate play. The Colby baseball team has not been particularly competitive in recent years, having gone winless in twenty-seven games in 2005. During the 1950s and 1960s the team was very competitive, frequently taking the Maine state championship, and participating in its first NCAA baseball tournament in 1958. The team earned another invitation the following season, but was forced to turn it down by the school administration, citing conflicts with final examinations. The team earned two more trips to the NCAA tournament in the 1960s.

The Colby baseball coach at that time was John Winkin, who had played for Coombs at Duke. When the Colby coaching job became vacant in 1954, Coombs recommended Winkin for the position. Winkin went on to coach at Colby for twenty years, doubling as the school's athletic director for the last ten years. He was selected by the National Association of Baseball Coaches for Coach of the Year honors in 1966. From Colby, Winkin moved to the University of Maine where he coached for another twenty-two seasons, leading the team to six College World Series tournaments. When Maine asked him to step down in 1997, the seventy-seven-year-old coach was hired by Husson College in Bangor, Maine, where he still served as baseball coach in 2006.

In recounting his association with Coombs, John Winkin claimed that "without question, he knew more about the game than any man I have ever known."[1] In a letter to Coombs' great-nephew, Nelson Wentworth, Winkin described his feelings for his former coach. "Jack Coombs meant a lot to me. I went to Duke because of him, and had four great years there. I also treasure the fact that all during my fifty-six months of action in World War II, I regularly heard from Jack Coombs by mail. He was also responsible for my landing the opportunity to coach at his alma mater. He was a wonderful person and a legendary coach."[2]

The baseball from Coombs' twenty-four-inning game is no longer in the Colby College trophy case, having been destroyed in a fire years ago. There is a large silver cup dedicated to Coombs in the athletic center, inscribed as follows: "Given by the alumni of Colby College to honor a great pitcher in college and professional baseball, and an outstanding college coach." On the occasion of the one hundredth anniversary of Coombs' graduation, special exhibits honoring Coombs were displayed in the college library and athletic center.

Coombs was instrumental in hiring a baseball coach for another educational institution. Following his last appearance for the New York Giants in 1943, Coombs' nephew Bobby joined the United States Navy, spending three years in the service. When Bobby was discharged from the navy, his Uncle John introduced him to the administration of Williams College, where the elder Coombs had coached for the three years following his retirement from major league baseball. Bobby was offered the baseball coaching job at Williams in 1946, and stayed there for the next twenty-eight years, leading the team to a record of 167–217 during that period.

John Wesley "Colby Jack" Coombs (courtesy Wentworth Family Personal Collection).

The baseball diamond at Williams is named the Bobby Coombs Baseball Field.

James B. Duke's vision of Duke University as a national university has become a reality, with Duke having emerged one of the premier educational institutions in the country at both the undergraduate and post-graduate level. The school competes at the Division I level in most sports. Basketball, under the leadership of renowned coach Mike Krzyzewski, rather than football or baseball, is now the premier athletic focus of the campus.

Following Coombs' retirement from Duke, his successor as baseball coach was Ace Parker, former Duke athlete and later professional football and baseball player. Parker led the team back to the College World Series in the following season, again being eliminated in three games. The team had its ups and downs during Parker's fourteen years as the coach, making one more trip to the College World Series in 1961. Following Parker's retirement, the fortunes of the baseball team slipped for the next twelve years.

For seven of those years, the team was under the direction of former major league outfielder Enos "Country" Slaughter. A lifetime .300 hitter in nineteen major league seasons, Slaughter had a reputation for hustle and hard work, a reputation epitomized by his famous "mad dash" from first base to score the winning run for the Cardinals in the 1946 World Series against the Red Sox. He was elected to the Baseball Hall of Fame in 1985. While coaching at Duke, however, he was very low-key and seemingly unenthusiastic about his job, and the team suffered under his direction, accumulating a record of 68–120. Coombs Field fell into disrepair as well, becoming so run down that opposing teams protested the playing conditions. Coach Tom D'Armi replaced Slaughter in 1978 and successfully went about the task of revitalizing both the team and its playing field.

Coombs Field at Duke University is a more substantial facility than its counterpart at Colby College. While small in comparison to the facilities available to other Atlantic Coast Conference schools, the field does have a covered grandstand that seats approximately 2,000 people. There is also a small grass-covered hill down the right-field line that provides excellent viewing for spectators. The outfield fences are surrounded by pine trees, giving a rural feeling to the field. The field was officially dedicated to Coach Coombs in 1978, and a bronze bust of Coombs was placed on a granite base at the entrance to the ballpark. Coombs is one of three people to be so honored on the Duke campus, the others being Wallace Wade, former athletic director and football coach, and James B. Duke, benefactor of Duke University.

Duke fields a competitive, though not dominant, baseball team. The school still sends players to the major leagues on a regular basis, although not with the frequency as during Coombs' tenure as coach. As of the close of the

2006 season, there were three Duke graduates on major league rosters — pitcher Chris Capuano of the Brewers, pitcher Scott Schoeneweis of the Reds, and outfielder Quinton McCracken of the Diamondbacks.

Coombs would probably get a chuckle out of the amount of support available to the team today. Back in his day, Coombs pleaded just to have an equipment manager to help keep track of balls and bats, necessary but expensive items during the Great Depression. Coombs and the players were responsible for the care and maintenance of the field. Coombs noted that he alone handled spring practices for nearly 100 aspiring ball players while football coach Wallace Wade and five paid assistants were handling workouts for half as many football players. Today, baseball still does not command the support of revenue-generating sports like basketball, but the Duke baseball team now has a full-time assistant coach plus an athletic department infrastructure that includes a strength coach, equipment manager, academic advisor, sports information director and fund raisers.

The dismantling of the Athletics roster following the 1914 World Series led to competitive hard times for Connie Mack's franchise. Starting in 1915, the club finished in the cellar of the American League for seven consecutive seasons, usually losing more than 100 games. Connie Mack the owner was patient with Connie Mack the manager and gradually rebuilt a roster that resulted in another dynasty. Led by a hard-hitting lineup that included four future Hall of Fame members — outfielder Al Simmons, catcher Mickey Cochrane, first baseman Jimmie Foxx and pitcher Lefty Grove — the 1929 Athletics deposed the Yankees' Murderer's Row as the American League's dominant team. Philadelphia went on to win the pennant in 1930 and 1931 as well, and captured the World Series in 1929 and 1930. Lefty Grove won thirty-one games for the Athletics in 1931, joining Coombs as the only thirty-game winners in the history of the franchise.

Economics forced Mack's hand once more, as the country found itself in the midst of the Great Depression in the early 1930s. Again unable to compete with some of the more financially independent owners, particularly Jacob Ruppert of the Yankees and Tom Yawkey of the Red Sox, Mack once more dismantled a championship team. Following the 1933 season, Grove was traded to the Red Sox and Cochrane was traded to the Tigers. Simmons had been traded to the White Sox a year earlier, and Foxx would be shipped to Boston in 1935. Beginning in 1935, the franchise finished last in nine of twelve seasons.

Connie Mack concluded his managerial career in 1950 at the age of eighty-seven, having been the sole manager of the Athletics since their inaugural season of 1901. During his career he captured nearly one thousand more victories than his nearest competitor, and went down in defeat two thousand more times than any other manager. By the time of his retirement, Mack and his children had the controlling interest in the Athletics. Disputes arose among the siblings, and the club was sold in 1954. Connie Mack died two years later, at the age of ninety-three.

At the time of Mack's death, the Athletics were no longer playing in Philadelphia. Baseball franchises had been remarkably stable for a period of fifty years, but starting with the move of the St. Louis Browns to Baltimore for the 1954 season, baseball began an eight-year period in which six franchises relocated to seemingly greener pastures. The Athletics moved to Kansas City for the 1955 season. While attendance improved in its new home, the fortunes of the team did not. The franchise was sarcastically referred to as a farm club for the New York Yankees, shipping young prospects to the Bronx, such as future home run champion Roger Maris, whenever the perennial champion Yankees appeared to be in need of additional talent.

While in Kansas City, ownership of the team passed to Charles O. Finley. A maverick among the owners and generally despised by his players and managers for his intrusive behavior, Finley moved the Athletics to Oakland, California, following the 1967 season. Finley realized that baseball was entertainment, outfitting his players in brightly colored green and yellow uniforms, encouraging them to grow mustaches and beards at a time when all ballplayers were clean-shaven, and creating nicknames for his players to make them more endearing to the fans. He also had an eye for talent and built another dynasty around slugger Reggie Jackson and pitchers Catfish Hunter and Rollie Fingers. The A's won the American League pennant and the World Series in 1972, 1973 and 1974, making them the only franchise other than the Yankees to win three consecutive World Series.

Following the team's run of success, Finley became frustrated with the advent of free agency for the players. Unwilling to pay the high salaries his charges commanded in what was now an open market, Finley tried to emulate Connie Mack by dismantling his team. He openly attempted to sell his star players to the highest bidder, a move that was blocked by baseball Commissioner Bowie Kuhn as not being in the best interests of baseball.

Finley eventually tired of the new economics of baseball and sold the Athletics in 1991. Since that time, the franchise has generally been competitive, winning its ninth World Series in 1989, although still struggling to compete with wealthier clubs.

Following Coombs' retirement, the Brooklyn Robins were managed by Wilbert Robinson for a total of eighteen years. The club captured the National League pennant again in 1920, but more typically finished between fourth and sixth place.

Lee McPhail was hired as general manager in 1938, and the fortune of the franchise, now officially known as the Dodgers, changed for the better. McPhail turned the club into contenders, capturing the National League pennant in 1941. McPhail left the club during World War II, and was replaced by Branch Rickey. Rickey had been general manager of the Cardinals when St. Louis considered Jack Coombs for its on-field manager. Rickey elevated the Dodgers from perennial contenders to the National League's most dominant team. Commencing in 1946, over an eleven-year period Brooklyn won six pennants and twice tied for first place, only to lose the pennant in a playoff. Their worst finish during this period was third place. Rickey's courageous decision to buck the baseball establishment's unwritten policy of discrimination by hiring black ballplayers — the policy that kept Fred Tenney from hiring William Matthews in 1905 — gave the Dodgers a talent edge they used to their advantage. In addition to the pioneering Jackie Robinson, the Dodgers boasted of such black stars as Roy Campanella, three-time league Most Valuable Player and future member of the Hall of Fame, and hard-throwing right-handed pitcher Don Newcombe, who won more than twenty games three times, including twenty-seven victories in 1956. The black ballplayers were not the only stars on the Dodgers' roster, which included future Hall of Fame members Pee Wee Reese at shortstop and Duke Snider in center field. While the Dodgers were the most dominant team in the National League during this period, they struggled in the World Series, playing the New York Yankees in all six of their trips to the October classic, but emerging as victors only once, in 1955.

During this run of success, ownership of the Dodgers transferred to Walter O'Malley. O'Malley realized that Ebbets Field, while beloved by loyal Brooklyn fans, had physical constraints that would limit the financial success of the franchise in the future. Tired of negotiating for a new stadium with the political leadership of the city of New York, O'Malley moved the franchise to Los Angeles following the 1957 season, and convinced fellow owner Horace Stoneham to move his New York Giants to San Francisco at the same time. The National Pastime was finally national in scope.

O'Malley negotiated an attractive land deal for his new ballpark, and Dodger Stadium, also known as Chavez Ravine, opened for play in 1962. Since that time, the Dodgers have enjoyed excellent attendance, becoming in 1978 the first team to sell more than three million tickets, and have usually enjoyed excellent baseball, capturing the World Series in 1959, 1963, 1965, 1981, and 1988.

Of all the major league ballparks where Jack Coombs performed, only two remain in use: Fenway Park and Wrigley Field. Both ballparks give the paying customer a feeling of intimacy with the game, given close proximity to the field of play, and with fellow fans, given the narrow seats and aisles in each facility. Baseball fans from throughout the country make pilgrimages to Boston and Chicago to see the fields (although some of the action can be obstructed by poles) where the legends of the game once played.

During Coombs' career, baseball went through its first "golden age" of ballpark construction, which was ushered in with the opening of Shibe Park in 1909. Shibe Park was later renamed Connie Mack Stadium when the Mack family took over the financial ownership of the franchise. Following the departure of the Athletics for Kansas City, the ballpark continued as the home of the National League Phillies through the 1970 season, when it was replaced by Veterans Stadium, a characteristic example of baseball's dark era of ballpark construction. Veterans Stadium was a "multi-use" facility for baseball and football, virtually indistinguishable from the ballparks in Cincinnati and Pittsburgh, with unobstructed views from seats well-removed from the perfectly symmetrical field of play, which was covered with a synthetic playing surface.

Baseball's second "golden age" of ballpark construction began with the opening of Oriole Park at Camden Yards in 1992. Like Fenway Park and Wrigley Field, Camden Yards is located in the heart of the city. The facility was built solely for baseball, having irregular dimensions to fit the urban landscape. The ballpark captures the feeling of intimacy of the classic ballparks, yet all seats are unobstructed, and the game is played on natural turf. Camden Yards demonstrated that a ballpark could be as much of an attraction as the team itself, and baseball's ownership caught on to the idea, especially when host cities were willing to contribute to the cost of construction of the new venues. As of the close of the 2006 season, only eight of baseball's thirty venues were built prior to 1990. Even storied Yankee Stadium, built in 1923, is scheduled to be taken out of commission as soon as a new facility is built next to "the House that Ruth Built." The old facility has a surfeit of mystique and aura, but the new facility will have plenty of luxury suites.

Although most of the ballparks where Jack Coombs plied his trade are gone, the farm that was the home for Coombs and his extended family is still standing on the outskirts of Kennebunk. The big farmhouse with its wraparound porch still sits on a rise above the road, overlooking Coombs Lane and the house where Coombs' brother Curtis lived for many years.

The house was almost destroyed by fire in 1947. Following a summer of severe drought, the state of Maine was struck by a series of wildfires that devastated over 200,000 acres throughout the state, severely damaging more than a dozen communities.[3] Coombs' great nephew Donald remembers being perched on the roof of the house with an Indian pump to keep the roof and building wet. The fire raged close by, but its path was split by nearby Alewife Pond, sparing the house and outbuildings. The contents of Coombs' den were moved for safekeeping, but some of his memorabilia were "lost" and never returned.

When Coombs died, he left the house and land to Colby College, with the transfer of the property to take place after the death of family members still living at the property. Mary Coombs died in 1965.

Some of Coombs' pitching records still stand. He holds the American League record for most shutouts in a season, with thirteen. He, along with Christy Mathewson, are the only two pitchers to capture three complete-game victories in a five-game World Series, and Coombs is alone in capturing back-to-back complete-game victories in a World Series.

In 1910 and 1911, Coombs led not only the American League, but both leagues, in victories. Since the founding of the American League, only fifteen pitchers, including Coombs, have led both leagues in victories for two or more consecutive seasons. Of the fourteen others, thirteen are already in the Baseball Hall of Fame, and the fourteenth, Roger Clemens, once seemed a virtual lock for election prior to baseball's steroid scandal.

Other marks of Coombs have been surpassed. His record for consecutive shutout innings was bested by Walter Johnson in 1913, and subsequently exceeded by Don Drysdale and Orel Hershiser, both of the Dodgers. Coombs won five World Series games without defeat, a mark later tied by Herb Pennock, and exceeded only by Lefty Gomez.

On May 1, 1920, Leon Cadore, a former Brooklyn teammate of Coombs, and Joe Oeschger, a pitcher on Coombs' 1919 Phillies team, locked up in a marathon pitching battle that ended in a 1-1 tie after twenty-six innings of play. It remains to this day the longest single-game pitching performance by any pitcher in major league history. Coombs, however, still holds the honor of the longest complete-game victory with his twenty-four-inning defeat of Boston in 1906.

The lot of a major league pitcher is quite different from the times of "Iron Man" Coombs. Coombs pitched 353 innings in 1910, including thirty-five complete games while on his way to thirty-one victories. League leaders in the early twenty-first century typically record 250–275 innings pitched, seven to ten complete games, and twenty to twenty-two victories.

The first indication of the extinction of the iron man pitcher came about during Coombs' career. The last time a major league pitcher totaled thirty-five complete games was in 1917, when both Grover Cleveland Alexander and Babe Ruth turned the trick. The last pitcher to have as many as thirty complete games was Catfish Hunter, with exactly thirty in 1975. During Coombs' career, managers became increasingly willing to remove a starting pitcher in favor of a fresh arm, although in Coombs' time that fresh arm usually belonged to another starting pitcher.

The last time a pitcher threw as many innings as Coombs did in 1910 was in 1973, when knuckleball pitcher Wilbur Wood tossed 359. The last to break the 300-inning plateau was Steve Carlton, with 304 in 1980.

The last thirty-game winner in major league baseball was Denny McLain, who notched thirty-one victories in 1968. Since that time only two pitchers, Steve Carlton and Bob Welch, have totaled as many as twenty-seven wins. In 2006, not a single pitcher in either league reached the twenty-victory plateau.

This is not to say the pitching was better back in Coombs' day; it was just different. Managers did not keep track of pitch counts, and the medical care for players was primitive in comparison to today, both for on-field injuries and off-field maladies. And ballplayers in Coombs' day were frequently treated as expendable assets, not multi-million-dollar investments like contemporary ballplayers. The dedicated relief pitcher was unheard of during Coombs' career, never mind the specialization of middle relievers, set-up men, and closers that populate baseball rosters today. Pitchers like Jack Coombs were given the ball and expected to go as many innings as needed. If that happened to be twenty-four innings in a single game, he went twenty-four innings and got a slap on the shoulder from your manager and thanks for doing a "great job." Four days later he was asked to toe the rubber again, with the expectation that he would go another nine innings.

Being an "iron man" was one of the measures of a great pitcher in Coombs' time, and Coombs demonstrated that he was equal to the challenge, achieving totals that made him one of the leaders of his era.

Jack Coombs was elected to several halls of fame during and after his lifetime. He is a member of the Iowa Sports Hall of Fame, the Maine Sports Hall of Fame, the North Carolina Sports Hall of Fame, the Duke Sports Hall of Fame, and the College Baseball Hall of Fame, to name a few. He never was selected for the highest honor of his profession — membership in the National Baseball Hall of Fame. His candidacy was considered again by the Committee on Veterans in 1959, but he did not receive sufficient support for election. Former Brooklyn teammate Zach Wheat was elected in 1959.

There were prominent people associated with the game of baseball who thought that Coombs was deserving of the game's highest honor. In 1959, J. G. Taylor Spink resigned as chairman of the Veterans' Committee in large part because he thought that the election procedures did not give sufficient opportunity for the election of players he thought deserving of the recognition. In his resignation letter Spink wrote, "I am strongly of the opinion that the rules for election of old-time stars need revision in order that more of these outstanding players might gain rightful recognition. As matters now stand, only one or two can be elected every two years, and many of these distinguished old-timers never will gain election under such a system. I have in mind men like Billy Hamilton, Bob Caruthers, Amos Rusie, Tim Keefe, Jack Coombs, and others of that character."[4] Hamilton, Rusie and Keefe eventually were elected to the Hall of Fame; Caruthers and Coombs are still waiting.

On the occasion of Coombs' retirement from Duke University, Connie Mack made a case for Coombs' election to the Hall of Fame, not only for his accomplishments on the playing field, but for his lifetime of service as a coach and educator. A few years earlier with the publication of *Connie Mack's Baseball Book*, Mack had selected Coombs to his "all-time major league team."[5] The pitchers that Mack considered "the greatest mound artists of all time" were Christy Mathewson, Lefty Grove, Walter Johnson, Chief Bender, Rube Waddell and Jack Coombs.[6] All but Coombs are in the Baseball Hall of Fame.

In January of 1925, having completed his eighteenth season with the Washington Senators by helping lead the club to its only World Series championship, Walter Johnson was asked to name those "pitchers who will live long in the history of baseball."[7] The men Johnson named were Rube Waddell, Ed Walsh, Bugs Raymond, Cy Young, Jack Coombs and Christy Mathewson. Raymond was the Giants pitcher with a world of talent marred by his addiction to alcohol, leading to his early departure from the big leagues and premature death at the age of thirty. All the others named by Johnson, with the exception of Coombs, are in the Hall of Fame. Johnson went on to compare Coombs and Mathewson for their clean living. "Matty was an honor to the game and the hero, perhaps, of more boys than any other ball player that ever lived. Jack Coombs, of the Philadelphia Athletics, also stands as another witness to the interdependence of big league baseball and clean living. He was an outstanding figure on the mound for years, which would not have been true had Coombs not taken good care of himself."[8]

In 1948, Shoeless Joe Jackson, considered by many to be one of baseball's greatest hitters and who was banned from baseball by Commissioner Landis for his involvement in the Black Sox scandal, named Coombs as one of the greatest pitchers he ever faced, including him with Smoky Joe Wood, Walter Johnson, Eddie Plank, and Vean Gregg.[9] Nap Lajoie, a .338 hitter over twenty-one major league seasons and one of the first members of the Baseball Hall of Fame, considered Coombs among "the greatest pitchers of all," along with Cy Young, Christy Mathewson, Chief Bender and Ed Walsh.[10]

Following his own election to the Hall of Fame, Home Run Baker publicly made his case for Coombs' election to the hall. "I have never said a word as to whether this player or that player should be in the Hall of Fame," Baker told the *Sporting News*. "I have confidence in the men who are selected to make the judgment. However, I think I ought to break the rule to put in a few words for the late Jack Coombs." According to Baker, "Coombs was a great pitcher, who could strike out Joe Jackson, one of the game's greatest hitters when he was with the Chicago White Sox, on three curve balls. He was as fine a fielding pitcher as you will see, a switch hitter who could deliver the run, and a man who never let down the team in a hard game."[11]

Illustrative of Baker's point, Coombs performed well against the best pitchers in baseball throughout his career, compiling a record of 21–8 against opponents who wound up in the Hall of Fame. He never lost to Mathewson, beating him in the 1911 World Series and twice during the 1915 season. He beat Walter Johnson three times in four decisions, and went 5–1 against Big Ed Walsh. Three of Coombs' World Series victories came against two of the greatest pitchers in the history of baseball — Christy Mathewson and Mordecai "Three Finger" Brown. The only Hall of Fame pitcher Coombs had a losing record against was Grover Cleveland Alexander, who beat Coombs in all four games they pitched against each other.

Writing for the *Sporting News* in 1957, sportswriter Francis Stann said, "Jack Coombs' death at 74 points up anew the frailties of the Hall of Fame at Cooperstown. He isn't in the Hall and should have been there long ago. Coombs was one of the real good pitchers as well as a gentleman and a scholar."[12]

With such prestigious advocates supporting his candidacy, why was Coombs not elected to the Hall of Fame? Noted sportswriter and baseball historian Lee Allen put it succinctly. "Bender, Plank, Baker, and Collins have all attained Hall of Fame recognition, and Coombs would almost certainly have made the grade also, had not injury and illness shortened his career."[13]

A career shortened due to misfortune does not by itself disqualify one from a place in the Hall of Fame. There are two pitchers in the Hall of Fame, Dizzy Dean and Addie Joss, who had their careers shortened by illness or injury. The table below compares some statistics from the careers of the three players.

Table 3. Career Pitching Comparison
of Coombs, Dean and Joss

	Games Won	Games Lost	Winning Percentage	Complete Games	Innings Pitched	Shutouts	Runs allowed per Nine Innings
Coombs	158	110	.590	187	2320	35	3.59
Dean	150	83	.644	154	1967	26	3.54
Joss	160	97	.622	234	2327	45	2.82

Addie Joss was a contemporary of Coombs; his career was tragically cut short when he contracted tubercular meningitis, leading to his untimely death at the age of thirty-one. Joss spent his entire career with Cleveland, and nearly pitched the team to the 1908 pennant when he tossed a perfect game against

Big Ed Walsh and the White Sox late in the season. He won twenty or more games in a season four consecutive years. Joss is best remembered for a remarkably low career earned run average, but it should be noted that he pitched in a time before earned runs were compiled as an official statistic, and his career ended in 1910, before the American League introduced its new baseball in 1911, leading to a nearly 25 percent increase in runs scored. Joss was elected to the Baseball Hall of Fame in 1978.

Jay Hanna "Dizzy" Dean achieved his fame pitching for the St. Louis Cardinals in the 1930s. A country boy from Arkansas with an outsized ego and unconstrained penchant for bravado, Dean won thirty games for the world champion Cardinals in 1934, the last National League pitcher to accomplish this feat. He followed that up with a twenty-eight-victory season in 1935, again leading the major leagues in wins, as Coombs had done in 1910–1911. In 1937, Dean's toe was broken when he was struck by a line drive while pitching in the All-Star game. Having returned to the rotation before the injury was healed, Dean altered his throwing motion and damaged his arm, and saw limited service on the mound for the remainder of his career. Following his major league career Dean became a broadcaster for major league baseball, entertaining fans around the country with his home-spun yarns and tortuous grammar. Dean was elected to the Baseball Hall of Fame in 1953.

Coombs had the advantage over both Joss and Dean in World Series play, having won five contests without defeat. Joss never had the opportunity to pitch in the World Series. Although Dean won the deciding game for the Cardinals against Detroit in 1934, his World Series career record is only 2–2.

Typhoid fever is still a scourge in those parts of the world lacking adequate infrastructure for water and sewage treatment. Millions of cases are reported annually, and more than 600,000 people worldwide are estimated to die from typhoid fever each year. The disease is virtually nonexistent in the United States, with most American victims having been exposed to the disease from overseas trips.[14]

One is left to wonder what might have been if John Wesley Coombs had not been exposed to typhoid fever in 1913. If there is a lesson to be learned, it is that one should listen to the admonishments of one's mother: always wash your hands thoroughly before eating; make sure your food is properly cooked; and, make sure all eating utensils are clean. You never know, failure to do so just might keep you out of the Hall of Fame.

Chapter Notes

Prologue

1. Except where noted, details of the game were drawn from the September 2, 1906, editions of the *Boston Globe, New York Times, Chicago Daily Tribune,* and *Washington Post.*
2. *Boston Globe,* September 2, 1906.
3. James M. Kahn, *The Umpire Story* (New York: G. P. Putnam, 1953), 45.
4. *Sporting News,* September 8, 1906.
5. In 1920, Joe Oeschger of the Braves and Leon Cadore of the Dodgers each pitched twenty-six innings in a game that ended as a tie.
6. Frederick Lieb, *Connie Mack: The Grand Old Man of Baseball* (New York: G. P. Putnam, 1945), 105. While Lieb quotes Mack by referring to Coombs as Jack, Mack invariably referred to Coombs as John throughout their long association.
7. Frederick Lieb, *Boston Red Sox* (New York: G. P. Putnam, 1947), 70.
8. Coombs file, Colby College Special Collections.
9. Dick Thompson, "In Name Only," *The National Pastime* (Number 20, 2000): 54.
10. Joe Dittmar, "'Doc' Powers' Shocking End," *The National Pastime* (Number 13, 1993): 62.
11. Lieb, *Connie Mack,* 121.

Chapter 1

1. Coombs family background based on discussions with Donald and Nelson Wentworth, December 10, 2005.
2. Joyce Butler, *Kennebunkport Scrapbook, Volume 1* (Kennebunk Landing, ME: Rosemary House Press, 1977).
3. J. D. Davis, *A Most Remarkable Mix: Sketches of Notable Freeporters* (Freeport, ME: Freeport Historical Society, 2000).
4. Earl H. Smith, *Mayflower Hill: A History of Colby College* (Hanover, NH: Colby College, 2006).
5. Ernest Cummings Marriner, *The History of Colby College* (Waterville, ME: Colby College Press, 1963).
6. Ibid., 438.
7. Ibid., 345.
8. Ibid., 283.
9. *Boston Globe,* April 12, 1903.
10. Ibid.
11. *The Colby Echo,* April 30, 1903.
12. Letter dated September 3, 1903, in Wentworth Family Personal Collections.
13. *Boston Globe,* February 18, 1911.
14. Unidentified newspaper clipping dated September 9, 1903, in Wentworth Family Personal Collections.
15. *The Colby Echo,* October 22, 1903.
16. *The Colby Echo,* April 8, 1904.
17. *The Colby Echo,* April 14, 1904.
18. Unidentified newspaper clipping in Wentworth Family Personal Collections.
19. *The Colby Echo,* June 17, 1904.
20. *The Colby Echo,* June 24, 1904.
21. Unidentified newspaper clipping in Wentworth Family Personal Collections.
22. *The Colby Echo,* December 2, 1904.
23. Wentworth Family Personal Collections.
24. Clifton Merrit, *Disorganized Baseball, Volume II: Baseball in Vermont (1887–1935)* (Monroe, CT: SAMISDAT, no date).

25. *Boston Globe*, July 23, 1905.
26. Karl Lindholm, "William Clarence Matthews," *The National Pastime* (Number 17, 1997).
27. Lee Allen, *The National League Story* (New York: Hill and Wang, 1961), 148.
28. Harry Grayson, *They Played the Game* (New York: A. S. Barnes and Company, 1945), 44.
29. Conflicting accounts exist as to when and how Coombs first came to the attention of Tom Mack. For example, Fred Lieb claims that Mack initially saw Coombs pitch in Worcester against Holy Cross, but the author can find no record of the Colby College team having competed against Holy Cross during Coombs' four years at Colby. Grayson's account seems more plausible.
30. *The Colby Echo*, October 18, 1905.
31. *The Colby Echo*, November 22, 1905.
32. *The Colby Echo*, March 7, 1906.
33. Ibid.
34. J. C. Kofoed, "Stars of Other Days — The Iron Man" (*Baseball Magazine*, Volume 13, No. 3, January 1915).
35. The *Washington Post*, February 20, 1911.

Chapter 2

1. Ira Smith, *Baseball's Famous Pitchers* (New York: A. S. Barnes and Co., 1954), 113–115.
2. Ibid. 104–105.
3. Lieb, *Connie Mack*, 95.
4. Smith, *Baseball's Famous Pitchers*, 46.
5. Lieb, *Connie Mack*, 102.
6. *Sporting News*, September 2, 1906, and September 15, 1906.
7. *Washington Post*, July 6, 1906.
8. *Chicago Tribune*, July 26, 1906.
9. Ibid.
10. *Sporting News*, July 21, 1906.
11. *Sporting News*, August 4, 1906.
12. Ibid.
13. *New York Times*, October 26, 1910.
14. Ibid.
15. Grayson, *They Played the Game*, 30.
16. *Sporting News*, September 2, 1906, and September 15, 1906.
17. *Chicago Tribune*, August 28, 1906.
18. *Washington Post*, March 31, 1907.
19. *Washington Post*, April 30, 1907.
20. *Washington Post*, June 23, 1907.
21. *Sporting News*, July 4, 1907
22. Lieb, *Connie Mack*, 113.

Chapter 3

1. *Sporting News*, March 12, 1908.
2. *Boston Globe*, March 13, 1908.
3. *Sporting News*, March 26, 1908.
4. *Sporting News*, April 2, 1908.
5. *Sporting News*, April 30, 1908.
6. Frederick Lieb and Stan Baumgartner, *The Philadelphia Phillies* (New York: G. P. Putnam, 1953), 84.
7. Ibid. 86.
8. Philip J. Lowry, *Green Cathedrals* (Reading, MA: Addison-Wesley, 1992), 209.
9. *Sporting News*, December 10, 1908.
10. *Sporting News*, April 29, 1909.
11. Dittmar, "Doc Powers' Shocking End."
12. *Washington Post*, May 8, 1909.
13. Lieb, *Connie Mack*, 126.
14. Al Stump, *Cobb: The Life and Times of the Meanest Man Who Ever Played Baseball* (Chapel Hill, NC: Algonquin Books of Chapel Hill, 1994), 176.
15. Ibid., 169.
16. *Boston Globe*, August 27, 1909.
17. Ibid.
18. *Washington Post*, August 27, 1909.
19. Ibid.
20. Stump, *Cobb*, 174.
21. Ibid., 304.

Chapter 4

1. *Boston Globe*, April 4, 1910.
2. Unidentified newspaper clipping, Wentworth Family Personal Collections.
3. Norman L. Macht, *Connie Mack and the Early Years of Baseball* (Lincoln: University of Nebraska Press, 2007), 385.
4. Unidentified newspaper clippings, Wentworth Family Personal Collections.
5. *Washington Post*, April 18, 1910.
6. Ibid., September 13, 1910.
7. *Chicago Tribune*, August 5, 1910.
8. Ibid.
9. *Washington Post*, August 5, 1910. Note that the "hall of fame" is a general term, and does not refer to the National Baseball Hall of Fame, which opened in Cooperstown, New York, in 1939.
10. *Washington Post*, August 10, 1910.
11. *Boston Globe*, August 11, 1910.
12. *Chicago Tribune*, September 25, 1910.
13. *Washington Post*, September 25, 1910.
14. *Boston Globe*, October 2, 1910.
15. Ibid.
16. Lee Allen, *100 Years of Baseball* (New York: Bartholomew House, 1950), 160.
17. *Chicago Tribune*, October 19, 1910.
18. Ibid.
19. Ibid.

20. Frederick Lieb, *The Story of the World Series* (New York: G. P. Putnam, 1949), 72.
21. Lieb, *Connie Mack*, 130.
22. *Chicago Tribune*, October 21, 1910.
23. Ibid.
24. Ibid.
25. *Washington Post*, October 23, 1910.
26. Unidentified newspaper clipping, Coombs file, A. Bartlett Giamatti Research Center.
27. Lieb, *Connie Mack*, 142.
28. *Washington Post*, December 11, 1910.
29. Lieb, *Connie Mack*, 144.
30. *Washington Post*, October 24, 1910.
31. *Sporting News*, October 27, 1910.
32. Raymond Gonzalez, "Pitchers Giving up Home Runs," *Baseball Research Journal* (1981): 18.

Chapter 5

1. *Los Angeles Times*, April 8, 1911.
2. *Boston Globe*, March 1, 1911.
3. *Boston Globe*, July 23, 1911.
4. Unidentified newspaper clipping, Wentworth Family Personal Collections.
5. *Washington Post*, December 24, 1910.
6. *Washington Post*, December 25, 1910.
7. *Boston Globe*, December 27, 1910.
8. Ibid.
9. Ibid.
10. Ibid.
11. *Washington Post*, May 14, 1911.
12. *Washington Post*, January 1, 1911.
13. Ty Cobb, *Busting 'Em and Other Big League Stories* (reprint, Jefferson, NC: McFarland & Company, 2003), 116.
14. Discussions with Donald and Nelson Wentworth, December 10, 2005.
15. *Washington Post*, July 11, 1911.
16. *Washington Post*, June 29, 1911.
17. *Boston Globe*, June 6, 1911.
18. Michael Gersham, *Diamonds* (Boston: Houghton Mifflin, 1993), 101.
19. Charles Alexander, *John McGraw* (Lincoln: University of Nebraska Press, 1988,) 155–156.
20. Ibid. 163.
21. Frank Graham, *McGraw of the Giants* (New York: G. P. Putnam, 1944), 59.
22. Frederick Lieb, *The Baseball Story* (New York: G. P. Putnam, 1950), 141.
23. For more on the Giants and the relationship between McGraw and Mathewson, see Frank Deford's *The Old Ball Game* (New York: Atlantic Monthly Press, 2005).
24. *Washington Post*, September 30, 1911.
25. *Washington Post*, October 17, 1911.
26. Ibid.
27. Ray Robinson, *Matty: An American Hero* (New York: Oxford University Press, 1993), 128.
28. Marty Payne, "Frank 'Home Run' Baker," *The Baseball Research Journal* (Number 29, 2000).
29. *Boston Globe*, October 18, 1911.
30. *Atlanta Constitution*, October 18, 1911.
31. *Washington Post*, October 18, 1911.

Chapter 6

1. *Washington Post*, November 7, 1911.
2. *Washington Post*, April 21, 1912.
3. Ibid.
4. *New York Times*, May 19, 1912.
5. "Ty Cobb vs. Ban Johnson," *Baseball Magazine* (Volume IX, No.3, July 1912).
6. *Washington Post*, May 19, 1912.
7. *Boston Globe*, May 26, 1912.
8. Colby College Special Collections.
9. Coombs file, Colby College Special Collections.
10. "Connie Mack Does Not Work Pitchers in Order," *Baseball Magazine* (Volume VIII, No.4, February 1912).
11. *Boston Globe*, July 4, 1912.
12. Lieb, *Connie Mack*, 161.
13. Ibid.
14. Lawrence S. Ritter, *The Glory of Their Times* (New York: Quill, 1985), 154.
15. *Boston Globe*, August 31, 1912.
16. Lieb, *Connie Mack*, 163.

Chapter 7

1. "The College Man as a Professional Ball Player," *Leslie's Weekly* (Volume 112, March 16, 1911).
2. Ibid.
3. H.G. Salinger, "The Path to Baseball Fame," *Leslie's Weekly* (Volume 116, June 5, 1913).
4. Charles E. Van Loan, "Big Leaguers in the Spangles and Out," *Munsey's Magazine* (Volume 47, July 1912).
5. *New York Times*, January 12, 1913.
6. *The Washington Post*, April 16, 1913.
7. Donald Emmeluth, *Deadly Diseases and Epidemics: Typhoid Fever* (New York: Chelsea House, 2004), 8.
8. For background on typhoid fever, see Emmeluth, *Typhoid Fever*, and Ausebel, Meyer and Wernick, "Death and the Human Environment: The United States in the 20th Century," *Technology in Society* (Volume 23, No. 2, 2001).
9. For a more thorough treatment of the subject, see Anthony Bourdain, *Typhoid Mary: An*

Urban Historical (New York: Bloomsbury, 2001).
   10. Ibid. 47.
   11. Wentworth Family Personal Collections, Diaries of Jesse Snow, June 4, 1913.
   12. "The Baseball Campaign up to Date," *Baseball Magazine* (Volume XI, No.3, July 1913).
   13. *Chicago Tribune*, July 24, 1913.
   14. *Sporting News*, July 31, 1913.
   15. *Washington Post*, August 5, 1913.
   16. Ibid.
   17. John B. Holway, "Louis Van Zelst in the Age of Magic," *The National Pastime* (1983).
   18. *Boston Globe*, October 31, 1913.
   19. *The Colby Echo*, May 13, 1914.
   20. Lieb, *Connie Mack*, 177.
   21. Ibid.
   22. *Boston Globe*, October 26, 1914.
   23. *Boston Globe*, November 1, 1914.
   24. *Boston Globe*, December 6, 1914.
   25. Coombs File, A. Bartlett Giamatti Research Center.
   26. Peter Williams, ed., *The Joe Williams Baseball Reader* (Chapel Hill, NC: Algonquin Books, 1989), 24.
   27. Frederick Lieb, *The Baseball Story* (New York: G. P. Putnam, 1950), 201.
   28. Lieb, *Connie Mack*, 183.
   29. For a more thorough discussion of this issue, see Norman Macht's *Connie Mack*.

Chapter 8

   1. *Los Angeles Times*, December 11, 1914.
   2. J. C. Kofoed, "Stars of Other Days — The Iron Man," *Baseball Magazine* (Volume XIII, No. 3, January 1915).
   3. Frank Graham, *The Brooklyn Dodgers: An Informal History* (New York: G. P. Putnam, 1945), 51.
   4. Robert W. Creamer, *Stengel: His Life and Times* (Lincoln: University of Nebraska Bison Books, 1996), 87.
   5. Ibid., 88.
   6. Jack Kavanagh and Norman Macht, *Uncle Robbie* (Cleveland: SABR, 1999), 74.
   7. *Washington Post*, April 7, 1915.
   8. *Boston Globe*, April 20, 1915.
   9. *New York Times*, May 1, 1915.
   10. Wentworth Family Personal Collections, Diaries of Jesse Snow, April 30, 1915.
   11. *Boston Globe*, May 20, 1915.
   12. Ibid.
   13. *Sporting News*, May 27, 1915.
   14. Ibid.
   15. *New York Times*, July 3, 1915.
   16. *Sporting News*, July 15, 1915.
   17. *Sporting Life*, July 31, 1915.
   18. *Washington Post*, October 20, 1915.
   19. *Los Angeles Times*, November 24, 1915.
   20. Ibid.
   21. *New York Times*, March 13, 1916.
   22. *Sporting News*, February 3, 1916.
   23. *Atlanta Constitution*, January 23, 1916.
   24. *New York Times*, April 10, 1916.
   25. *Boston Globe*, May 8, 1916.
   26. *New York Times*, July 4, 1916.
   27. *New York Times*, August 21, 1916.
   28. *New York Times*, September 6, 1916.
   29. Coombs file, unidentified newspaper clipping, Colby College Special Collections.
   30. *Atlanta Constitution*, October 3, 1916.
   31. *Boston Globe*, October 5, 1916.
   32. *Boston Globe*, October 6, 1916.
   33. Ibid.
   34. Ibid.
   35. Ibid.
   36. *Boston Globe*, October 7, 1916.
   37. *New York Times*, October 7, 1916.
   38. Wentworth Family Personal Collections, Diaries of Jesse Snow, October 3, 1916.
   39. *Washington Post*, October 9, 1916.
   40. *Boston Globe*, October 11, 1916.
   41. Ibid.
   42. *Los Angeles Times*, October 11, 1916.
   43. "What the Players Thought of the Series," *Baseball Magazine* (Vol. XVIII, No. 2, December 1916).
   44. *Sporting News*, October 19, 1916.

Chapter 9

   1. Creamer, *Stengel*, 116.
   2. *Washington Post*, November 6, 1916.
   3. *New York Times*, May 4, 1917.
   4. *Boston Globe*, May 7, 1917.
   5. *Sporting News*, September 13, 1917.
   6. *Sporting News*, December 6, 1917.
   7. Smith, *Baseball's Famous Pitchers*, 166.
   8. *New York Times*, May 22, 1918.
   9. *New York Times*, July 5, 1918.
   10. Ibid.
   11. *Boston Globe*, April 23, 1917.
   12. Multiple versions of this story exist, all related by people who were not participants in the game. An alternative version, probably emanating from Robinson, implies that Coombs suggested to Robinson that he could use the glove in a manner that would require removal by a proctologist.
   13. *Washington Post*, November 5, 1918.
   14. *Washington Post*, December 17, 1918.
   15. *Sporting News*, December 19, 1918.
   16. *Sporting News*, December 26, 1918.
   17. Ibid.

18. *Sporting News*, April 17, 1919.
19. *Sporting News*, June 26, 1919.
20. *Boston Globe*, July 9, 1919.
21. Ibid.
22. Ibid.
23. *Washington Post*, July 14, 1919.
24. *Sporting News*, July 17, 1919.
25. *Boston Globe*, July 9, 1919.
26. *Sporting News*, December 18, 1919.
27. *Sporting News*, March 11, 1920.
28. *Sporting News*, June 10, 1920.
29. Unidentified newspaper clipping, Wentworth Family Personal Collections.

Chapter 10

1. Discussions with Donald and Nelson Wentworth, December 10, 2005.
2. *Boston Globe*, November 5, 1920.
3. Amherst Graduates Quarterly, "The First Collegiate Baseball Game," *The National Pastime* (Number 16, 1996).
4. *New York Times*, May 24, 1923.
5. Robert F. Durden, *The Launching of Duke University, 1924–1949* (Durham, NC: Duke University Press, 1993), 28.
6. Ibid., 24.
7. Ibid., 209.
8. Ibid.
9. Coombs File, Colby College Special Collections.
10. *Duke Alumni Register*, April 1952.
11. Richard M. Groat, with Frank Dascenzo, *Groat: I Hit and Ran* (Durham, NC: Moore Publishing, 1978).
12. *Washington Post*, October 31, 1941.
13. Text of speech by J. W. Coombs (date unknown), Duke University Archives.
14. Ibid.
15. Ibid.
16. *Washington Post*, October 23, 1955.
17. "The Legend of the Real Crash Davis," Philadelphia Athletics Historical Society website.
18. Groat, *I Hit and Ran*, 31.
19. Bill Werber, *Circling the Bases* (Self-published, 1978), 47.
20. Letter from Charles E. Jordan to Dr. Cecil W. Clark, November 9, 1945, Colby College Special Collections.

Chapter 11

1. Discussions with Donald and Nelson Wentworth, December 10, 2005.
2. Add Penfield, "Colby Jack," (unpublished paper), Duke University Archives.
3. Ibid.
4. *Duke Alumni Register*, May 1948.
5. Coombs File, Duke University Archives.
6. John W. Coombs, *Baseball: Individual Play and Team Strategy* (New York: Prentice Hall, 1951), ix.
7. Coombs file, Duke University Archives.
8. Coombs, *Baseball*, x.
9. Ibid,. 83.
10. Ibid., 146.
11. Ibid., 60.
12. Ibid., 171.
13. Ibid., 320.
14. Add Penfield, "Colby Jack," (unpublished paper), Duke University Archives.
15. *Sporting News*, June 11, 1952.
16. *New York Tribune*, February 6, 1939.
17. Letter from Coombs to Freeport High School Class of 1917, May 14, 1917, Colby College Special Collections.
18. Ibid.
19. *Durham Herald*, January 22, 1937.
20. *New York Times*, September 17, 1937.
21. Letter from Charles E. Jordan to Dr. Cecil W. Clark, November 9, 1945, Colby College Special Collections.
22. Coombs File, Colby College Special Collections.
23. Ibid.
24. Ibid.
25. *Durham Sun*, May 13, 1952.
26. *Sporting News*, August 27, 1952.
27. Letter from John W. Coombs to Lew Slaw, March 2, 1957, Wentworth Family Personal Collections.
28. Coombs file, Colby College Special Collections.
29. Ibid.
30. Ibid.
31. *Sporting News*, April 24, 1957.
32. *Sporting News*, March 20, 1941.
33. *Sporting News*, November 11, 1943.

Epilogue

1. Unidentified newspaper clipping, Wentworth Family Personal Collections.
2. Letter from John Winkin to Nelson Wentworth, Wentworth Family Personal Collections.
3. Joyce Butler, *Wildfire Loose: The Week Maine Burned* (Camden, ME: Down East Books, 1997).
4. *Sporting News*, August 5, 1959.
5. Connie Mack, *Connie Mack's Baseball Book* (New York: Alfred A. Knopf, 1950), 200.
6. Ibid., 203.

7. *Washington Post*, January 4, 1925.
8. *Washington Post*, January 11, 1925.
9. *Sporting News*, February 13, 1952.
10. *Sporting News*, November 16, 1955.
11. *Sporting News*, August 19, 1959.
12. *Sporting News*, May 15, 1957.
13. Lee Allen, *The American League Story* (New York: Hill and Wang, 1962), 71.
14. Emmuleth, *Typhoid Fever*.

Bibliography

Books

Alexander, Charles C. *John McGraw*. Lincoln: University of Nebraska Press, 1988.
_____. *Ty Cobb*. New York: Oxford University Press, 1984.
Allen, Lee. *The American League Story*. New York: Hill and Wang, 1962.
_____. *The National League Story*. New York: Hill and Wang, 1961.
_____. *One Hundred Years of Baseball*. New York: Bartholomew House, 1950.
_____. *The World Series: The Story of Baseball's Annual Championship*. New York: G. P. Putnam, 1969.
Bourdain, Anthony. *Typhoid Mary: An Urban Historical*. New York: Bloomsbury, 2001.
Brown, Warren. *Chicago Cubs*. New York: G. P. Putnam, 1946.
_____. *Chicago White Sox*. New York: G. P. Putnam, 1952.
Browning, Reed. *Cy Young: A Baseball Life*. Amherst: University of Massachusetts Press, 2000.
Bucek, Jeanine, ed. *The Baseball Encyclopedia*, tenth edition. New York: Macmillan, 1996.
Butler, Joyce. *Kennebunkport Scrapbook, Volume I*. Kennebunk Landing, ME: Rosemary House Press, 1977.
_____. *Kennebunkport Scrapbook, Volume II*. Kennebunk Landing, ME: Rosemary House Press, 1989.
_____. *Wildfire Loose: The Week Maine Burned*. Camden, ME: Down East Books, 1997.
Clifton, Merritt. *Disorganized Baseball, Volume II: Baseball in Vermont (1887–1935)*. Monroe, CT: SAMISDAT, no date.
Cobb, Ty. *Busting 'Em and Other Big League Stories*. Reprint, Jefferson, NC: McFarland, 2003.
Cobb, Ty, with Al Stump. *Ty Cobb: My Life in Baseball*. Reprint, Lincoln: University of Nebraska Press, 1993.
Cohen, Richard M., David S. Neft, and Roland T. Johnson. *The World Series*. New York: Dial Press, 1976.
Coombs, John W. *Baseball: Individual Play and Team Strategy*. New York: Prentice-Hall, 1951.
Creamer, Robert W. *Stengel: His Life and Times*. Lincoln, NE: Bison Books, 1996.
Davis, J. D. *A Most Remarkable Mix: Sketches of Notable Freeporters*. Freeport, ME: Freeport Historical Society, 2000.

Davis, Ted. *Connie Mack: A Life in Baseball.* Lincoln, NE: Writers Club Press, 2000.
Deford, Frank. *The Old Ball Game.* New York: Atlantic Monthly Press, 2005.
Dickey, Glenn. *The History of the World Series: Since 1903.* New York: Stein & Day, 1984.
Durant, John. *Baseball's Miracle Teams.* New York: Hastings House, 1975.
Durden, Robert F. *The Launching of Duke University, 1924–1949.* Durham, NC: Duke University Press, 1993.
Emmeluth, Donald. *Deadly Diseases and Epidemics: Typhoid Fever.* New York: Chelsea House, 2004.
Gershman, Michael. *Diamonds.* Boston: Houghton Mifflin, 1993.
Goldstein, Richard. *Spartan Seasons.* New York: Macmillan, 1980.
Graff, Henry, ed. *The Presidents: A Reference History.* New York: Macmillan, 1997.
Graham, Frank. *The Brooklyn Dodgers: An Informal History.* New York: G. P. Putnam, 1945.
_____. *McGraw of the Giants.* New York: G. P. Putnam, 1944.
_____. *The New York Giants: An Informal History.* New York: G. P. Putnam, 1952.
_____. *The New York Yankees: An Informal History.* New York: G. P. Putnam, 1948.
Grayson, Harry. *They Played the Game.* New York: A. S. Barnes, 1945.
Groat, Richard M., with Frank Dascenzo. *Groat: I Hit and Ran.* Durham, NC: Moore Publishing, 1978.
Jordan, David M., *The Athletics of Philadelphia.* Jefferson, NC: McFarland, 1999.
Kahn, James M. *The Umpire Story.* New York: G. P. Putnam, 1953.
Kalinsky, George, and Bill Shannon. *The Ballparks.* New York: Hawthorn Books, 1975.
Kashatus, William C. *Money Pitcher: Chief Bender and the Tragedy of Indian Assimilation.* University Park: Pennsylvania State University Press, 2006.
Kavanagh, Jack. *Ol' Pete: The Grover Cleveland Alexander Story.* South Bend, IN: Diamond Communications, 1996.
_____. *Walter Johnson: A Life.* South Bend, IN: Diamond Communications, 1995.
_____, and Norman Macht. *Uncle Robbie.* Cleveland: Society for American Baseball Research, 1999.
Lieb, Frederick. *The Baseball Story.* New York: G. P. Putnam, 1950.
_____. *Baseball as I Have Known It.* New York: Coward McCann, 1977.
_____. *Connie Mack: Grand Old Man of Baseball.* New York: G. P. Putnam, 1945.
_____. *Boston Red Sox.* New York: G. P. Putnam, 1947.
_____. *Detroit Tigers.* New York: G. P. Putnam, 1946.
_____. *The Story of the World Series.* New York: G. P. Putnam, 1949.
_____, and Stan Baumgartner. *The Philadelphia Phillies.* New York: G. P. Putnam, 1953.
Light, Jonathan Fraser. *The Cultural Encyclopedia of Baseball.* Jefferson, NC: McFarland, 1997.
Lowry, Philip J. *Green Cathedrals.* Reading, MA: Addison-Wesley, 1992.
Macht, Norman L. *Connie Mack and the Early Years of Baseball.* Lincoln: University of Nebraska Press, 2007.
Mack, Connie. *Connie Mack's Baseball Book.* New York: Alfred A. Knopf, 1950.
_____. *My 66 Years in the Big Leagues.* Philadelphia: John C. Winston Company, 1950.
Marriner, Ernest Cummings. *The History of Colby College.* Waterville, ME: Colby College Press, 1963.
McConnell, Bob, and David Vincent, eds. *The Home Run Encyclopedia.* New York: Macmillan, 1996.
Okkonen, Marc. *The Federal League of 1914–1915.* Garrett Park, MD: Society for American Baseball Research, 1989.
Ostrander, Kathleen. *Images of America: Kennebunk.* Charleston, SC: Arcadia, 2005.
Ritter, Lawrence S. *The Glory of Their Times.* New York: Quill, 1985.
_____. *Lost Ballparks.* New York: Viking, 1992.
Robinson, Ray. *Matty: An American Hero.* New York: Oxford University Press, 1993.

Seib, Phillip. *The Player: Christy Mathewson, Baseball, and the American Century.* New York: Four Walls Eight Windows, 2003.
Smith, Earl H. *Mayflower Hill: A History of Colby College.* Hanover, NH: Colby College, 2006.
Smith, Ira L. *Baseball's Famous First Basemen.* New York: A. S. Barnes, 1955.
_____. *Baseball's Famous Outfielders.* New York: A. S. Barnes, 1956.
_____. *Baseball's Famous Pitchers.* New York: A. S. Barnes, 1954.
Solomon, Burt. *The Baseball Timeline.* New York: DK Publishing, 2001.
Stout, Glenn, and Richard A. Johnson. *The Dodgers.* Boston: Houghton Mifflin, 2004.
_____ and _____. *Red Sox Century.* Boston: Houghton Mifflin, 2000.
_____ and _____. *Yankees Century.* Boston: Houghton Mifflin, 2002.
Stump, Al. *Cobb: The Life and Times of the Meanest Man Who Ever Played Baseball.* Chapel Hill, NC: Algonquin Books, 1994.
Thorn, John, et al. *Total Baseball: The Ultimate Baseball Encyclopedia.* Toronto: Sports Classic Books, 2004.
Werber, Bill. *Circling the Bases.* Self-published, 1978.
_____, and C. Paul Rogers III. *Memories of a Ballplayer.* Cleveland: Society for American Baseball Research, 2001.
Williams, Peter, ed. *The Joe Williams Baseball Reader.* Chapel Hill, NC: Algonquin Books, 1989.

Newspapers/Periodicals

Atlanta Constitution
Baseball Digest
Baseball Magazine
The Baseball Research Journal
Boston Globe
Chicago Tribune
Leslie's Illustrated Weekly Newspaper
Los Angeles Times
Munsey's Magazine
The National Pastime
Pearson's Magazine
New York Times
Sport Magazine
Sporting News
Technology in Society

Archives/Collections

A. Bartlett Giamatti Research Center, Cooperstown, NY.
The Brick Store Museum, Kennebunk, ME.
Colby College Special Collections, Waterville, ME.
Duke University Archives, Durham, NC.
Wentworth Family Personal Collections

Web Sites

www.aafla.org
www.baseballhalloffame.org
www.baseballlibrary.com
www.baseball-links.com
www.baseball-reference.com
www.colby.edu
www.duke.edu
www.goduke.com
www.paperofrecord.com
www.philadelphiaathletics.org
www.princeton.edu
www.proquest.com
www.retrosheet.org
www.tsha.utexas.edu
www.sabr.org
www.wikipedia.com
www.williams.edu

Index

Adams, Franklin Pierce 55
Alexander, Grover Cleveland 76, 122–123, 128, 137, 142–143, 147, 183, 186
Allen, Ernest 147
Allen, Lee 186
Ambler, Wayne 160
American League 24, 34, 57, 68, 70, 81, 83, 92, 102, 114–115, 148, 179, 183
Ames, Red 79, 87
Amherst College 15, 151
Anson, Cap 84
Apperius, Sammy 18
Appleton, Ed 120
Archer, Jimmy 62–63
Arizona Diamondbacks 179

Baker, Frank "Home Run" 2, 41, 45, 68, 75, 84–86, 103, 112, 114–115, 174, 185–186
Baker, William 142–147
Baker Bowl (Philadelphia) 146
Ballplayer's Fraternity 92
Baltimore Orioles 34, 80–81, 116, 119, 121, 152
Bancroft, Frank 47
Barker, Dr. Lenox 166
Barley, George 160
Barry, Jack 41, 50, 60, 68, 111, 131, 139
Baseball: Individual Play and Team Strategy 166–167
Baseball Magazine 96, 107, 118
"Baseball's Sad Lexicon" (Adams) 55–56
Bates College 12, 15–16, 18, 20
Bender, Charles "Chief" 2, 26–28, 30, 32, 37, 40, 50, 57, 59, 61–62, 66, 70–71, 73–75, 82–84, 86–90, 96–97, 99, 101, 103, 108–109, 113–118, 127, 134, 148, 151, 174, 185–186
Bennett Park (Detroit) 75
Bevens, Bill 58

Bixler, Seelye 172
"Black Sox" scandal 150, 185
Bobby Coombs Baseball Field (Williams College) 178
Boland, Bernie 147
Bonser, Frank 67
Boston Americans/Red Sox 3–7, 23, 30–31, 41, 50–52, 54, 74, 91–93, 96–98, 102–103, 105, 109, 116, 130–134, 147, 157, 179
Boston Braves 113, 121, 127, 129, 145
Boston Globe 5, 53, 66, 77, 123, 130–131
Bowdoin College 12–13, 16, 18, 21
Braves Field (Boston) 132
Bresnahan, Roger 81
Briggs Stadium (Detroit) 75
Brooklyn Dodgers (football) 160
Brooklyn Dodgers/Robins/Superbas 58, 83, 100, 119–122, 124–134, 136–137, 139–142, 145, 147, 150, 172, 180–181
Brown, Carroll 92, 97, 99, 109
Brown, Mordecai "Three Finger" 54, 56, 58, 62–63, 103, 186
Brush, John 77
Bucknell University 78
Bull Durham 160
Bush, Joe 99, 109
Byrne, Tommy 155

Cadore, Leon 139, 183
Cameron, Eddie 174
Campanella, Roy 181
Capuano, Chris 179
Carlisle Indian School 27
Carlton, Steve 184
Carrigan, Bill 5, 130–131
Caruthers, Bob 185
Chance, Frank 55–56, 58–62, 82, 103

199

Chapman, Ray 133, 148
Chase, Hal 84
Chavez Ravine (Los Angeles) 181
Cheney, Larry 126–127, 139
Chesbro, Jack 24, 30
Chicago Cubs 54–64, 77, 80, 82 126, 128, 130, 140, 142–143, 147
Chicago Tribune 26, 52, 54, 60, 108, 140
Chicago White Sox 3, 25–26, 28–29, 32–33, 38, 40, 50–51, 53, 60, 69, 75, 91, 93, 102, 115, 147–148, 173, 179, 186–187
Cincinnati Reds 112, 123, 142, 145, 158–159, 179
Clarke, Bill 152
Clemens, Roger 183
Cleveland Naps/Indians 33, 53, 99–100, 104, 109, 130–131, 133, 148, 160
Coakley, Andy 27
Cobb, Ty 35–36, 38–41, 44–46, 57, 68–71, 73–75, 84, 86, 91–92, 102–103, 125, 130, 147, 150, 164, 167
Cochrane, Mickey 2, 179
Colburn Classical Institute 11
Colby College 1–2, 4, 7–8, 11–21, 50, 67, 86, 93–95, 112, 151–153, 155, 168–169, 171–172, 176–178, 183
Colby Echo 12–16, 20
Cole, Leonard 56, 62
College Baseball Hall of Fame 184
College of the Holy Cross 16, 43
Collins, Eddie 2, 18, 29, 38, 40–41, 50, 63, 66, 68, 73–75, 84, 86, 102, 106, 114–116, 139, 164, 173, 186
Collins, Jimmy 5
Collins, Ray 97
Columbia Park (Philadelphia) 23, 28, 42
Columbia Presbyterian Hospital 29
Columbia University 29, 38
Comerica Park (Detroit) 75
Committee on Veterans 174, 184
Connie Mack: Grand Old Man of Baseball (Lieb) 2, 23
Connie Mack Stadium (Philadelphia) 182
Connie Mack's Baseball Book (Mack) 185
Connolly, Tommy 36
Considine, Bob 160
Coombs, Alice (sister) 9
Coombs, Curtis (brother) 9–10, 182
Coombs, Ellen Snow "Nellie" (mother) 9, 73
Coombs, Ernest (brother) 9
Coombs, Frank (father) 9–10, 13, 66–67, 73
Coombs, Harry (brother) 9
Coombs, John Wesley "Colby Jack": 1–2, 46, 118, 179, 181; arrival in Philadelphia 23–24; author of *Baseball: Individual Play and Team Strategy* 1, 166–168; barnstorming tours 47–48, 68–69, 103; baseball clinics and presentations 168–169; baseball coach at Duke University 152–156; baseball coach at Princeton University 152; baseball coach at Williams College 151; baseball season of 1906 4, 25–26, 28–30; baseball season of 1907 30–35; baseball season of 1908 37–42; baseball season of 1909 43–44; baseball season of 1910 50–54, 65; baseball season of 1911 70–77; baseball season of 1912 90–93, 97, 99–100; baseball season of 1913 103–105, 107–109; baseball season of 1914 112–113; baseball season of 1915 121–126; baseball season of 1916 126–130; baseball season of 1917 136–137; baseball season of 1918 139–142; birth 9; bronze bust at Duke University 178; candidate for Baseball Hall of Fame 2, 172–174, 184–187; candidate for Baseball's proposed board of control 150; characteristics of a good college baseball coach 160–161; childhood 10–11; college baseball player 13–21; college basketball player 12, 15, 20; college football player 12, 15; college student 12; comparing McGraw and Mack as managers 136; compensation in major leagues 21–22, 48, 66, 88, 103, 111, 115, 117, 119, 126, 139, 143, 146; death 174–175, 183; develops new pitch 44, 47, 49; Federal League 114–116; first major league game 25–26; golf 48; honors from Colby College 50, 93–96, 112, 155, 171–172, 176–177; hunter 20, 114, 118, 169–170; injuries 15, 33–34, 52–53, 71, 86–87, 90, 92, 103, 107, 124–125; Kennebunk, Maine 66–67, 72–73, 170–171, 182; manager of Philadelphia Phillies 142–146; managerial candidate for Detroit 150; marriage to Mary (Russ) Coombs 68, 164–165, 173; member of Duke University community 164–166; member of sports halls of fame 184; mentor to college baseball players 157–163; national magazine articles 102–103; nicknames 10, 15, 57, 128, 171; Palestine, Texas 49, 90, 173; pitching coach of Detroit Tigers 147–149; pitching "in a pinch" 15, 33, 50–51, 58, 64, 92; record against Hall of Fame pitchers 186; recruiting college baseball coaches 176–177; religion 12; retirement from major league baseball 142, 149; semiprofessional baseball 11, 14–17; shutout record in American League 65, 76, 128, 183; signs contract with Brooklyn 118–121; sixteen inning shutout against Chicago 51–52; stage performer 17, 20, 88–90; statistical comparisons with other pitchers 101–102, 186–187; teaching at Duke University 166; track and field accomplishments 20; twenty-four inning victory against Boston 4–8, 28–31, 43, 51, 106, 177, 183; typhoid fever 8, 105–109, 111, 139; World Series of 1910

Index

57–65, 88; World Series of 1911 82–87, 124–125, 128, 134, 171; World Series of 1916 132–134
Coombs, Mary Elizabeth Russ (spouse) 49, 68, 87, 90, 103, 109, 111, 121, 164–165, 173–174, 183
Coombs, Raymond "Bobby" (nephew) 158–159, 170, 177
Coombs Field (Colby College) 172, 176
Coombs Field (Duke University) 153–154, 178
Cork-centered baseball 64, 70, 76, 82
Coveleski, Stan 99–100
Craft, Harry 155
Crandall, Doc 79
Cravath, Gavvy 146
Crawford, Sam 35–36, 73, 75, 174
Criger, Louis 7
Cross, Monte 5, 28, 30
Cutshaw, George 139

D'Armi, Tom 178
Daubert, Jake 120, 131
Dauss, George 147
Davidson College 153
Davis, Harry 6, 27, 32, 36, 43, 72
Davis, Laurence "Crash" 160, 162
Day, Walter 66
Dean, Chubby 160
Dean, Dizzy 186–187
Dell, William 120
Delta Upsilon Fraternity 17
Detroit Tigers 34–37, 40, 43–45, 47, 49–50, 52, 54, 63, 68–69, 71–76, 83, 91–92, 96–98, 112, 147–148, 150, 158, 172, 187
Diamond Café 119
Dodger Stadium (Los Angeles) 181
Dolan, Cozy 106
Donovan, Bill 52–53
Doyle, Larry 47, 141
Drysdale, Don 183
Duke, James B. 152, 178
Duke Alumni Register 166
Duke University 152–164, 166, 168, 170–174, 176, 178–179, 185
Duke University Sports Hall of Fame 184
Dunn, Jack 116
Dygert, Jimmy 27, 35, 37
East Texas National Bank 173

Ebbets, Charlie 83, 118–119, 121, 123, 126, 133, 135–137, 139, 150
Ebbets Field (Brooklyn) 119–120, 140, 181
Ehmke, Howard 147
Evans, Billy 69, 126
Evers, Johnny 55–57, 113
Exeter Academy 158

Ezell Mercantile Company 173

Fanwell, Harry 53
Faust, Charles "Victory" 79–80, 111
Federal League 114–117, 126, 135
Fenway Park (Boston) 43, 92, 132, 181–182
Ferris, Hobe 46
Few, William Preston 152–153, 161, 165
Fingers, Rollie 180
Finley, Charles O. 180
Fogel, Horace 38–39, 78
Forbes Field (Pittsburgh) 42
Ford C. Frick Award 162
Foster, Rube 131
Foxx, Jimmie 2, 158, 179
Frazee, Harry 147
Freedman, Andrew 81
Freeman, Buck 5, 31
Freeport High School 10–11, 67, 94, 169
Fullerton, Hugh 131

Gainer, Del 71, 83
Gardner, Larry 131, 134
Gehrig, Lou 98, 158
Gettysburg College 27
Gilmore, Jim 114
Gomez, Lefty 183
Goodwin, Forrest 95
Graham, Frank 120
Grant, Eddie 19
Gregg, Vean 185
Grimes, Burleigh 139–140
Grimshaw, Moose 4–5, 7
Groat, Dick 155–157, 162–163
Grove, Lefty 2, 179, 185

Hamilton, Billy 185
Hanlon, Ned 34, 80
Hanrahan, Red 136
Harris, Joe 4–8, 51, 106
Hartsel, Topsy 6, 27
Harvard College 13, 16, 18–20, 151
Harwell, Ernie 174
Hershiser, Orel 183
Heydler, John 81
Hill, Dr. J.F. 11, 19, 50, 176
Hilltop Park (New York) 29, 77
Hoey, John 6, 16
Hofman, Solly 56, 58, 62
Holy Cross College 43
Hooper, Harry 130, 133
Hopkins, Stephen 9
Hornsby, Rogers 125
Houck, Byron 97, 99, 109
Hunter, Catfish 180, 183
Huntington Avenue Grounds (Boston) 3–5
Hurst, Tim 6–7

INDEX

Husson College 177

Inter-City Athletic Association 18
Iowa Sports Hall of Fame 184

"Jack Coombs — As a Pitcher" 143–144
Jackson, Joe S. 52, 62, 64, 76
Jackson, Reggie 180
Jackson, "Shoeless Joe" 185–186
James, Bill (baseball analyst) 1
James, Bill (baseball player) 113
Jennings, Hughie 34–35, 45, 69, 80, 84, 92, 119, 147, 150, 152
Johnson, Ban 34, 81, 91–92
Johnson, Walter 41, 44, 47, 49, 57, 65, 70, 90, 98–102, 109, 183, 185–186
Jonnard, Claude 147
Jordan, Charles E. 163, 171
Joss, Addie 33, 186–187

Kavanagh, Jack 121
Keefe, Tim 185
Keeler, Willie 34, 80
Kennebunk, Maine 9–10
Killefer, Bill 142
Kling, Johnny 56
Knight, John 5–7, 28
Koob, Ernie 52
Koufax, Sandy 24
Krause, Harry 97
Krzyzewski, Mike 178
Kuhn, Bowie 180

La Grand, Iowa 9
Lajoie, Napoleon 33, 102, 185
Landis, Kenesaw Mountain 60, 150, 154
Lapp, Jack 63, 85, 91, 106, 114, 143
Lardner 52, 54, 108
Law, Ruth 121
Lazzeri, Tony 158
"Learning the Game" 88–89
Leonard, Dutch 131, 147
Leslie's Weekly 102
Leukers, Claude 91
Lewis, Duffy 130
Lewiston Athletic Club 13
Lieb, Fred 23, 59, 81, 116, 174–175
Life 168, 173
Livingston, Paddy 45
Lord, Bris 5–6, 37
Los Angeles Times 118

Macht, Norman 48, 121
Mack, Connie 2–6, 8, 19, 21, 23–26, 28–31, 33–45, 48–51, 53–54, 57, 59, 62–66, 68–69, 71–77, 83, 86–87, 90, 96–100, 103–105, 108, 111–118, 124, 130, 136–137, 139, 142, 144, 147–148, 153–154, 156, 158, 162, 164, 166, 172–173, 179–180, 185
Mack, Connie, Jr. 153
Mack, Earle 54, 68
Mack, Roy 68
Mack, Tom 19, 21, 29
Maine Literary & Theological Institution 12
Maine Sports Hall of Fame 184
Mallon, Mary "Typhoid Mary" 106–107
Mamaux, Al 139
Maple Hill Farm (Kennebunk, Maine) 66, 72, 182
Maranville, Rabbit 113
Maris, Roger 180
Marquard, Rube 47, 78–80, 83–87, 99, 103, 125–127, 130–132, 139
Martin, Alfred M. 1
Massachusetts Institute of Technology 21
Mathewson, Christy 24, 39, 56, 64, 78–80, 82–88, 101–103, 111, 123–124, 127–128, 130–131, 134, 143, 150, 164, 171, 183, 185–186
Matthews, William Clarence 18–19, 181
Mays, Carl 131, 133, 149
Mazeroski, Bill 157
McCahan, Bill 160
McCarthy, Joe 174
McCracken, Quinton 179
McGinnity, Joe 81
McGraw, John 24, 34, 78–83, 86–87, 102, 106, 111, 119, 125–126, 129, 136–137, 152, 162, 164
McGuire, Deacon 92
McInnis, Stuffy 41, 82–83
McIntire, Harry 56, 60
McKechnie, Bill 114
McLain, Denny 184
McPhail, Lee 180–181
Merkle, Fred 55, 85
Merriwell Frank, 17
Meusel, Emil 145
Meyers, Chief 47, 126, 131
Millett, Ellsworth 174
Milwaukee Brewers 179
Minnesota Twins 162
Moore, Earl 103
Moran, Pat 142–143, 145
Morgan, Cy 75, 88–89, 96–97, 99
Morgan, Red 5, 7
Mowrey, Mike 126
Mullin, George 82–83
Munsey's Magazine 102
Murnane, Tim 54, 130
Murphy, Danny 27, 36, 38, 40, 43, 58, 60, 114–118
Myers, Hy 132, 135

National Association of Baseball Coaches 176
National Baseball Hall of Fame 2, 27, 29, 56,

78, 80, 91, 98–100, 103, 119–120, 123, 140, 162, 173–174, 178, 181, 183–187
National Collegiate Athletic Association (NCAA) 153, 173, 176
National Commission 150
National Football League 160
National League 24, 34, 39, 57, 70, 81, 83, 102, 114, 125, 129, 142, 181
Navin, Frank 34, 92, 147
Navin Field (Detroit) 75
Navy Pre-Flight School 155
New England League 4, 7–8
New York Giants 24, 31, 34, 39, 47, 54–55, 77–87, 98, 102–103, 109, 111, 113, 119, 121, 124–129, 131, 134, 136–137, 140–141, 144–145, 158, 171, 177, 181
New York Herald 84
New York Highlanders/Yankees 7, 25, 28–30, 35, 39–40, 43, 46, 50, 58, 64, 73–74, 76–77, 91, 97–99, 112–113, 117, 120, 147, 157–158, 160, 179–181
New York Times 124, 126, 128, 151
Newcombe, Don 181
Nicholls, Simon 30, 37–38, 43
North Carolina Sports Hall of Fame 184
North Carolina State University 153, 155
Northampton, Massachusetts 16–17
Northern League 17–19
Northey, Ron 160
Northwestern Hospital 107
Noyes, Thomas 94

O'Day, Hank 55
Oeschger, Joe 183
Oldring, Rube 28, 37, 40, 57, 86
O'Loughlin, Silk 36
Olson, Ivy 126
O'Malley, Walter 181
Oregon State University 156
Oriole Park at Camden Yards (Baltimore) 182
Ott, Mel 1
Overall, Orval 56–57

Palestine, Texas 48–49
Parent, Freddy 5
Parker, Ace 160, 174, 178
Pearl, Kathryn 88, 90
Pearl, Violet 88, 90
Pearlstone, Hyman 48–49, 68, 118
Penn State University 156
Pennock, Herb 91–92, 99, 114, 183
Pesky, Johnny 155
Pfeffer, Jack 120, 124, 127, 130–131, 133–135, 139
Phelon, William 107
Philadelphia Athletics 2–6, 21, 23–25, 27–37, 39–54, 56–60, 62–66, 68–78, 82–87, 90, 92–93, 97–105, 108–115, 118–119, 122, 124, 127, 130, 137, 142, 147–148, 154, 156–160, 172–173, 179–180, 185
Philadelphia Phillies 31, 38–39, 44, 70, 76, 78, 103, 122–123, 125, 127–129, 137, 142–147, 182
Phillips Andover Academy 19
Pittsburgh Pirates 54, 64, 68, 137, 157
Plaisted, Frederick 86, 94
Plank, Eddie 2, 27–28, 30–31, 35–37, 40–43, 49–50, 53, 57, 59, 61, 66, 68, 71–72, 74, 77, 82–84, 87, 96–99, 101, 103–105, 107–109, 114–117, 148, 151, 173, 185–186
Polo Grounds (New York) 77, 83, 85, 88, 128, 141
Powell, Jack 74
Powers, Doc 4–5, 7–8, 23, 43, 50
Princeton University 151–152
Pro Football Hall of Fame 160
Progressive Party 118
Providence Grays 47

Rath, Morrie 50
Ration League 155
Raymond, Arthur "Bugs" 79, 185
Reese, Pee Wee 181
Reulbach, Ed 18, 56, 60
Rice, Grantland 123, 130, 136
Rice University 137
Richie, Lew 56
Rickey, Branch 181
Rigler, Charles 58, 141
Rixey, Eppa 122–123, 143
Roberts, Jim 147
Roberts, Kenneth 9
Robinson, Jackie 181
Robinson, Ray 84
Robinson, Wilbert 34, 80–81, 119–121, 124–127, 129–130, 132–133, 137–142, 152, 180
Rollins College 156
Rucker, George 120, 127
Rudolph, Dick 113
Ruppert, Jacob 179
Rusie, Amos 185
Ruth, Babe 46, 98, 116–117, 131–133, 147–148, 158, 183

Sain, Johnny 155
St. Joseph's College 92
St. Louis Browns 36, 47, 52, 74, 76, 96, 100, 113, 122, 180
St. Louis Cardinals 124–125, 137, 140–141, 144, 157, 178, 181, 187
Schoeneweis, Scott 179
Schreckengost, Ossee 6, 8, 24–25, 28
Schulte, Frank 56, 58, 62–63
"Seeing Coombs at Waterville" (Noyes) 94–95
Sewell, Joe 157
Seybold, Socks 27, 37–38, 40

204 INDEX

Shawkey, Bob 114
Sheckard, Jimmy 56, 58, 62
Shibe, Ben 42, 48, 72–73, 83
Shibe, Tom 83
Shibe Park (Philadelphia) 8, 42–43, 50, 68, 158, 182
Shore, Ernie 131–132
Sicking, Eddie 145
Simmons Al, 179
Slaughter, Enos "Country" 178
Sloane Hospital for Women 107
Smith, Sherry 120, 127, 132–133, 135, 139
Snider, Duke 181
Snodgrass, Fred 85–86
Snow, Jesse (uncle) 122, 132
Society for American Baseball Research (SABR) 1
Soper, Dr. George 106
Speaker, Tris 57, 84, 130–131
Spink, J.G. Taylor 174, 184
Sport Magazine 157
Sporting Life 125
Sporting News 7, 25–26, 28, 33, 38, 64, 108, 123, 125–126, 134, 137, 143, 146–148, 168, 173–175, 185–186
Stahl, Chick 5–6, 8, 31
Stahl, Jake 97, 102
Stallings, George 113
Stein, Fred 1
Steinfeldt, Harry 56, 58
Stengel, Casey 120–121, 125, 135–136, 139
Stoneham, Horace 181
Story of the World Series (Lieb) 59
Stump, Al 44, 46
Sugden, Joe 92
Summers, Oren 52

Taft, William Howard 49
Tannehill, Jesse 31
Tarkington, Booth 9
Taylor, John 5
Tenney, Fred 19, 23, 181
Thomas, Ira 43, 63, 68, 72, 87, 111, 151, 168
Tiger Stadium (Detroit) 75
Tinker, Joe 55–56, 61, 63, 103, 114
Tipton, Eric 155, 159
Trinity College 152
Tyler, Lefty 113
Typhoid fever 8, 91, 105–107, 125, 139, 187

University of Florida 156
University of Maine 15–16, 18, 20, 176
University of New Hampshire 12
University of North Carolina 153–155
University of Notre Dame 43
University of Tennessee 156
University of Virginia 123
Updike, John 92

Van Zelst, Louis 111
Veterans Stadium (Philadelphia) 182
Vickers, Rube 38
Virginia League 78
Virginia Polytechnic Institute 160

Waddell, Rube 2, 6, 24–28, 30, 33, 35–36, 39, 78, 117, 185
Wade, Wallace 152, 159, 178–179
Wagner, Honus 103
Wake Forest University 153, 155
Walker, George Herbert 171
Walker, Tilly 131
Walker Cup 171
Walsh, Ed 28–29, 44, 51–53, 57, 72, 75–76, 93, 100, 102, 123, 185–187
Ward, Chuck 139
Warner, Charles Henry 106
Washington Nationals/Senators 25, 29, 40, 47, 49, 90, 97, 109, 112–113, 158, 160, 162, 185
Washington Post 26, 30, 32, 52, 54, 62, 64, 69–70, 76, 84, 88, 90, 121, 133, 142–143, 146
Waterville, Maine 11, 14
Welch, Bob 184
Wentworth, Donald 2, 182
Wentworth, Nelson 2, 177
Werber, Bill 153–154, 157–158, 161, 163, 172
Wesleyan College 151
West Side Grounds (Chicago) 60
Western Michigan University 156
Wheat, Zack 120, 125, 133, 135, 140–141, 184
Wheeler, John 84
White, Charles 8
White, Doc 53, 102
Whitted, George 145
Williams, Joe 116
Williams, Ted 155
Williams College 151, 153, 177–178
Wiltse, Hooks 79, 87
Winkin, John 176–177
Wolff, Bob 162
Wood, Joe 54, 92–93, 97–98, 100, 104, 131, 185
Wood, Wilbur 184
World Series of 1910 54, 57–65, 70, 128
World Series of 1911 82–88, 124–125, 128, 134, 171
World Series of 1914 113
World Series of 1916 132–136
Wrigley Field (Chicago) 43, 181–182

Yale University 98, 126, 151
Yankee Stadium 182
Yawkey, Tom 179
Young, Cy 6, 31–32, 47, 106, 139, 185

Zimmerman, Henry "Heinie" 57–58

www.ingramcontent.com/pod-product-compliance
Ingram Content Group UK Ltd.
Pitfield, Milton Keynes, MK11 3LW, UK
UKHW042002140426
5217IPUK00015B/940